THE INVISIBLE ARAB

ALSO BY MARWAN BISHARA

Palestine/Israel:
Peace or Apartheid: Prospects for Resolving the Conflict

The Invisible Arab

The Promise and Peril
of the
Arab Revolutions

MARWAN BISHARA

NATION
BOOKS

NEW YORK

Copyright © 2012 by Marwan Bishara

Published by
NATION BOOKS, A Member of the Perseus Books Group
116 East 16th Street, 8th Floor
New York, NY 10003

NATION BOOKS is a co-publishing venture of the Nation Institute
and the Perseus Books Group.

Books published by NATION BOOKS are available at special discounts for
bulk purchases in the United States by corporations, institutions, and
other organizations. For more information, please contact the Special
Markets Department at the Perseus Books Group, 2300 Chestnut Street,
Suite 200, Philadelphia, PA 19103, or call (800) 255-1514, or e-mail
special.markets@perseusbooks.com.

Editorial production by Lori Hobkirk at the Book Factory.
Designed by Cynthia Young at Sagecraft.

"Identity Card" by Marmoud Darwish, translated by
John Mikhail Asfour, copyright John Mikhail Asfour, appears by
permission of the publisher, Dar el Awda, as well as the translator.

Cataloging-in-Publication Data is available at the Library of Congress.
ISBN-13: 978-1-56858-708-0

10 9 8 7 6 5 4 3 2 1

To Azmi

CONTENTS

PREFACE | 20/20 Vision

This is an essay about the fall and rise of the Arabs. It is an attempt to understand how their revolution evolved, what went right, why it is paramount, and how it could still go terribly wrong.

In much of the world's media, the narrative goes like this: an oppressed people who have suffered passively suddenly decide that enough is enough and, thanks to Western technology and inspiration, spontaneously rise up to reclaim their freedom, inspiring what is called the Arab Spring.

Like most revolutions, however, this one was a long time coming. The historic takeover of Tunis's November 7 Square, Cairo's Tahrir Square, and Manama's Pearl Square, among others, were the culmination of a long social and political struggle—countless sit-ins, strikes, pickets, and demonstrations by people who risked and suffered intimidation, torture, and imprisonment.

What started as a desperate act of self-immolation by Mohamed Bouazizi, a street vendor, soon became a viral event on the Internet, one that led angry Tunisians to pour into the streets by the thousands. Demonstrations turned into national upheaval and culminated in a full-fledged revolution that toppled the Tunisian dictatorship and spread east to other countries to kindle the greatest Arab transformation in memory. Never had the region witnessed such collective vigor and yearning for change.

Within a few weeks, millions of Arabs filled their streets and squares, giving new meaning to the claim that there's power in numbers. The silent majority finally spoke, breaking the psychological barrier of fear erected by regimes through decades of oppression, and discovering in record time that, as the fairy tale foretold, the emperor had no clothes.

If we are to do justice to the immense courage of those who stood up to—and in some cases brought down—their regimes, we need to not only recognize their determination, but also listen to what they have said and are saying about how to bring justice and democracy to the Middle East. We also need to back their efforts in every way possible. They have earned the right—with their blood and, in many cases, lives—to be respected and supported.

This story begins with the young Arabs whose networking and organization brought the people out into the streets. The youth, who make up 60 percent of all Arabs, have been looked upon as a "demographic bomb," an "economic burden," or as a "reservoir for extremism." However, unlike previous generations, this group heralded change.

The young Arabs were not alone, though. Their "awakening" has been inspired by political, community, labor, and national leaders who offered countless sacrifices in years past. They have been influenced by the experiences and successes of others around the world who have suffered from similar challenges arising from globalization, while at the same time taking advantage of its byproducts: the information revolution and the popularization of technology. Important as these technological advances are, however, sensationalizing the role of Facebook or Twitter and crediting them with the revolution is like crediting the inventor of portable cassettes—the Dutch conglomerate Phillips—with the Islamic revolution in Iran, which relied heavily on mass circulation of the Ayatollah's recorded messages. There is no doubt new media played an important role in the Arab uprising, but the heart of the revolution was made up of people who had long been deemed invisible by dictators as well as by their international sponsors.

For decades these Arab citizens and their social and political movements have been either unfairly demonized or totally ignored in the West—by both its leaders and the media—who saw the region through the prisms of Israel, oil, terrorism, or radical Islamism. But today's Arabs are presenting a stark contrast to the distortion, disinformation, and outright humiliation heaped upon them. Characterized as unreceptive to democracy and freedom, they are now giving the world a lesson in both.

For decades, Arab underdevelopment was blamed on cultural distinctness and dreamy pan-Arabism or insolent Islam. Countless books and studies in the West spoke of "the Arab exception," which cast doubt on Islam's or Muslims' capacity to cope with or integrate into modern democratic societies. Few ever bothered to understand the societal evolution in the Arab and Islamic world, preferring to look at Islam exclusively without also taking notice of Muslims, and to build stereotypes about a "captive Arab mind" while failing to understand today's Arabs.

Since September 11, 2001, international media coverage of Arabs has continued to degenerate, portraying them as a hateful, chronically underdeveloped, and violent people who loathe modernity and freedom. And when the robust, creative, and mostly peaceful revolutions in Tunisia and Egypt proved the media wrong, the Western media credited U.S. presidents, Western technology, and politicians as modern-day Lawrences of Arabia. Some media went as far as to credit "Israel's justice system" and "Chinese development" for inspiring the Arab Spring.

But the Arab Spring is exclusively Arab, and this essay traces its roots by looking at the complex factors peculiar to Arab society as well as the universal influences that made it possible. It explains why the inclusive, pluralistic nationalism that motivated the revolution has been brewing for some time and is indispensable to its long-term success.

THE INVISIBLE ARAB is a voyage in time and space from the "liberation generation" of the 1950s, through the "defeated generation" of the 1970s and '80s, the "lost generation" of the 1990s, onto today's "miracle generation." The book examines how this demographic "time bomb" has proved to be the carrier of progress, unity, and freedom, how social networks of people have demanded social justice, and how new and satellite media intertwined to reconnect Arabs across borders, ethnicity, and religion.

Above all, this book is a reflection on Arab defiance and hope against all odds; on how a new generation of Arabs overcame decades of fear, oppression, torture, and outright slaughter at the hands of some of the cruelest and bloodiest dictatorships of the twentieth century; on how the revolution exposed Western clichés about Arabs as neo-colonial farce, some of which were internalized by many of the West's "good Arabs" over the decades.

These issues are why this revolution will ultimately be judged on how it scores with freedom and justice and on whether it can pave the way for accommodating the various ideological, religious, political, and civic trends, as well as reconciling nationalism and Islam with democracy as the indispensable trinity of stability and progress in the Arab world. Whether this revolution will culminate in an Arab, modern, and universalistic vision of the future remains to be seen.

This essay begins with events leading up to the revolution in Tunisia and finishes in the autumn of 2011. Along the way, it attempts to investigate the root causes of many of the components of the Arab upheavals.

NOTE: I realize as this book goes to press, in December 2011, that the situation in many of the countries I am writing about remains fluid. Egyptians have returned to the streets and public squares of their major cities, forcing the military to apologize for its policies, to appoint a new government with full authority, and to promise to vacate its executive role after presidential elections by the middle of 2012. Forty-two people died in the anti-military riots. The situation will remain fluid for some time in Egypt and elsewhere. The ebb and flow of the Arab revolutions is producing further political storms that could flood the Arab world with chaos. However, I sincerely believe that the peoples of the region have made a decisive break with the past.

INTRODUCTION |
The Promise of a New Dawn

They took everyone by surprise, including themselves. T-shirted youths filled public squares, cheered and sang, chanted and demonstrated peacefully, and, in the process, turned the tables on their violent regimes. People of other generations joined them—not as moderates or extremists, jihadists or atheists, Muslim or Christians, rich or poor, young or old, men or women, conservatives or liberals, but as citizens united for freedom and justice.

A long nightmare, shaped by political oppression, military defeats, social regression, and economic stagnation, finally gave way to a new dream of national unity, development, stability, legality, transparency, and accountability. Like Eastern Europeans, Latin Americans, and others before them, the Arabs at last took matters into their own hands.

Their long-held motto *Insha'Allah* or "God willing" was replaced with *Masha'Allah* or "God willed it." "Down with the regime" overtook "Long live the leader." Arabs offered their blood for the freedom of their homelands instead of sacrificing it for the leader whose praises they'd been forced to chant.

1

Their revolution has brought the best out in Arabs—their collective conscience, their deeds and slogans, which have been peaceful but firm, elegant but revolutionary, poetic but strategic—and it has energized millions. Never has personal and national dignity been so intertwined and mutually reinforcing. Never has a transformation come so fast when the stakes were so high, the people so daring, or the change so within reach.

If it was Tunisia that lit the Arab imagination, it was the determination of the people of Egypt, the Arab world's largest country, that served as the catalyst. Never has the power of the people appeared so humane, so inspiring, so personal, so determined as in Tunisia, so daring as in Syria, so diverse as in Yemen, so humble as in Bahrain, so courageous as in Libya, or so humorous as in Egypt. If, as one keen observer noted, every joke is a tiny revolution, the Arabs, and most notably the Egyptians, are revolutionaries par excellence.

No longer would revolutionaries fear change in accordance with the Arab dictum, "Better one hundred years of tyranny than one day of chaos." Considering that the Arabic word for "regime" and "order" is one and the same—*nitham*—any attempt to bring down a regime is equated with chaos, along the lines of France's Louis XV's *après moi le deluge*. Over history, this fallacy has been internalized by many, even by opposition parties that allowed themselves to be domesticated through blackmail and bribery. The end result was stagnant regimes, subservient oppositions that acted as mere puppets, and continuous social and economic regression.

The youth-led upheaval has embarrassed "loyal opposition" groups in Tunisia, Egypt, and other countries. The speed and efficiency with which the demonstrations have been organized and maintained have shamed the old establishment parties that have boasted large memberships and state controlled media outlets. Unlike the timid demands of the "domesticated" opposition parties that advocated for limited reform, or worse, colluded with despots in order to gain power, the new revolutionaries have insisted on wiping the slate clean, demanding regime change and constitutional reform.

By illustrating the power of the people, the revolutionaries have marginalized the extremists who ran amok in the region and the world, claiming to speak for all Arabs and Muslims through violence and terrorism. No longer would those who terrorized Arabs, polarized their societies, and gave rulers and foreigners justification to use excessive force be the only Arab face visible on the international stage. The millions that have filled the Arab political and metropolitan landscape have ridiculed and shrunk the megalomania of the few hiding in faraway hills, using the passion of believers to commit some of the worst atrocities.

Forced to choose between despotic regimes and foreign intervention, between oppressive stagnation and the threat of Islamist tyranny, Arabs have chosen an even more radical third option: freedom—freedom of expression, freedom from want, freedom from humiliation. The threat of "either dictatorship or chaos" was exposed and confronted. The Arab revolution has taken on regimes, bypassed the traditional opposition (and then incorporated them once their protests reached critical mass), marginalized extremist movements, and put foreign powers on notice. And, in the process, it has begun to reverse decades of colonial myths and authoritarian thinking.

THE PERILS OF A RUDE AWAKENING

But as time has gone by and the new Arab awakening has swept through complex societies that have been ruled by ruthless dictators who handle their states like private estates, the Egyptian and Tunisian "honeymoons" have given way to difficult and bloody confrontations in Libya, Bahrain, Yemen, and Syria. It soon became clear that the swift beginnings of peaceful transition in Tunisia and Egypt were the exceptions to the rule; in other tribally entrenched, ethnically divided, religiously diverse societies, the state had been marginalized by canny, oppressive regimes and the national military subordinated to better-trained, loyal units under the direct control of leaders—units that were all too ready to use naked and disproportionate force against unarmed and peaceful protestors.

In spite of everything, a new, more courageous, and individualistic Arab seemed to break out of restrictive, patriarchal loyalties. This Arab was ready to make sacrifices for a brighter, less-haunting future. One young Syrian activist wrote on Facebook, "I am going to demonstrate, knowing that I might not come back." Demonstrating became synonymous with sacrifice and even martyrdom, as the protestors reclaimed the word from the jihadis. It became clear that the Arabs' struggle for freedom was by definition national and personal.

Many important events will follow and continue to unfold after I finish writing this essay. But as Zhou Enlai joked when asked by U.S. president Richard Nixon's entourage in 1972 about his opinion of the French revolution, "It is too early to tell."

I doubt it will take us that long to evaluate the Arab revolution, and we might now draw some very basic and general conclusions. The way back is not the way forward, and in a relatively short time, people will have a greater say in the making of their future than ever before. It is the nature of this participation that will, in the end, define the very transformation of the Arab region.

The absence of a unifying political agenda or revolutionary philosophy behind the uprisings beyond general demands for democratic change leaves the door wide open for interpretation of the meaning of the revolutions and their specific goals. Seeking change and attaining freedom is one thing; building democracy and modern nationhood is a different matter.

The harder part of this revolutionary journey will come as the Arabs, sooner rather than later, discover that democracy and freedom come with greater responsibility. Defeating dictatorship is a prerequisite for progress but does not guarantee it, especially in the absence of functional state institutions, democratic traditions, and modern infrastructure. The prevalence of poverty, inequality, and rising regional and international competition present huge challenges.

Transnational cooperation can open the way toward greater unity, economic integration, and the strengthening of pluralism in each and every Arab country. That will require Arabs to revisit and reshape their national identity, adapt religion to modern statehood, and reconcile to a pluralistic, democratic process for regional stability, unity, and good governance.

Be that as it may, the Arab uprising has already reinvented, indeed revolutionized, the region's political reality, thinking, and discourse.

A MELANCHOLIC AUTUMN

On a sunny day in December 2010, my colleagues and I stood outside the Al Jazeera English cafeteria, looking toward the Al Jazeera Arabic building. We were wondering what to do after a particularly depressing week. One frustrated executive whispered that producers couldn't find enough interesting images to adequately capture the gloom of the evening news hour. Television is a 24/7 beast that needs to be fed constantly with image-rich dramas. We could do only so much with leaked documents, as the network had done with WikiLeaks in the late summer of 2010.

Al Jazeera Arabic had gained prominence with its breaking news and live coverage of events in its own backyard—the Arab and Muslim worlds—through a vast network of journalists, as well as through engaging talk shows and controversial debates. Its coverage of the 2000 Palestinian Intifada, the U.S. wars in Iraq and Afghanistan, and the Israeli wars in Lebanon and the Gaza Strip provided, for the first time, a real alternative to Western-dominated satellite media networks. Since Al Jazeera English aims to uphold the same courageous principles that made the Arabic brand so globally celebrated, we felt duty-bound to make our coverage as exciting and insightful as our sister Arabic network.

But the autumn of 2010 had been particularly long and melancholic. A mélange of political chaos, geopolitical paralysis, and economic depression had taken hold of the region. The tension in the air was palpable. The Israeli-Palestinian "peace process" had deadlocked yet again, Iran was full of bombast, the United States menaced the region with its imperial ambition, Iraq was paralyzed, conflict was brewing in Lebanon, the Horn of Africa suffered from insurrection, drought, and civil war, Afghanistan and Pakistan were heating up, Yemen and Sudan, like Somalia, were disintegrating. The region was heading to the abyss with little fanfare.

None of these pent-up tensions interested international media outlets that had long turned their attention away from the war-ravaged Middle East. Even the few U.S. networks left in Iraq were closing or scaling down their bureaus, despite the deterioration of conditions and the continued presence of more than one hundred thousand soldiers and contractors. Instead, the summer was one of overwhelming banalities, such as the controversy over the plan of a rather opportunistic Arab American Feisal Abdul Rauf—a realtor and an imam who had long toured on behalf of the U.S. State Department's public relations division—to build a community center near Ground Zero that would include a swimming pool, auditorium, and sports facilities. It was befitting of the media affair that the imam's wife, Daisy Khan, an interior designer, became the authority to turn to for insight into U.S.-Muslim relations, acting as a spokeswoman for Islam and as the executive director of the American Society for Muslim Advancement, which was founded by her husband.

The fact that the community center wasn't a mosque, wasn't grand, and wasn't going to be built on the 9/11 site, didn't prevent the "sensitive affair" or the "provocative act" from taking over the headlines and "inflaming passions," threatening a religious backlash in the West and East alike. Republican leader Newt Gingrich compared the "mosque" to a Nazi memorial, inflaming emotions and, in the process, covering up for and perhaps justifying U.S. wars in the Islamic world.

And if that wasn't enough of a silly side show, an unknown American pastor, Terry Jones, whose idea of getting attention consisted of burning Qurans in front of TV cameras, became the next big media story to shake already fragile U.S. relations with the Arab and Muslim world. Jones asked people around the world to join him in burning the Quran on September 11, 2010—a demented plea that required the intervention of President Obama, Secretary of State Hillary Clinton, General David Petraeus, NATO chief Anders Fogh Rasmussen, and former Alaska governor Sarah Palin to get Jones to cancel his action. But attention grabbing wasn't limited to eccentric pastors from obscure churches in America's South. As often happens during dark and depressing times, false prophets and populist leaders cashed in on the fear and anger in a variety of ways, making a bad situation untenable.

The strongest example of this has been Osama bin Laden's al-Qaeda and other al-Qaeda branches that have masterfully exploited modern communications to incite violence and carry out sensational terrorist acts and, in the process, grab headlines that misrepresent the reality of the Arab and Muslim worlds. The latest salvo came from the mountains of Yemen where Anwar al-Awlaki, then figurehead of al-Qaeda in the Arabian Peninsula, and a dual U.S. and Yemeni citizen, called in November 2010 for killing Americans "without hesitation." The fact that he spoke American English made his media sideshows compelling viewing for an audience spellbound by threats since the 9/11 attacks. (Al-Awlaki would be silenced in the summer of 2011 by a drone attack, apparently President Obama's weapon of choice in his war against al-Qaeda—an extrajudicial killing of a U.S. citizen without trial, justified on national security grounds.)

Alas, one falling tree makes more noise than a whole growing forest. Away from the media creations such as Abdul Rauf and Terry Jones and media grabbers bin Laden and al-Awlaki, the region was going through some of the darkest moments of its recent history as new powers and international configurations were defining the future of the greater Middle East and North Africa.

In the absence of real alternatives, many have placed bets on dangerous populist leaders (or as the Arabs say, "For lack of horses, they put saddles on dogs"). Bin Laden was only the latest and most surrealistic attempt to overcome the despair and impotence of a lost generation. Iraq's Saddam Hussein and Libya's Muammar Gaddafi had all made similar attempts to champion the cause of Arabs against the backdrop of constant failure. The lack of development, unity, and robust public opinion led to further failures that sowed even more disappointment and bitterness. As the Arab world became hostage to destructive forces from within and without, pent-up tensions were brewing under the gathering of a winter storm.

FORECASTING A HOT WINTER

"This is going to be a hot winter," I wrote in a memo in November 2010, forecasting the political temperature of the coming season. Warning of a possible deterioration in the region, I recommended that special plans be drawn up to strengthen Al Jazeera's presence in various conflict zones.

"The Middle East's falling temperatures will do little to cool off what appears to be a hot winter season. As a number of fragile or deadlocked states heighten tensions toward major crisis, conflict, and possibly terrible violence, it's paramount that we at Al Jazeera reflect and prepare for various scenarios including the worst, war."

The list of countries was long, but they shared similar characteristics: deepening division, frustrated populations, compromised sovereignties, instability, and the threat of violence and inter- and intra-national conflicts. The modern Middle Eastern state had always been in crisis, but at no time in recent memory had the region looked so gloomy, its politics so cynical, official disagreements so stark, tensions so high, and impoverishment so widespread. Despair lingered on every street corner.

In occupied Palestine, bottled-up frustrations two years after Israel's 2008 war in Gaza gave the impression that we were seeing the calm before the storm. Israel carried out aerial bombardments against "suspected targets" in the Gaza Strip killing hundreds, issued threats to Hamas—the democratically elected Islamist movement in control of the besieged strip—and warned that the situation would lead to military action if any rockets launched from the strip fell on Israel. Hamas's relative respect of the ceasefire agreement with Israel made little difference. The closed-off Gaza Strip—one of the world's most densely populated and impoverished areas—had turned into a pressure cooker. In the West Bank, the diplomatic deadlock between the Ramallah-based National Authority of Mahmoud Abbas and the Binyamin Netanyahu government created a dangerous political vacuum in which Palestinians were discredited further as "peace partners," and Israeli settlers were allowed to continue building in the occupied territories. The result dangerously escalated tensions between Palestinian inhabitants and settlers. The Obama administration's inability or unwillingness to put the necessary pressure on Israel to halt its destabilizing colonization of Palestine had further alienated Palestinians and radicalized Israelis. Mind you, no previous U.S. administration had managed or was willing to resolve this perennial problem.

Internal Palestinian papers revealed by Al Jazeera underlined what had been long known of Israel's humiliation of their Palestinian counterparts. The papers exposed the futility of negotiations, with every Palestinian compromise being met with arrogant rejection and the promise of continued Israeli occupation. Unprecedented Palestinian compromises on Jerusalem, borders, and refugees were met with Israeli intransigence and chutzpah. Furthermore, the U.S.'s indifference as sponsor of the talks embarrassed the Arab "peace partners"—Egypt and Jordan—which had been all too willing to provide political cover for the failed negotiations.

Lebanon, in a constant state of political turmoil since its civil war in 1975, was edging toward another major national crisis among its leading ethnic elites. Five years after a U.N.-mandated international investigation into the assassination of Prime Minister Rafik Hariri, the United States and its allies were eager for the Special Tribunal for Lebanon to issue indictments of four Hezbollah fighters. Such a development threatened to further inflame the situation in the divided country and possibly present Israel with a pretext for restoring the strategic deterrence it lost against Hezbollah in the 2006 war.

Hezbollah had confronted and rebuffed the Israeli invasion in a way not seen before in six decades of Israeli-Arab conflict. As a result, the group's popularity and that of its leader rose rapidly in the Arab world. The Arabs, who had lost the June 1967 war against Israel in six days, watched with wonder as a small but well-trained and dedicated group broke the myth of Israeli invincibility. Its leader, Sheikh Hassan Nasrallah, warned that any indictments against Hezbollah fighters, based mainly on telephone records, were part of an Israeli-U.S.-engineered conspiracy against the resistance group. He issued unmasked threats from his secret bunker that raised the stakes for the U.S.-supported government and Lebanon's neighbors.

Sudan, too, was suffering instability and violence as the country approached the January referendum over the secession of the south, which was clearly set on splitting away from the north (and has since become independent). In western Darfur, conflict continued as President Omar al-Bashir, who has ruled since his military coup d'état in 1989, was indicted on genocide charges by the International Criminal Court in The Hague and issued arrest warrants against him. Under the shadows of al-Bashir's dictatorship, and with many outstanding and contentious issues unresolved, Sudan's countdown toward division was saturated with tension.

Yemen fared no better. President Ali Abdullah Saleh's opponents in the south continued to call for secession two decades after Saleh imposed the capital Sana'a's will on the region, following a civil war against the former self-declared "Marxist" rulers in Aden. Meanwhile, a series of confrontations against the Houthis in the north of the country provoked Saudi military intervention in the border region and exposed the fragility of the tribal Yemeni state and the weakness of its sovereignty. This weakness allowed al-Qaeda to establish a foothold in the country, a development that Saleh used to his advantage by parlaying the incursion into U.S. support for his dictatorship. Hiding behind the all-purpose bogeyman provided by al-Qaeda, President Saleh responded to Washington's requests to confront and curtail the group's presumably growing influence in the country by escalating the use of force in various tribal areas alongside U.S. drone attacks on suspected al-Qaeda havens. To make matters worse, widely publicized WikiLeaks revelations exposed the president's complicity with the U.S. bombing of Yemeni territory. Saleh reportedly asked U.S. officials to allow his forces to take responsibility for the aerial attacks to defuse public anger at the carnage wreaked by Americans conducting anti-terrorism activities. The disclosure of the president's lies further embarrassed the regime and infuriated the opposition.

The same went for Iraq. Seven years after its invasion, the torn nation continued to suffer from instability, conflict, and signs of de facto secession by the Kurds in the north of the country. Ethnic and political divisions, dismal economic performance, and a deadlocked parliament, coupled with mounting bomb attacks, an ever-increasing death toll in Baghdad's Sunni areas, and deepening insecurity against the backdrop of conflicting regional pressures, all seemed to pave the way for another showdown. Under the leadership of the increasingly autocratic Nouri al-Maliki, Shia political parties continued to dominate the government and in the process alienated Sunni parties and the Sunni Awakening, or *Sahwa* councils that had switched sides in favor of the U.S. occupation. They began to abandon the new Iraqi military and state security structures, threatening to return to the dark days of sectarian violence. The silent majority that had voiced its opposition to sectarian parties in the local elections was ignored as tensions brewed in the political void.

Frustrated by the escalation, the Iraqi government renewed its warning to Syria, demanding that it stop supporting Iraqi opposition groups. Syrian denials did little to dispel the tensions as Iraq's neighbors continued to show more than brotherly interest in the evolution of its post-occupation political landscape while the United States began to pull out of Iraq.

Similar escalation continued across the Red Sea in Somalia, against the background of increased tensions in the Horn of Africa. The country has long suffered from the secession of Somaliland, the U.S.-supported invasion by Ethiopia, and protracted civil war, to which there is no end in sight. The Islamist Shabab militias made advances against the U.S.-supported coalition government, which was on the verge of breaking down in Mogadishu.

These areas might seem like discrete examples of political instability, but in this region things never happen in isolation.

ROT AND DECAY

The tragedy of the Arab world took a bitter, comic twist with the release of a new batch of WikiLeaks documents, following those released the year before on the subject of the U.S. wars in Iraq and Afghanistan. The so-called Wiki cables exposed political corruption, decadence, and cynicism in the corridors of power throughout much of the Arab world. U.S. reports from various Arab capitals revealed a plethora of politically bankrupt, financially corrupt, and conspiring Arab regimes. Written by U.S. diplomats, the cables were perhaps more political, even anthropological, than historic, decrying inept, indifferent, and contemptuous leaders with lavish lifestyles that the United States "had" to tolerate in order to maintain and expand its economic and strategic interests. The wide dissemination of these cables, which aired the dirty laundry of so many Arab leaders, was further humiliation. I could see from the responses we were getting on air the degree to which the new revelations, shocking but hardly surprising, had completely and utterly undermined the already discredited regimes.

Cables from secretive Tunisia a few weeks before the revolution offered a glimpse into the inner workings of a repressive regime bent on robbing the country of its wealth for the gain of the ruling family and its close business partners. They describe how Tunisia's brutal and corrupt regime, one of the most repressive in a rather oppressive neighborhood, was kept afloat by a network of primordial relations. President Zine Abidine Ben Ali's twenty-nine-year-old son-in-law, Sakher el-Materi, acted as the country's de facto banker. He owned, among other things, a shipping cruise line, concessions for Audi, Volkswagen, Porsche, and Renault, a pharmaceutical manufacturing firm, and real estate companies.

In one cable from July 2009, U.S. Ambassador Robert Godec wrote

> Tunisia has been ruled by the same president for 22 years. He has no successor. And, while President Ben Ali deserves credit for continuing many of the progressive policies of President Bourguiba, he and his regime have lost touch with the Tunisian people. They tolerate no advice or criticism, whether domestic or international. Increasingly, they rely on the police for control and focus on preserving power. . . .
>
> Corruption in the inner circle is growing. Even average Tunisians are now keenly aware of it, and the chorus of complaints is rising. Tunisians intensely dislike, even hate, First Lady Leila Trabelsi and her family. In private, regime opponents mock her; even those close to the government express

dismay at her reported behavior. Meanwhile, anger is growing at Tunisia's high unemployment and regional inequities. As a consequence, the risks to the regime's long-term stability are increasing.[1]

Apparently the writing was on the wall, but nobody bothered to read it. Alas, such corruption and greed were hardly limited to Tunisia.

THE SUCCESSION THAT TRIGGERED A REVOLUTION

In November 2010, Egypt held its first round of parliamentary elections. However, it soon became clear that heated and energetic election campaigns would lead nowhere. The eighty-one-year-old Egyptian president, Hosni Mubarak, had no intention of sharing power after three decades at the helm, at least not until he would install his son Gamal as his successor.

For the majority of Egyptian youth, Mubarak was the only ruler they had known. "Through him everything was done, and without him nothing was done that was done." For three decades, this former air force general refused to appoint a vice president, even though the consitution required him to. And despite an assassination attempt on his life in 1995 in Ethiopia, and his collapse in front of the national assembly in 2003, he kept the position of president empty for his son to fill. Gamal Mubarak, a London-based investment banker during the 1990s, moved back to Egypt and got involved in national politics in 1998, becoming adviser to his father and later deputy head of the National Democratic Party (NDP), responsible for its Policies Committee—a euphemism for the new influential business elite branch in the party. Gamal, like his counterparts among dictators-in-waiting, was seen by the Western establishment as a liberal, modernizing partner. Gamal and his brother are thought to have $340 million worth of deposits in Swiss banks, according to Assem el-Gohari, head of Egypt's Illicit Gains Authority; in contrast, 40 percent of the country's 80 million people live on two dollars or less per day.

The November 2010 elections were the Mubaraks' last chance to secure an absolute majority in parliament, a feat that that would have paved the way for Gamal's succession. Reportedly, no more than 10 to 15 percent of the electorate bothered to vote, despite official claims of a majority turnout. Indeed when voters did turn up at polling stations in opposition strongholds, they found that some of the voting centers had been closed by the NDP's armed thugs. Those who were able to enter polling stations were given ballots with the names of opposition candidates removed. While observers from the opposition were excluded from the counting process, independent election observers reported that envelopes and lists were stuffed and switched. It came as no surprise then that the Muslim Brotherhood, which held 88 out of the 518 seats in the outgoing parliament, did not win a single seat in the first round.

Most of the opposition quit before the second round of voting, giving the NDP free reign. By the end of the rigged process, the ruling party—predictably— had an absolute majority of seats that allowed Mubarak and his cronies to pass any constitutional resolution they deemed necessary. Hailed by the regime as democratic, everyone else thought the elections were little more than a farce. The rigging was so flagrant that Egypt's High Administrative Court couldn't turn a blind eye, and it annulled the first and second round of voting in twenty-four districts, making clear in a statement that the "High Election's Commission's nonimplementation of previous rulings nullifies the results [in these districts], making the composition of the People's Assembly fraught with the suspicion of invalidity."[2]

While Mubarak couldn't have cared less about the judiciary, his government was worried about popular anger at the brazen and humiliating way in which it had confiscated the Egyptian people's right to vote.[3] I could sense that anger from my Egyptian colleagues at Al Jazeera Arabic during our regular chat over coffee at the modest second-floor cafeteria, which overlooks the parking lot but offers a 360-degree view of the Arab world. The atmosphere in this cafeteria is always bristling with the exchanges of those entering and leaving the world's conflict zones. And now, in mid-December, the atmosphere was one of shock. Many argued that there was no point to the futile voting theatrics anywhere in the Arab region, let alone in Egypt. But some were bullish about the future of the Arab world: they won't succumb to this circus lying down; the regime will not get away with it; not this time; Mubarak has gone too far to ensure a succession that most Egyptians just didn't sign on to.

Feeling the threat of growing mass opposition, Egypt's state security services undertook the usual measures to preempt an outbreak of protest, including rounding up political activists under the country's old emergency laws. This wasn't a massive campaign of arrests, as the regime remained confident then that the people were quiescent. The preparations for the anti-government protest could have been hampered by a car bomb that exploded in front of a church in Alexandria on New Year's Eve, killing twenty-one people and triggering a new cycle of sectarian violence in the country. On January 23, 2011, two days before the first major Tahrir Square demonstration was to take place, Habib el-Adly, the interior minister, declared that he had exclusive evidence indicating that an unknown fringe Palestinian Islamist group in the besieged Gaza Strip had carried out the operation. The minister was later jailed on corruption charges for ordering the killing of unarmed demonstrators in the subsequent protests. His security services destroyed and burned much of their archives before the revolutionaries got to them, but some among opposition groups and journalists suspected that the minister of the interior was behind the New Year's Eve explosion that turned public attention away from the election results.

IN THE NEXT PART OF THIS ESSAY, I will look into what went wrong in the Arab world over the last decades. How, as in Egypt and Tunisia, most of the Arab world had come to suffer from unscrupulous ruling families at the helm of repressive regimes supported by private armies. How post-colonial optimism gave way to a cohort of totalitarian leaders of Arab republics who were often more cynical and bloody than their authoritarian monarch couterparts. And, how these *gom-lokiyyahs*, or republic-monarchies, have been as preoccupied with family succession as the monarchies.

Indeed, in this surreal post-republican order, leaders looked beyond two-, three-, or four-term presidencies to life-terms. They sat at the helm for decades, running their countries like family businesses that are passed down from father to son, sharing a ruling philosophy with the likes of Louis XIV of France, who claimed, "*L'État, c'est moi.*" Worse, as I will show, these kleptocracies acted as the agents of Western neoliberalism, robbing Arab nations of their wealth and presiding over terrible impoverishment and deepening disparities.

Despite the regime's attempts to contain simmering discontent, Egyptian youth were clearly determined to take on the regimes that oppressed them. And they were ready for the task. Helped by years of practice in organizing, protesting, and picketing, and inspired by their Tunisian neighbors' success in the bringing down of their dictatorship and the exiling of Ben Ali, they were unafraid and undeterred. They planned their protest for January 25, 2011, with two very specific demands in mind: democracy and social justice. Thousands took hold of Cairo's Tahrir Square and, from then on, in the words of Nobel Peace Prize–winner and former director general of the International Atomic Energy Agency (IAEA) Mohammad el-Baradei to the cheering crowds only three days later, "What we started can never be pushed back."

As I discuss later, Egyptians, like the Tunisians and other Arabs, had reached their limit. They were no longer willing or able to endure political and economic humiliation. So a new generation of Arabs came together to resist ignominy and tyranny. They inspired millions from all social strata, including outlawed labor unions, civil society, and women to join, and in the process and turned their demonstrations into national uprisings. In no time these full-fledged revolts brought down the frail but violent *ancien regimes* as they mutated through the Arab world.

No longer would autocrats be able to silence their people. After decades of oppression, the invisible victims made themselves visible, and the masses made themselves heard. The promise of a better future healed past wounds, fulfilling that long ignored national slogan, "If the people want to live, destiny must respond."

But what explains the contagion? Why did the revolution spread so quickly from Tunisia to Egypt, and then on to Yemen, Libya, Syria, and Bahrain, causing people across the region to fill the main streets and public squares with their calls for social justice and reform? Yemenis first demonstrated in solidarity with Tunisians and Syrians in support of their fellow Arabs in Libya. The first slogan I heard coming out of Syria was "Syrian germs salute Libyan rats." It mocked the official Libyan response and underlined the solidarity among the various upheavals. Paradoxically, Islamist and Western leaders that have made the most noise over the future of the region during the last few decades were caught in the headlights. But their determination to catch up and support the revolutions has complicated the process toward democracy.

To be sure, three transregional factors—nationalism, Islamism, and Western interventionism—have had major influences on the transformation of Arab societies, including the makeup and the undoing of Arab regimes. In the final part of this essay, I will discuss the effects of these three dynamics on the success or failure of the Arab revolution.

O people

I am the first, the fairest

And the finest among the rulers

I am the full moon and the whiteness of jasmine

I am the inventor of the first gallows, and the best
*   divine messenger*

Whenever I think of retiring from power, my conscience
*   holds me back*

Who, I wonder, will govern after me this good people?

Who, after me, will heal the lame, the leper, and the blind . . .

And who will revive the bones of the dead?

Who, I wonder, will take out the moon from his coat?

Who, I wonder, will send the rain to people?

Who, I wonder, will flog them ninety lashes?

Who, I wonder, will crucify them above the trees?

Who, I wonder, will force them to live like cows?

And die like cows?

Whenever I thought of leaving them

My tears overflowed like a cloud

And in God I trusted . . .

And decided to mount the people . . .

From now until the day of resurrection . . .

—NIZAR QABBANI (1923–1998), "THE JOURNAL OF AN ARAB EXECUTIONER," TRANSLATED BY GAELLE RAPHAEL

1 | L'Ancien Régime

What went so wrong? How did the dream of liberation from colonialism turn into a nightmare for Arab states of north and northeast Africa and the Middle East? How did sovereignty designed to keep the West out turn into an alibi for keeping the people down? How did self-declared political leaders become national criminals? Why did they last so long and become so brutal, frequently even more so than their colonial predecessors?

In tracing the ills of the modern Arab world, some pundits have highlighted religion as the main source of its "backwardness," while others have underlined Arab cultural deficiencies that prevented the region from embracing rational policies and democratic principles—a mindset known as cultural exceptionalism, or its latest media term, "the caged Arab mind." But it's not within the scope of this essay to expose these and other fallacies about an intrinsic Arab backwardness, or analyze racist views of Arabs and Islam.

What is important to remember is that the Islamic world counts for some of the world's economically successful and democratic nations, and to recall the great historical periods in Arab civilization, including the period when Arabs documented, translated, and revived interest in the achievements of the classical world, while Europe was mired in the Dark Ages. It's also important to remember that full universal suffrage was adopted by the West as late as the twentieth century, with many other countries implementing it only over the last few decades, and recognize how Arabs have embraced the idea of elections whenever possible, even under military occupation, as in the case of recent Iraqi and Palestinian elections, where citizens voted with little hesitation in the hope that their ballots would count.

It's my contention that the roots of Arab problems are not civilizational, economic, philosophical, or theological *per se,* even if religion, development, and culture have had great influence on the Arab reality. The origins of the miserable Arab reality are political *par excellence.* Like capital to capitalism, or individualism to liberalism, the use and misuse of political power has been the factor that defines the contemporary Arab state. Arab regimes have subjugated or transformed all facets of Arab society.

Since gaining liberation from Western colonialism, the Arab world has been ruled mostly but not entirely by regimes whose practice has been antithetical to any sense of human progress, unity, democracy, and human rights. Those who tried, albeit selectively to chart a better way forward on the basis of national security and national interest, were dissuaded through pressure, boycotted, or defeated on the battlefield. The political backwardness of the larger postcolonial transformation soon became the plague that infected everything else. The guardians of the state who were entrusted with the welfare of their nations monopolized power, controlled the economy, and ignored the civil liberties of the majority in order to privilege the few.

That is why twenty-first-century Arab revolutionaries need to go beyond changing leadership and actually reinvent state structures if they want to transform Arab society.

BORN OUT OF SIN

The birth of the new Arab state began with the arbitrary division of the Arab world, when Western colonial interests began to break up the Ottoman Empire around the beginning of the twentieth century. France and Britain insisted on the formation of weak client states with obedient monarchies, rejecting the demands of the Arab elites for a relationship of equals. When, in the mid-1920s, the leaders of the "greater Syrian revolution" embraced the French Revolution's slogan of "*liberté, égalité, fraternité*" from the late eighteenth century, they were repressed violently.

The desire of English and French leaders was either to prevent outright independence, as in the case of Algeria, or to make Arab nations dependent on them, as in Iraq, Syria, Jordan, and the Arab peninsula. U.S. president Woodrow Wilson's fourteen-point doctrine for national self-determination was noticed in the Arab world but wasn't taken seriously by U.S. allies.

European powers systematically undermined efforts to evolve parliamentary democracies in favor of propping up autocratic systems helmed by influential elites who supported their military presence against the popular will. This held true, first, in Iraq and Syria, then in Lebanon, Jordan, and Yemen, and finally in Egypt and Algeria. In the process, colonial powers cracked down on mass uprisings in Egypt in 1919, Iraq in 1920, and in Syria in 1925. It was not a coincidence that the question of a homeland for the Jewish people in Palestine gained real traction only after the British Empire's Balfour Declaration of 1917, further frustrating Arab national sentiments and the aspiration for independence. From then on and until the establishment of Israel in 1948, Zionists used the British to help them settle in Palestine.

According to historian Rashid Khalidi in *Resurrecting Empire*

By the time they had disappeared from the Arab world, with the sole exception of Lebanon, these deeply flawed parliamentary democracies had become largely discredited. This was in part because of their manipulation by entrenched elites, endemic corruption, and a widespread failure to address deep domestic problems, but also because of their inability to end a foreign occupation and resist Western powers' intervention in these states' domestic affairs. The systems were therefore understandably little mourned by most of their peoples. Thus foreign intervention, which was designed primarily to defend Western military presence and maintain substantive control over these Middle Eastern countries, repeatedly sabotaged fragile democratic or proto-democratic governments in the Arab world that were unable to achieve full-fledged national independence. Their ramshackle parliamentary systems were overthrown one by one and replaced by nationalist, military-dominated, one-party regimes, the descendant successors of which still blight many Arab countries.[1]

Colonial European interference went so deep as to influence the making of modern Arab states and politics in the first half of the twentieth century and beyond. French and British powers might have disagreed on many issues, but they harbored similar hostility to the modern Arab metropolis, considering it the epicenter of radicalism. They encouraged Arab minorities and those on the periphery of Arab society to step up their involvement in the modern Arab state—its politics, institutions, and military—in order to neutralize the civic majority.[2] It takes a certain kind of chutzpah to speak of an "Arab exceptionalism" or aversion to democracy, condemn the Arabs for falling behind, and lecture them on the rights and wrongs of international relations, considering the fact that Western intervention in the Arab region has blocked democratic change and left a trail of bitterness, hostility, and division that continues to influence the national political culture and temperament to this day.

It took much for the Arabs to gain independence from the colonial powers. The last French colonialists were dislodged from Algeria in 1962 in a bloody conflict that claimed hundreds of thousands of lives. This history isn't so easily forgotten; it is featured in the history curriculum of Arab schools and emphasizes the resistance to European and Israeli colonialism. This history is also a main component of visual arts, poetry, and folklore, and it is all too often revisited in television documentaries and soap operas. The most popular drama series that was broadcast in 2010, the year the revolution broke out in Tunisia, told the story of a Syrian village's resistance to French occupation. It featured charismatic and courageous Syrians, as well as collaborators and heartless French soldiers. It had obvious allegorical resonance. Tens of millions of Arabs identified with the characters and the plot as if it were a recent occurrence. I would venture to guess that this message resonated with the inhabitants of Dera'a, the southern Syrian town that first rose against Assad and rejected humiliation at any cost, including death.

During the early post-colonial period, Western powers maintained pressure on the newly independent states in order to ensure their subservience well beyond the Second World War, beginning with Iran in which the English and Americans conspired to bring down the democratically elected Mossadeq government in 1953, and then against Egypt in 1956, when the British, French, and Israeli invaded after Gamal Abdel Nasser nationalized the Suez canal. But France and Britain began to show signs of weakness when the United States forced them to withdraw their forces from occupied Egyptian territories and, for all practical purpose, took on their imperial responsibilities and privileges in the region. In the 1950s, the Eisenhower administration concentrated its efforts on the Baghdad Pact, which included Britain, Turkey, Pakistan, Iran, and Iraq, as a bulwark against Arab nationalists like Nasser. In 1958 Eisenhower sent thousands of U.S. troops into Lebanon to back Christian president Camille Chamoun against a Muslim rebellion sympathetic to Nasser.

The continued Western humiliation and exploitation of dependent Arab monarchies throughout the Cold War led to the destabilization of the young Arab states, where popular opposition was brewing. The monarchies grew heavily dependent on their military to crack down on upheavals and various opposition groups such as the Druze in Syria and Shias in Iraq. As a result, the military grew in influence and prestige, allowing leaders to usurp power, a pattern exemplified by the Pan–Arab Nasserites in Egypt in 1952, the Ba'ath in Syria and Iraq in 1958, and the National Liberation Front (FLN) in Algeria after 1962.

An anecdotal joke about these agonizing years tells of an old and bitter Syrian who wondered how long independence was going to last. As long as the Ottoman or French occupation? Indeed, internal repression has proved no less violent or humiliating than foreign aggression. It has worked by imposing military rule through emergency laws with the vindictiveness of an enemy.

OFFICERS TAKE OFFICE

The populist military officers who took power in the 1950s and '60s began their reign by nationalizing major state assets and distributing land to the poor peasants. These leaders espoused modern secular, socialist, and nationalist agendas and preached patriotism, dignity, and justice. But they had a penchant for conspiracy, were often enamored with the Soviet model of statehood, and, as most were in their mid-twenties and thirties, tended to be naïve and inexperienced with regard to politics. Conversely some were dangerously ambitious.

Most of the leading army officers eliminated their fellow "revolutionaries" and began to rule with an iron fist. Many of these purges were later justified as necessary due to the state of emergency caused by wars against Israel and its Western allies. In the process, militaries were supersized, reaching four or five times the ratio of soldiers per capita compared to other nations.[3] Exceptionally high military spending began to drain between one-third and one-half of government budgets. Despite their continued humiliation and paralysis on the world stage, the Arab regimes didn't succumb or admit failure; instead they deployed populist rhetoric to win popular support and legitimacy and reinforced domestic control through greater investment in security. For example, while the Yemeni army numbered around 64,000 at the turn of the twenty-first century, its central state security forces numbered more than 70,000. It is no surprise then that when generals look at political challenges, they see military problems. Even the Palestinian leadership came under the control of its fighting factions after 1968—notably the Yasser Arafat–led Fatah, which tried to establish a military presence, even after being defeated by the Jordanians in 1970.

The Arab ruling officers were ruthless and regularly conspired against one another, assassinating and imprisoning their rivals. Military coup d'états peaked at several per annum during the 1950s and '60s. By the end of that rocky and bloody period, those associated with sectarian loyalty or dependent on tribal allegiances won the day. From the Alawites that controlled the Syrian military, and the Sunnis that were dominant in Iraq, to Lebanon where the Maronites took control of the military (and even ruled between 1958 and 1964) onto Iraq, Libya, Algeria, and Yemen's ethnic, tribal, and clan-based rulers, sectarianism became a central animating force in the Arab world.

In the new postcolonial Arab state the military was expected to fulfill three important functions. First, it served as a melting pot for all segments of society—religious, tribal, and ethnic—using national conscription to create a national identity with loyalty first and foremost to the state. Second, it was to provide a high-tech environment that would function as a modernizing force in society. And, finally, it was to defend the nation against foreign invasion. In other words, it was expected to be a defining, grooming, and protective backbone of the new Arab state.

Alas, reality bore no resemblance to expectation. Instead the military has perpetuated sectarianism, division, and backwardness. Because of Arab disunity and the struggle for power among ruling parties, Israel continued to win on the war front, not because of its special powers or divine intervention, but rather because of the impotence of Arab militaries. When the Arab militaries did get their act together, as in October 1973, it was able to mount a preemptive war and eventually began to recover occupied territory. The mere fact they kept its war strategy secret was seen as an achievement.

During those same formative decades of the 1950s and '60s, a similar militarization process took place in Israel based on the same assumptions that the military is a melting pot to harmonize, "Zionize," and whip into shape new, soft immigrants that fit a martial Israeli identity. From 1950 to 1980 this process was under the aegis of the Ashkenazi Labor Party, but in recent decades, rightwing coalitions became more representative and domineering in the society as a whole. And the same militarization process was also dominant in Turkey. But unlike others, Israel democratized its political process and went on to win on the battlefield against Arab military regimes that were incapable of defending their nations, let alone ruling them.

THE TANK AND
THE OLIVE TREE

The new Arab autocrats imposed their primordial, archaic, tribal, or Bedouin mentality and culture on modern state institutions. This ruralization of the state authority or "Taryeef As-Sulta" was first introduced by the colonialists to weaken cosmopolitan elites who sought a relationship based on parity with Europe. In the following decades, ruralization of civic and political life took on a life of its own.

As with many other parts of the developing world, demographic explosion coupled with poverty and bad governance led to serious population displacement through migration from rural areas to the cities as citizens began an arduous search for work. Most major Arab cities saw a five- to tenfold population increase from the first to the fourth quarter of the twentieth century, tipping the balance in a number of countries in favor of urban areas. This concentration of the population made it easier for the militaristic regimes to exert control over people. However, this social transformation also led to ruralization of certain aspects of urban life.

Unrecorded, uncounted, and unaccustomed to urban life, the subaltern settled chaotically within and on the immediate periphery of towns and cities, changing the human and architectural landscape. In many Third World cities, random construction created slums without adequate infrastructure. Their inhabitants comprised a new reservoir of cheap labor that took whatever was available, from street vending to crime, while bitterly awaiting divine intervention. Their lack of integration into city life preserved their village and tribal habits, mentality, and loyalties and ensured their acceptance of the chaotic ways of governance. Indeed many joined the local party branch or the security services and in no time made it to the top of the government or military echelon. But they never succeeded in assimilating into modern city life. Instead, they brought their customs to bear on the Arab metropolis, creating tensions between old elites and the newcomers. That the city elites weren't completely innocent is extraneous here.

The new social mosaic strengthened the Arab regime's staying power as it drew heavily on the periphery of society for fresh recruits based on blood relations and tribal loyalties. Overriding national and military loyalties, these neophytes were allowed to form their own clusters within the army and eventually paved the way for takeover of civilian governments and ruling political parties through coercion and coup d'états.

To maintain a grip on power, the regimes depended on the same bonds and mindsets that brought them to power in the first place, putting tribal, rural, or Bedouin mentality and relations at the heart of government, security, and state. When making policy, loyalty took precedence over merit, emotions over rationality, approximation over precision, blood relations over citizenship, loyalty to tribe over patriotism, belief in the leader over belief in the government, appreciation of charisma over professionalism, rhetoric over documentation, clan over individualism, and so on. The regime relied on tribal coalitions and divisions rather than coalitions of political parties to expand the base of authority. Within a few years these so-called outsiders had deformed local government and national institutions, distorted political and parliamentary systems, and dominated the security organizations.

This was no way to govern a modern state. But most Arab republics lacked republicans, let alone democrats. They espoused modern ideas, but in reality they were primordial in power. And the results were surreal at best; indeed as time went by, the political and security managers of the state had totally undermined the very principles of socialism, nationalism, and republicanism they had long boasted about. This was particularly evident when leaders treated their republics as if they were private estates.

It's perhaps important to mention that traditional opposition parties have suffered from similar ruralization or ideological paternalism. Their leaders maintained control at all cost, at times paving the way for succession of sons or siblings. It has been the norm to have opposition dinosaurs serving even longer at the helm of their political parties than the dictators themselves.

TOTALITARIAN AND AUTHORITARIAN (YOU SAY TOMATO, I SAY TOMAHTO)

By the beginning of the twenty-first century, Arab autocracies represented some of the oldest dictatorships in the world. Zine el-Abidine Ben Ali's dictatorship in Tunisia, the most recently established in the region, ruled for twenty-five years, followed by thirty years for Egypt's Muhammad Hosni Sayyid Mubarak, thirty-three years for Yemen's Ali Abdullah Saleh, forty-three years for Libya's Muammar Gaddafi, and forty-three years for Syria's Bashar al-Assad dynasty. Saddam Hussein was removed in 2003 after twenty-four bloody years ruling Iraq. Only the Arab authoritarian monarchies precede these dictatorships in longevity. Bahrain, a repressive Sunni monarchy, has ruled over a Shia majority since its independence from Britain in 1971.

Arab regimes have differed in the degree of control and violence they have exercised—from relatively open authoritarian regimes to terribly closed totalitarian autocrats. The former allowed for limited diversity, semi-political organization, and tempered freedom of expression, but didn't allow for change of governments or power-sharing through free and fair elections. So, for example, Egypt allowed parties to compete in parliamentary elections but set strict criteria for the eligibility of candidates and voters, ensuring that the results favored the ruling party whose leader remained president through phony referenda. And in the monarchies of Morocco, Jordan, Kuwait, and Bahrain, parliamentary elections were held, paving the way for certain degrees of representation in parliament, and, at times, an elected government. Alas, these parliaments were curtailed or summarily dismissed by royal decree. The fact that some of these authoritarian regimes didn't try to define, micromanage, or determine every aspect of their societies made them more tolerable for the average citizen.

Despite Mubarak's and Ben Ali's authoritarian regimes and their hold on their countries' institutions and military, state and society were kept relatively separate from the regime, just as loyalties to regime and state were kept separate. In comparison to their Arab peers, Egypt and Tunisia have had strong middle and working classes, durable national institutions, and a cohesive modern identity within a long-established nation-state backed by thousands of years of collectively shared history. Tunisia has one of the highest rates of literacy in the Arab world and has had a modern constitution since 1861, two decades before the French colonized it. Gender equality was established in the mid-1950s, long before other Arab and European women enjoyed the same rights and privileges.

Egypt, with five thousand years of civilization along the Nile, is even more steeped in history. The nation sits on strong institutions that were developed during the nineteenth century, after

Mohammad Ali took over in 1805 and began to modernize the country and its main metropolis. It's this cohesiveness, strong national identity, and culture that have been missing from the other Arab states swept by the Arab revolt.

More totalitarian Arab regimes, on the other hand, have aimed to erase features of plurality and diversity in order to establish a uniform political society based on the ruling ideology. Exercising direct censorship over the media, they monopolized political thought and all aspects of civil and political society. In Syria and Iraq, the Ba'ath party monopolized government, the economy, and the armed forces, and enshrined its singular control of government in the constitution, not allowing for alternation of power.

The totalitarian regimes couldn't be distinguished from their militaries and, to a large degree, the national institutions. Little space was left between the naked force of the clan-based regime and the defenseless citizens, as various protective state agents and mediators—whether legal, civic, or welfare-related—were scrapped, definanced or simply ignored.

The lines between state and regime were blurred, as were the buffers between regime and family, security, military, civic, and religious institutions. The neutrality and independence of national institutions, such as judiciary and parliament, were totally compromised. States were, for a lack of better words, turned into the private estates of the ruling families. While these regimes boasted of secular republicanism, they were run similar to the Wahhabite kingdom of Saudi Arabia and the United Arab Emirates, where no political activism was allowed and where the ruling families dominated all facets of political life.

Totalitarian regimes justified their total monopoly of power on the basis of holistic ideologies and bombastic visions, deceptive or unrealistic as they might be. The Syrian constitution's Article 8 makes it clear that only the Ba'ath party can govern the country. In Libya, the leader of the republic who referred to himself as the "king of kings," dismantled all political parties and instated his rather ludicrous *The Green Book* as the country's de facto constitution or bill of rights. The more ostentatious the cult of personality, the more secretive the mechanization of its security services became.

It's as if the greater-than-life statues of esteemed leaders and regime symbols were meant to replace the people who were ejected from the public space altogether. Similarly, the welfare state was removed from communities at large.

These are the factors at play in countries like Syria (and, until recently, Libya), where falling leaders threaten to take their countries down with them, unlike the authoritarian regimes in Tunisia and Egypt, which seemed to crumble with the downfall of their leaders. For decades, totalitarian rulers exploited all resources and facets of their nations to consolidate power and authority, rendering their regime indistinguishable from the state. For them, the fall of the regime could mean no less than the end of the state.

The totalitarian Arab republics have deteriorated into Mafiosi-type rule. Their motto: (brother) leader first, country second, and people third, or as they said in Libya, "Allah, Moa'mar, Libya." In one of the most disgusting scenes, which occurred in mid-2011, Syrian security thugs tied a middle-aged man's hands behind his back, slapped him, and demanded he repeat after them, "There is no god but Bashar!"

Arab regimes depended mainly on force for their survival. The names and responsibilities of their security organizations under the direct control of the inner circle of the regime varied from one country to another, but the principle remained the same: servicing and defending the regime at any cost. And from the way these security services responded in Libya, Yemen, and

Syria, they also risked plunging their respective country into civil war. The first priority of internal security, state security, security services, intelligence services or their military counterparts, the Republican Guards, Presidential Guards, and special units—not so dissimilar from Royal Guards in Saudi Arabia—was to prevent a coup against the regime.

Preventing a coup is achieved by placing these special units on top of all national military services, police, and other state institutions—all of which explains why, since the 1989 takeover by Sudan's al-Bashir, no regime change has taken place in the Arab world. Before the 1980s, though, the Arab world witnessed many coup d'états. Of course, in the monarchies, such as those in Bahrain and Saudi Arabia, royal family members were in control of the military.

For decades, Arab autocrats cited foreign and international threats to justify their resistance to reform; that included the constant state of war in the region, involving notably Israel, Iran, and the United States, especially in the post–Cold War period. Domestically, Arab leaders justified their tight grip over state power on the basis of defense against Islamic fundamentalism and ethnic secession and conflict. But as these leaders grew more confident and arrogant, they no longer bothered to explain why they continued to rule people "until death sets them apart." Indeed, the Arab world knows no former Arab leaders, only dead ones.

This was best articulated by an army officer in the southern Yemeni city of Taiz, where Republican Guards attacked protestors in Horriyah (Liberty) Square using water cannons, bulldozers, and live ammunition, killing at least twenty of peaceful Yemenis in the process. In response to the protestors' slogan "the people want to bring down the regime," the officer brazenly wrote on a wall: "The regime wants to bring down the people."

Controlling Religion

While mosque and state were separated along the lines of a modern, European-style project in the "republics," the dictators imposed repressive secularism from above. They kept religion out of (their) state affairs, but brought their regime to bear on religion in all its forms. In that way, the Tunisian regime, for example, intimidated the deeply religious or religious fundamentalists and discouraged any appearance of religiosity in the public sphere. Some of the regime nudged people to eat during the fasting month of Ramadan and forbade women from wearing headscarves in public places. Their coercive methods weren't any different from the despotic Ayatollah-led or Wahhabi regimes in Iran and Saudi Arabia, respectively, that coerce people into specifically conservative ways of practicing religion.

Gaddafi went further to enforce *The Green Book* as the *modus operandi* for Libya. It was taught in schools as a modern philosophical substitute for democracy and socialism, and implemented through the popular committees that covered up the regime's totalitarianism. He also traveled abroad to promote his philosophy as a way forward for the world, spreading a belief system that was, for lack of a better word, bullshit.[4]

In countries where religious freedoms are guaranteed by a constitution, the regimes tried to control religion by tightening its grip on the main religious institutions and by banning religious political activism, such as that of the Muslim Brotherhood. Regimes have maintained close control and surveillance of official religious authorities, imposing edicts from their palaces on the grand muftis—the official state interpreters of Islamic law. Whether they wanted to wage war, make peace, or lift subsidies, dictators made sure that the muftis and their official religious institutions acquiesced. Instead of ensuring separation between state and mosque, the regimes hijacked both to fit their policies and preserve power.

Like racist Western Islamophobes, Arab dictators believed there was no such thing as a temperate or good Islamist. In fact, they believed moderate Islamists posed greater danger to their rule than extremist and violent jihadists. While the latter posed a security threat, the more popular Muslim Brotherhood posed political challenges to their rule, especially when they raised socio-economic grievances that the general public could identify with. But the regimes exploited the security threat posed by the jihadists in order to repress all political Islamists and tame their philosophical or ideological stance.

In countries with substantial religious and ethnic minorities, the regimes resorted to classical divisive propaganda to instill fear of the Islamists' agenda. To make matters worse, the Muslim Brotherhood and notably the Salafi groups did little to calm the fears of those sectors of the society worried about the consequences of a Sharia'a controlled state. Indeed, regimes also succeeded in dividing political opposition groups by playing on the sensibilities of the liberal and leftists fear of the Islamists' agenda, even though all have fallen victims to the same dictatorial policies. Sadly this seemed to work in many occasions as various secular groups turned a blind eye to crackdowns on Islamists, as was the case in Tunisia, Morocco, and Algeria. And the Islamists, in turn, ignored the regimes' crackdown on leftists and nationalists, as was the case in Egypt, Yemen, and Sudan.

Locking Intellectuals

The distinction between authoritarian and totalitarian regimes was accentuated and altered during the Cold War. Washington favored what it called "moderate" authoritarian regimes and supported them militarily, while Moscow rooted for what it called "progressive" totalitarian systems that found support and inspiration in the Soviet Union's model of dominant one-party rule. With one or two exceptions, the East-West polarization led the republics to lean toward Moscow, while the monarchies leaned toward the United States. Saudi Arabia has since been considered a moderate and friendly monarchy despite its repressive totalitarian and theocratic rule.

The perks from these relationships were plentiful for the Arab dictators. Aside from arms and strategic and economic support, their security apparatuses were equipped and trained in the most venal techniques of repression. It helped them turn their nations into big prisons, figuratively and literally. They incarcerated an entire people for their political views in uglier ways than their colonial predecessors. The number of Egypt's political prisoners jumped tenfold between 1981 and 2003, reaching more than eighteen thousand, according to the Egyptian Organization of Human Rights (EOHR). In some countries there were no verifiable estimates of the number of prisoners, and some, such as Libya, categorically denied the existence of any political prisoners (perhaps because Gaddafi killed them all). As if Israel holding eleven thousand Palestinian political prisoners was not enough, Fatah and Hamas have also started doing the same.

And no segment of the society has been as jailed, abused, and bruised as intellectual activists, writers, artists, and political and community organizers—the people who influence public opinion. Needless to say, if the role of an intellectual is to probe power, it's not the role of a leader to jail intellectuals. But in his review, "Torture, Imprisonment, and Political Assassination in the Arab Novel," Egyptian writer and academic Sabry Hafez argued, "Arabic literature is perhaps one of very few literary traditions that have a distinct literary genre known as the 'prison novel.' This is not only because a great majority of writers have themselves lived the experience of arrest, imprisonment, and even torture, but also because the history of the contemporary Arab intellectual is one of constant struggle with the authorities." Indeed there are countless novels about the prison and the experience of prisoners who tend to suffer along with countless other people among their family, friends and loved ones.[5]

Moreover, in addition to habitual violations of civil liberties, Arab regimes took it upon themselves—under the guise of the "war on terror"—to expand their abuses of the peaceful opposition. Worse, under the secret U.S. rendition program, Arab regimes did Washington's dirty work as "torturers for hire." According to former CIA agent Robert Baer, "If you want a serious interrogation, you send a prisoner to Jordan. If you want them to be tortured, you send them to Syria. If you want someone to disappear—never to see them again—you send them to Egypt."[6] Whether that's an accurate description or an exaggeration is beside the point; Arab prisons are infamous for their excessive injustices, torture, and other human rights violations. Not only have the number of political prisoners increased in certain countries, but so did the inhumane methods used to coerce and humiliate prisoners of conscience to deter them from speaking their minds.

The case of Abdul Kareem Belhaj is instructive. When the dust began to settle in the Libyan desert in the summer of 2011, the CIA realized that one of those leading the fight against Gaddafi was a young man whom they had helped arrest and sent to be tortured for a year in Thailand. He was captured, then shipped off to Libya, courtesy of the CIA and the British MI6 rendition program, where he was imprisoned and tortured for seven years. Now that Gaddafi is gone, it's the likes of Belhaj that Washington will need to coordinate with.

Arbitrary arrest, torture, and violations have been used all too often to deter the people from trespassing into the public sphere. The idea is to keep them as isolated as possible, to make them prisoners of their own fears. Dictators don't like to share the public space with their subjects, and they try their best to banish ordinary citizens from the political landscape, which they want to remain a sovereign space for their families to exploit.

Subsidizing Despotism

The energy-producing Arab nations have sustained rentier-type economies, characterized by a trade-off between economic welfare and political representation. Whereas the modern democratic state was founded on the cry of "No taxation without representation," a statement that demanded true participatory democracy in exchange for the government helping itself to a share of the public's wealth, the modern Arab state has turned that notion on its head. With free-flowing petrodollars pouring into their countries, Arab leaders have been able to sell off national resources and enrich themselves without having to turn to their citizens for personal taxation. Without the pressure of taxation trickling up to elites, these governments—whether they were monarchies or secular dictatorships—have demanded total fealty from their citizens. The resulting dependency between the people and regimes, and between the regimes and the industrial world, notably the West, relieved the rich from developing social economies or pursuing industrial development. They were also freed from the need to expand the civic role of the state, relying instead on their abundant natural resources, which they have sold in return for consumerist and military imports. It became a ritual in the wealthy monarchies, for the kings, emirs, or princes to provide small sums of money to their "subjects," and the poor in particular, as a *makrama* or "generous gift"—money that was generated from the natural resources of their land.

Even those countries without oil wealth have followed this model, as wealthier Arab states have purchased the support of these poorer allies to gain leverage or in exchange for military support. The Persian Gulf countries, for example, gave Egypt, Iraq, and Syria financial support.

However, the fall of oil prices in the 1980s and '90s diminished state welfare and paved the way toward a shift from public sector–based economies to privatized economies through liberalization of investment and trade, especially in the less resource-rich states. The process, which coincided with the end of the Cold War and the victory of liberal capitalism over communism, accelerated the unplanned privatization and liberalization of the Arab economies, leading to greater gaps between rich and poor and to economic and social instability.

The lack of accountability and transparency with regard to government economic policy meant that much of the windfall from selling state assets and liberalizing trade went to the ruling families, their friends, and associates who were centered, in many cases, around the "heirs to the throne." These heirs apparent, who had no ideological or moral pretenses, were trigger-happy when it came to doing the West's economic and strategic bidding.

This became evident in everyday life. According to the United Nation's Development Programme's (UNDP) first *Arab Human Development Report*, written exclusively by Arab experts, "Arab countries have not developed as quickly as comparable nations in other regions. Indeed, more than half of Arab women are illiterate; the region's infant mortality rate is twice as high as in Latin America and the Caribbean. Over the past twenty years, income growth per capita has also been extremely low."[7]

DEVELOPING UNDERDEVELOPMENT

As more job seekers moved from the neglected, marginalized, and impoverished countryside into population centers, new belts of poverty were created around most metropolitan areas, and these soon developed into hotbeds of crime and fanaticism. Those who stayed behind in peripheral areas suffered away from the limelight, and their protestations went unheard and unreported. Until, that is, protestors in Tunisia's Sidi Bouzid clashed violently with police and publicized their resistance online for the whole world to see. Such was also the case in Syria's Dera'a, and Yemen's Taiz, where protestors demonstrated against shortsighted and wrong-headed economic policies adopted by the ruling families who basically presided over an accelerated development of underdevelopment.

Unlike the traditional poor, who depended on the land and immediate family and clan for their basic subsistence, the newly displaced and impoverished had little or no support system in the absence of land, family, and state welfare programs. The disparities between the center and its immediate periphery, the affluent and the marginalized, the nouveau riche and the destitute only deepened toward the end of the twentieth century and early in the twenty-first century, leading to bitterness and pent-up tensions.

Slowly but surely, new barriers were erected to keep the poor out of sight of the decadent rich, which deformed the human landscape, physically and culturally. And to placate the angry poor, preventive security measures were augmented throughout the populated areas, with authorities at times using the guise of combating terrorism to take exceptional measures against the poor.

Gated communities, which were unheard of only a few years earlier, became the preferred paradise of the new rich, who bought sea resort homes and erected high walls around the privileged housing that sprung up everywhere. In Egypt, coastal resorts such as Ghardaga Villa City contrasted sharply with the "cemetery city" in the middle of Cairo, where more than a million homeless lived on top of the dead. The same type of absurd progress was duplicated in other Arab countries, at times in the most vulgar of ways as tribal leaders, warlords, and mass murderers reveled in their ill-gotten luxuries.

The UNDP's Arab Human Development Project concluded that the causes of underdevelopment in the Arab world are political suppression, economic corruption, discrimination, gender politics, instability, and war. Even among the rich, Arab countries have produced more waste, fraud, and underdevelopment than they have attracted investment, modernization, and stability. Libya is a good example of a republic small in population and rich in oil that, nonetheless, suffered from high rates of unemployment—reaching a third among the young—all the while lacking decent hospitals.

As their debt-laden economies deteriorated in the late 1980s, most Arab countries interested in foreign loans and investments had to take new austerity measures and "reform" their economies in line with Western diktats. This can be compared to the Latin America of past decades when dictatorships, income disparities, and poor development led to drug wars—Arabs have turned to religion, with similar results.

THE NEW NOBILITY

Arab ruling families have been the leading force and focal point of a new and corrupt elite, which has vested interests in the survival of the regime. Made up of rich bureaucrats and generals, they are "partners" in the business community along with their relatives, friends, and clans. Their control and management of the state's two main facets of power—national resources and security—enabled them to shape the business community according to a system of patronage that encouraged nepotism and alienated the traditional bourgeoisie that tended to be far more productive, competitive, and responsible—three indispensable features of a successful economy that the ruling elites lacked.

As ruling families monopolized activity in the major economic fields of energy, communication, transportation, and security, they blocked free competition and abused laws, deepened stagnation, and in the process created lots of waste. Indeed economic corruption and waste of resources have cost these countries a substantial percentage of their gross national product (GNP)—far exceeding their expenditure on education and health care. It was incumbent upon the younger generation of Arab autocrats to build bridges with the nouveaux rich to create a loyal and influential power base for them within the regime. Indeed, Gamal Mubarak—the younger of the two sons of ousted Egyptian president Hosni Mubarak—brought the new Egyptian nobility to the party leadership through the so-called Higher Policies Council, the platform for the new rich inside the party that used its influence to pass laws and regulations in its favor. Similarly, Saif al-Islam Gaddafi—the second son of former Libyan leader Muammar Gaddafi—became the face of Libya's new economic liberalism, serving as the intermediary between multinational corporations and the corrupt business community at home.

The following are examples of family members who stood at the major nerve centers of these regimes:

In Yemen, Ali Abdullah Saleh's family gave him a strong power base that he spent years consolidating.

Saleh's son, Ahmed, heads the army's special forces, the country's Republican Guard, and an elite commando unit. When the uprising swept through Yemen, the forty-two-year-old operated from the presidential palace and his father's main office in a military compound in the capital of Sana'a, relegating Vice President Abed Rabbo Mansour Hadi to work from his home or office in the defense ministry.

Saleh's half brother is head of the air force, and several other brothers hold key positions in the military and intelligence services as well.

Saleh's nephews also command major security posts: Tareq Mohammad Saleh is head of the Presidential Guard and head of Saleh's personal bodyguards; Yahia Mohammad Saleh is head of the central security services, the counterterrorism unit, and the riot police; and Amar Mohammad Saleh is deputy director for national security.

Collectively, Saleh's family commands tens of thousands of troops, many of them the best-trained and equipped in Yemen.

In Libya, the ruling family was so powerful and so in control of the country's resources that to speak of the rule of Popular Committees is no more than a bad joke.

Gaddafi's second son, Saif al-Islam, positioned himself as a "champion of reform," which meant opening up to the West. He headed the Gaddafi International Charity and Development Foundation through which he projected his influence and normalized relations with Western powers and businesses.

Gaddafi's fifth son, Mu'tassim, followed in his father's footsteps into the army and was appointed head of the country's National Security Council. WikiLeaks cables claimed that

Mu'tassim had demanded $1.2 billion from the chairman of Libya's national oil corporation in 2009 to establish his own militia.

Gaddafi's eldest son, Muhammad, the only child of Gaddafi's first wife Fathia Khaled, headed the country's Telecommunication Committee and the Libyan Olympic Committee.

Gaddafi's third son, Al-Saadi, served as an officer in a special forces unit, headed a military battalion, and reportedly played a role in crushing the early protests in Benghazi. The WikiLeaks cables claimed that Al-Saadi, who has a turbulent past, has used military forces under his control to intimidate business rivals. He was the head of the Libyan National Football Association, in addition to owning a share of the Libyan Al Ahli Football Club, as well as the Italian Serie A giants Juventus.

Gaddafi's fourth son, Hannibal, was a major player in Libya's maritime shipping industry, which was responsible for shipping Libyan oil abroad. Known for his long history of unstable behavior, he was arrested in Switzerland for his mistreatment of two servants at a Geneva hotel, leading to the disruption of diplomatic relations between Switzerland and Libya.

Gaddafi's sixth son, Khamis, was commander of a special forces unit—known as the 32nd Brigade—which, according to the one of the WikiLeaks cables, "effectively serves as a regime protection unit." This unit was reportedly involved in suppressing unrest in Benghazi.

Gaddafi's only daughter, Aisha, used nongovernmental organizations—especially the United Nations, where she was a goodwill ambassador— to advance her interests and held the rank of lieutenant general in the Libyan army.

Gaddafi's brother-in-law, Abdullah Sannusi, was the head of military intelligence.

In Syria, President Bashar al-Assad, who took over from his father in 2000, has since been surrounded by military and intelligence figures, composed of members of the family, clan, or the Alawite community. Together they control the country with an iron fist.

Bashar's brother, Maher al-Assad, is Syria's second most powerful man. He heads the Republican Guard, the elite force that protects the regime from the army and domestic threats and that is the only force permitted to enter Damascus. He also commands the fourth armored division.

Assef Shawkat, Bashar's brother-in-law, was appointed in 2010 as head of military intelligence and deputy chief-of-staff of the armed forces.

Rami Makhlouf, a first cousin of Bashar's, was the family's banker and hence the most powerful economic figure in Syria. He was the popular subject of persistent accusations of corruption and cronyism.

Col. Hafez Makhlouf, Bashar's cousin, has headed the Damascus branch of the General Security Directorate, the overarching civilian intelligence service in Syria.

Mohammed Nasif Kheirbek, a relative, is the deputy vice president for security affairs.

General Dhu al-Himma Shalish, the head of Presidential Security, is Bashar's cousin.

Manaf Tlas, a Republican Guard commander and son of the former long-serving defense minister Mustafa Tlas, is said to be one of the president's closest friends. He's been a member of the ruling Ba'ath Party's Central Committee since 2000, and along with his brother, Firas, has strong connections to Syrian businesses.

Autocrats-in-Waiting

As their grip on power reached new and unprecedented heights, leaders of Arab republics across the region focused less on the utility of their leadership and more on the continuity of their legacy. Syria took the lead, which was most evident in the regime's violent crackdown on the Islamist uprising in the city of Hama in the 1982, when the military under the command of the president's younger brother, Rifa'at al-Assad, dispatched tanks to the city to put down "the Islamist rebellion." Everything in sight was destroyed. Images of the ruined city played on national television as a salutary lesson for all to watch. Similar images were broadcast on national television in July 2011—three decades later—after more than two hundred tanks entered the city, this time under the command of President Bashar Assad's younger brother, Maher. However, this time around, people from all walks of life—secular and Islamist, leftists and liberals of all ages—rose in defiance. Even a friend of the Syrian regime, Turkish Prime Minister Recep Tayyip Erdogan, condemned the regime's killing machine, as international outcry built up against the mass murder.

Bashar al-Assad's succession in 1999 was the first in an Arab republic. After his designated older brother, Bassel, died in a car accident, Bashar, an ophthalmologist by training, was the most unlikely candidate to succeed his father at the helm of a country at war. And yet, he was speedily promoted through the echelons of the military establishment, becoming a tank battalion commander in 1994, then lieutenant colonel in 1997, before being promoted to colonel in January 1999. In the process, ground was laid for quick constitutional amendments to bypass the age requirement and secure a place for the inexperienced Bashar at the helm of the "revolutionary republic." Hardly a revolutionary act, this was the first succession in a so-called progressive republic led by a "modern" Ba'ath party for whom, according to the constitution, half of the seats in parliament are allocated.

The absurdity of the succession process did little to tone down the republican, socialist rhetoric of the ruling Ba'ath party that by then had all but turned into the propaganda tool of the regime. In an effort to calm the fears of the business community, as well as the remnants of the country's civil society and opposition groups, the regime promised to renew efforts at liberalizing the country's policies and economy once Bashar was confirmed. The "Damascus Spring" at the beginning of the new millennium was seen as an opening, a way toward national dialogue about reform and a new, more democratic direction for the country. Most of it centered on ending the state of emergency and the Ba'ath party monopoly enshrined in the constitution, which made possible its uninterrupted rule since 1963. All of this opened the door for political plurality, new party laws, and free and fair parliamentary and presidential elections.

But, in the end, this new agenda proved to be no more than a charade. As soon as Assad junior strengthened his regime, he torpedoed all hopes by declaring that no serious change to the political system was desirable or permissible for the sake of "national unity." However, limited economic liberalization did get underway in 2005, allowing the regime's new lieutenants to strengthen their grip on the economy. This generation of Syrian autocrats was referred to as "the Tunisian trend," in reference to Tunisia's own Western-imposed privatization and trade liberalization that brought in foreign investment while maintaining a police state.

When Bashar al-Assad tried to explain the delays in political reform he promised more than a decade before the revolutions swept the Arab world, he justified it on security grounds, naming 9/11, the 2003 invasion of Iraq, the Lebanese debacle, and Israel's 2006 and 2008 war on Lebanon and Gaza, respectively. It seems there's never a good time to reform. The incongruity of the Ba'ath theatrics was exposed during Bashar's speech, following the outbreak of the popular Syrian uprising of 2011 when a fawning Syrian parliamentarian told the chuckling Assad, amid the cheering of his colleagues, "Bashar, you should be, not only the leader of Syria, but the leader of the whole world."

Similar dynastic politics were underway in Libya as Gaddafi's sons ran the day-to-day economic and security affairs in the "peoples' republic," with Saif al-Islam the designated successor to his father. In Tunisia, Ben Ali entrusted much of the "family business" to his and his wife's family, especially their twenty-nine-year-old son-in-law, Sakher el-Materi, whom he groomed as a possible successor. In Yemen, Ali Abdullah Saleh invested heavily in his tribe, Hashed, and especially in his sons, Ahmad and Khalid, and his brothers to run the country. The most outrageous of these nepotistic ventures was Mubarak's attempts to crown his son as his successor despite the public's bitter opposition in a republic with a modern state tradition. For years, the Mubarak's family oversaw Gamal's rise in the party and in parliament, feeling he was the promising figure that could succeed his father.

WORST OF BOTH WORLDS

The excesses and eccentricities of one generation of ruling family were reproduced in the next. But a division of labor soon emerged between members of the ruling families: the elders managed the conservative, authoritarian, and centralized state politics and security. In essence, they controlled all facets of the state. The juniors spearheaded decentralization, privatization, and liberalization of their countries' economies and societies. Little wonder that the younger generation led by Gamal Mubarak, Saif al-Islam, Sakher el-Materi, Ahmed Saleh, Rami Makhlouf, and the crown prince in Bahrain were feted in the West and received with open arms as the promised reformers. They were not military types like their fathers; they were educated, Western-influenced. Perhaps their English wasn't perfect, but they said "Cool," "Awesome," and "You Guys," so the West was comfortable with them.

With the growth of globalization through financial markets and open border policies, these and other largely unqualified junior dictators became power brokers, or power mediators, between the three pillars of influence: the regimes' old guard, the "business whales" or the new oligarchs who devoured everything they had access to, and Western governments and multinationals with interests in the region's emerging markets.

Many of the Western-leaning, affluent class and their entourage became the enthusiastic advocates of Washington consensus–style policies. In essence, the American establishment suggested a dozen or so principles to developing countries that they promised would stave off economic stagnation and decline but, in reality, opened the countries' markets and economies to international conglomerates. This allowed both the young oligarchs and Western companies to reap lucrative benefits.

The heirs apparent of these Arab countries advocated deregulation, liberalization of trade and interest rates, and redirected state expenditures toward short-term projects with high-financial yields. They ignored fiscal discipline, tax reform, or securing copyrights—all of which led to greater economic disparity and bankrupt states. This explains why the national indicators might show 3 to 7 percent annual growth in some of the non-oil-producing countries, such as

Tunisia and Egypt. This was not only due to favorable international investments, but also at times somewhat creative accounting done with the assistance of Western accounting firms.

Much of the money went into the pockets of the newly rich and powerful and their bankers and patrons overseas. These states were receiving favorable credit evaluations from the International Monetary Fund (IMF) and other institutions, which fed the myth of an economic miracle in some Arab countries. These faulty valuations masked the anguish felt by the majority, an anguish caused by rising prices and the rising cost of essentials such as water and electricity. The end result was a mix of nepotism, corruption, waste, stagnation, major disparities in wealth and influence, rising unemployment, and an atmosphere of repression, fear, and intimidation.

At a terrible disadvantage, the Arab leaders had little choice but to step down or acquiesce to a triumphant West, which was able to blackmail and impose its ultimatum: join us or be condemned to the margins of the international system that's managed by Western institutions such as the IMF, the World Bank, the World Trade Organization, and the G-7 countries. It is not a surprise that Arab states figure at the bottom half of the list of countries evaluated by Transparency International.

The Arab world's established oligarchs acted under or, more likely, above the radar of the national judiciary as they formed new shadow elites that escaped accountability by the state or the public. These elites secured favorable investment and trade conditions for multinationals and became informal mediators for the Coca-Colas, BMWs, and McDonalds—big businesses that monopolized important facets of the new financial services and communication industry, securing military contracts through fraud, and giving away oil concessions. In Egypt, they went as far as to gamble with the savings and retirement plans of state employees.

These parvenus, promoted as the "liberal" elite, were liberal only in their interpretation of the law and the public interest. Liberalism for them was a mode of governance and living that entailed decadence. Seen as immoral and exhibitionist playboys by the common men or women living in a world poisoned by their profligacy, they were referred to in the West as secular, modern, and, worse, flamboyant. Indeed, they superseded their counterparts among the royal families in terms of excesses, when all the while their subjects suffered from unprecedented impoverishment and insecurity. Their habits extended from traveling on private jets, buying expensive real estate and yachts, throwing wild parties, and treating aides like slaves, in the process generating disgust and bitterness among the better-informed populace. Gaddafi's sons, for example, were reportedly notorious for wasting their country's oil wealth on investing in their favorite Italian football team Juventus. They also flew private jets to New Zealand on New Year's Eve to be the first to celebrate the New Year, and paid American pop singers hundreds of thousands of dollars to sing at their decadent, far-off island parties.

DIVIDE, CRUSH, AND SUBJUGATE

Repression left people with little or no protection and hardly any credible or capable party to rally around for security or true change. Even national armies were either tamed by despots or bribed into silence. The concentration of power in the hands of ruling families and their cronies blurred the lines between authoritarian and totalitarian regimes. These dictatorships used their special forces and security services to crush, subjugate, or domesticate the pillars of their nations' societies, including religious, military, judiciary, business elites, labor unions, civil society syndicates, or the political parties, including the ruling parties. By 2008, the Ba'ath party presumably emulating the 1970 "Corrective Movement"—the name for the faction fight within the Ba'ath Party that saw Hafez al-Assad and his military faction assume power—had turned the Ba'ath into the "amen party" of the Assad clan, just as the ruling Egyptian National Party became a rubber-stamp instrument of Mubarak and company.

The regimes domesticated, alienated, or divided entire ethnicities, tribes, and sects, turning them against one another. If the regimes could claim any success, it would be taming public opinion through fear, patronage, and propaganda, destroying the vitality of their societies, and undermining their economies.

Organizations with substantial followings such as the Muslim Brotherhood, which tried hard to join the political process, were either outlawed or deterred by severe repression. Likewise, the political parties that pursued any compromise in order to share power were shunned, banned, or forced to be the regime's junior allies. And attempts to object by the judiciary or middle-class professional organizations were either largely ignored or marginalized. People's alienation from the civic and political life of the state was exploited by the regimes to drive a deeper wedge among various identities, keeping them preoccupied by divisions, for example, Sunni versus Shia, Christian versus Muslim, Kurd versus Arab, and Berber versus Arab.

In the absence of modern elites to bridge the gap between regime and citizen, people looked to their clans, tribes, and ethnicities for refuge and identity, dealing a greater blow to civic and national identity within the Arab states. Most were able to escape in the new consumerist culture sustained by economic liberalization and encouraged by the regimes' cronies. This included an abundance of entertainment, ranging from hundreds of satellite channels to cheap made-in-China goods, and culminated in the sort of fancy new shopping malls built in such places as Dubai, which would be envied and copied throughout the Arab world. And yet, many more Arabs gave up on worldly answers or salvation and instead found sanctuary in the mosque in the hope of a divine intervention.

By the time the regimes finished off much of the organized leftist, liberal, and pan-Arab oppositions, the only ones left standing were the violent fundamentalist groups. The polarization between military rule and extremist Islamists dealt another terrible blow to civic and political life in the Arab world, with reckless generals and sheikhs having the last word.

PEDDLERS

As Arab regimes have failed miserably to build successful, modern, and democratic post-colonial states, they've also failed to establish a united and useful pan-Arab block. They peddled "country first" slogans in order to justify their regional failures and subservience to Western patrons; they peddled Arab nationalism in order to extract support from the bitter majority; and then they used conflict and war in order to justify emergency laws. So for example, the Syrian regime justified its police state by its nationalist stance and state of war with Israel, while the Egyptian regime justified turning its back on the Palestinians and the Iraqis by presumably putting "country first."

Worse than this, though, were the ways in which the regimes peddled pan-Arab solidarity and national cohesiveness in public but undermined each in practice. The Syrian regime's insistence on a "special relationship" with Lebanon meant dominating it, as a part of greater Syria, while at the same time denying its own Kurdish citizens—hundreds of thousands of them—citizenship in their own country. Likewise, the Iraqi regime justified the invasion and occupation of Kuwait in 1991 as a way of making it the country's eighteenth province, leading to terrible consequences for both countries for the region that has continued to suffer from Saddam's wars.

Blueprints on common defense and plans for a common market have been gathering dust on the Arab League shelves. These autocracies have clearly benefited from their divisive strategies domestically, and from the continuous state of war or siege that provided them the excuses to monopolize power. What began in the period following the Second World War as an attempt by patriotic and nationalist leaders to break away from Western domination and Israeli aggression, has turned into an attempt to preserve power at any cost, justifying repression on national security considerations. What could have been and, in some cases, started as cooperation and coordination—even unity in the case of Egypt and Syria in 1958–1961—turned into zero-sum relationships that undermined one another.

The leaders of the Ba'ath movement peddled secular nationalism to justify their rule of Syria and Iraq, but tensions and competition between the regimes killed whatever hope was left for cooperation and unity. For decades, Hafez Assad and Saddam Hussein bypassed their ruling parties' hierarchies, using their cadres as nothing more than cheering bureaucracies for their despotic rule. Their ruling families eventually gained precedence over party leadership as siblings took over the privileged Republican Guards.

Nasserism, for example, might have been the most pragmatic, most rational anti-colonial movement in the region's modern history, but it was inefficient, undemocratic, and paternalistic and therefore incapable of prosperity at home and across Arabia. What began as a promising revolution in Egypt in 1952 turned undemocratic when the popular army officers maintained their rule over the country through a mélange of populist, nationalist, and pseudo-socialist rhetoric. Gamal Abdel Nasser did attempt to tackle issues of social justice, such as the redistribution of land and privatization, but in the process he paved the way for greater state control as his efforts formed a bureaucratic bourgeoisie that presided over economic stagnation. Nasser's paternalist nationalism met the same fate as party and state bureaucrats, who were charged with promoting pan-Arabism through slogans and clichés rather than truly strengthening the ties among Egyptians and the rest of the Arab world. His successors fared no better. They gave up the pan-Arab dream and Egypt's strategic independence in favor of U.S. support. Despite $2 billion in annual aid, Egypt continued to suffer from chronic stagnation and backwardness.

Similar failures characterized the evolution of the Arab West. In the Maghreb—the North African Arab countries of Morocco, Libya, and Tunisia—parliaments tried to unite in the 1950s but were met with skepticism, and efforts at North African unity eventually died with the change of regimes. Eventually subregional Arab councils were created in the Maghreb, including in Morocco, Mauritania, Algeria, Tunisia, and Libya, but failed to chart a new way forward because of political and territorial disputes, notably between Morocco and Algeria over the Sahara Desert, but mostly for lack of will and vision.

Less of a failure was the attempt by Saudi Arabia to establish the Gulf Regional Council following the Islamic revolution in Iran in order to coordinate economic policy. Thanks to oil revenues, the council was maintained, but it remained limited because of its members' political differences and narrow interests. Attempts at subregional Arab configuration could have been a stepping-stone toward greater Arab unity. But, instead, its limitations and failures created a greater setback for solidarity, cooperation, and integration.

The end result should have come as no surprise to anyone: those who began their post-colonial journey as a powerful voice in the developing world and the non-aligned movement no longer counted. Collectively, Arabs were relegated to the sidelines of the world system—mere observers of history passing them by. They watched with envy as Western Europeans united and Eastern Europeans were liberated from totalitarianism and integrated into a larger European Union. All the while, Arab leaders continued with their silly bickering. They also watched with jealousy as Latin America got rid of its dictators and certain African nations began to democratize.

PEDDLERS CLUB

To be an Arab meant belonging to a collective that had no strategic weight and made no scientific, artistic, or cultural contribution to world civilization. A collective organized in an official league, the League of Arab States, established after the Second World War to coordinate Arab policies, hardly counted when it came to important regional issues. They were kept out of negotiations with Iran over its nuclear program, despite their proximity, and they were coerced to sign the Nuclear Non-Proliferation Treaty despite Israel's nuclear arsenal.

The culmination of Arab failure was most evident in the performance of the Arab League. It failed to deliver on any of its major principles and objectives. In fact, its members, dictators, and monarchs made a mockery out of potential Arab unity by peddling "common defense," a "charter for human rights," and "common market" initiatives without any intention of seeing them through. As their agreements collected dust on the shelves of the Arab League, their summits unraveled either as boring, sighing sessions with leaders dozing off as others spoke aimlessly and endlessly, or as tragicomedies with shouting matches, conspiracies, improvised speeches, walkouts, curses, and insults. Absent from meetings was the voice of the common Arab citizen or any consideration for his or her wellbeing.

Incapable of facing up to the dangers engulfing their region since the end of the Cold War and especially since 9/11, devoid of unity of purpose, lacking leverage or independent initiative, the only things Arab states agreed on was lowering people's expectations and limiting their objectives to the bare minimum. The Arab League occasionally rubber-stamped American initiatives, especially those concerned with reviving the moribund "peace process." In the case of the war on terror, the leaders agreed to security coordination to combat terrorism, without paying much attention to the root causes of extremism—as that would have meant dealing with their own failures. Usually the interior ministers of the league spent more time coordinating repression and border security than they did trying to improve the civil rights of citizens. Mostly they came out empty handed. Once President Mubarak answered with dismay at a perfectly normal question about the results of a summit meeting, "Why do you expect something will come out when we meet?!" Indeed, you shouldn't.

DICTATORSHIP FATIGUE

Once the Arab dictators destroyed the state from within, they were left with stagnation, polarization, and bitterness coupled with underdevelopment and impoverishment. As they grew older and failed to provide the people with minimum sustenance and basic political rights, their "I am the state" rule began to run out of steam. Eventually a weaker nation meant less important and less influential leadership.

But the fatigue wasn't just political; it was also personal. After ruling for so many decades, these dinosaurs grew impatient, insolent, and exhausted. Their dyed hair and dark sunglasses didn't help much. They mostly looked senile or so sick they could hardly rule. Others grew so undeniably cynical and so indifferent, they lost touch with the people.

Their attempts to crown their juniors were met with vehement rejection from the people who no longer could stand more of the same. Having spent decades monopolizing the sovereign and political pillars of the state, hardly anyone else would be able to replace them, certainly not those who lacked the experience and the charisma to lead, unless they turned their republics into absolute monarchies.

Eventually, the expired regimes not only lost all credibility and legitimacy as state managers, but also the capacity to deter people from reclaiming their citizenship, humanity, and dignity. As soon as people rose in defiance, the fearsome leaders began trying to justify themselves, underlining their "sacrifices" to the nation, emphasizing their willingness to reform, and denying any desire to extend their rule. But fear had switched sides. Long haunted by the fear of domineering and sadistic paternalism of those who continuously molested their nations, a brave young generation, undaunted by their leaders' violence, showed themselves to be a force to be feared and reckoned with.

2 | The Miracle Generation

THE MAKING OF ARAB YOUTH

The modern history of the Arabs has four clear-cut phases: liberation from colonial rule and the building of a post-colonial state that ushered in optimism and hope through to the mid-1960s; state economic failure and military defeat, notably against Israel, from the 1960s to the '80s; the resulting humiliation and isolation that paved the way for two decades of degeneration, division, and widening economic disparity from the rest of the world; and then, as the darkest hour approached, a new generation came forward to reverse the drift toward stagnation and desperation.

Political repression and economic deprivation left a deep scar on this generation. In virtually every Arab country, more than half of the population is under thirty years of age—that's 140 million people—while a quarter are between the ages of fifteen and twenty-nine, making this generation the largest youth cohort in the history of the Middle East. This underemployed and increasingly angry demographic has given traction to the "youth bulge" theory, which posits that when population growth outstrips that of jobs, social unrest is inevitable. There are, however, a number of other strategic, political, and social factors that have also come into play.

Unemployment was extremely high in 2010—nearing close to 25 percent in many countries in the region and reaching 45 percent in some, such as Algeria and Iraq. Most of the unemployed were young. For example, four out of every five unemployed Egyptians are under thirty, and 95 percent of them have at least a secondary school degree. The same goes for Jordan and Syria, where the unemployment rate for people under thirty is four times higher than that for those over thirty.

For a long time, the centralized Arab state, or in some cases as I discussed earlier, the *rentier* state, was the largest employer, whether through centralized state capitalism—often wrongly referred to as socialism—or through state-provided services such as health care, education, and security. However, the hasty and ill-advised liberalization and privatization of state enterprises, coupled with increased global competition from the world's emerging economies, forced states to reduce employment opportunities faster than the private sector could create new jobs. Indeed, a substantial part of state hiring reflected nepotism or "masked unemployment." All of which begs the question: If Arab states have struggled to create an adequate number of jobs thus far, how will they be able to deal with the bulging youth population that's about to enter the job market—a demographic shift that will create a need for 51 million jobs by 2020, according to the UNDP?

The more university degrees young Arabs hold, the less likely they will find employment in the absence of robust state investment in skill-based industries. In Tunisia, for example, unemployment has risen sharply among the highly educated—it was 10.9 percent in 1994 and reached 18.4 percent between the years of 2001 and 2007. As a result, many young, educated Arabs have become very concerned about the rising cost of living, affordable housing, and the lack of job opportunities.

Unemployment and repression began to alter the structure of Arab family life, as a whole generation could not afford to marry or have children. With previous generations, 63 percent were married by the time they reached their mid-twenties; by 2010 only 50 percent of those under twenty-nine were married, and more couldn't live independently because of rising housing costs.

As a result of these demographic and societal changes, youth is no longer a fleeting phase between troubled childhood and forced adulthood—a period shortened by a rather conservative and traditional society suspicious of its "wild" aspirations, individual ambitions, and revolutionary ideas. It has now become an extended generational stage that presents both new opportunities and a different set of challenges and responsibilities to young people and the society at large. This generation, because of shrinking distances, faster communication, and permanent connectivity, has added weight, influence, and voice to this tech-savvy youth. The dynamics of what had long been a speedy transition from one's teenage years to marriage had changed in Arab society.

No longer nudged to the next safe chapter of their lives, the young Arabs had begun to take risks and make themselves visible in public spaces—not through suicide bombings, but rather through the affirmation of life, dignity, and liberty through their protests. The presence of cameras, social media, and satellite television only helped them become a force to be reckoned with.

The youth have grown disenchanted with the ruling establishment. In one poll, 99 percent of those questioned said that democracy was very or somewhat important to them. "Surveys showed that Arab public opinion was no different from those of other societies in its definition of democracy and citizenship, providing answers comparable to responses in the United States and Japan," said Fares Braizat, the head of the Public Opinion Program at the Arab Center for Research and Policy Studies, commenting on these polls. "Surveys conducted before the Arab uprisings revealed that participation in governance and demands of oversight and combating corruption got top priority amongst Arabs, with some variations in regions witnessing an increase in sectarian tensions."

BATTLE FOR THE BULGE

Arab patriarchy and Western paternalism have long assumed that a "naïve" and "easily manipulated" Arab youth poses a potential threat to security and order.

Muslim clerics saw this supposedly vulnerable group as being threatened by premarital sex, drugs, HIV, and vulgar pop culture delivered by the West. Radical Islamist leaders visualized them as the best possible recruits for their causes. Pentagon strategists also believed that the unemployed youth were "easy recruits to radicalism" or a "natural source of instability and violence" as was argued by former U.S. secretary of defense Donald Rumsfeld. Likewise, Arab autocrats have also feared that their frustrated young citizens are a source of instability and disorder, who must therefore be contained.

The liberal Western establishment has argued that the increasingly interconnected and globalized youth are promising interlocutors for the West in the Middle East and should therefore be cultivated. It reckons they are free of colonial baggage and more prone to "universalist ideals" as propagated and promoted by the United States and its allies. And since the Internet is the centerpiece of globalization, Arab youth, it was assumed, are natural byproducts of a cyber environment.

Predictably, the battle for the young hearts and minds of the region heated up over the last couple of decades—with dictators, Islamists, and imperialists each trying to soft-sell themselves. In a 2005 special issue on the youth, the Middle East Research and Information Project (MERIP) delineated new fault lines imposed on the youth by the regimes, and the rest of the society through a number of studies that were prescient and are worth revisiting.

Grooming
Loyal Subjects

The latest Arab dictators haven't exactly been "philosopher-kings." In the absence of a moral compass, their appetite for control has been their guiding force. Since dictatorships and the public interest haven't really synced, the dictatorships have had to resort to desperate propaganda and deception to cover up the repression and lack of strategic vision that characterize their regimes.

They have deployed a number of strategies to strengthen their patronage and authority over the youth by establishing military conscription or other forms of national service, while expanding indoctrination programs and rewriting school textbooks in the name of national unity. They have also targeted universities where students have historically played an important role in most of the social and political upheavals of the twentieth century, using repressive measures and propaganda to prevent dissent.

For example, the Egyptian student union elections, which were conducted at the same time as the national elections in 2010, were also rigged by the education ministry. The ministry banned or disqualified Islamist and leftist candidates in favor of

National Democratic Party–affiliated (NDP) students—allowing them to win easily. With three million students in private and public universities, the Egyptian government was more than keen to pacify any activity against the regime through a system of patronage that offered enticements, educational placements, and promises of jobs.[1]

The regimes also took special interest in the youth's favorite pastime: sport. This task was delegated to younger members of the ruling families, with potential successors, siblings, and associates leading the initiatives. New ministries for youth and sport were established and placed under the control of the dictators-in-waiting. In Iraq, Saddam Hussein's sons Qusai and Odai presided over their country's youth institutions, Olympic committee, and national soccer team, while in Libya, Saadi Gaddafi was touted as a soccer star, playing for Udinese, Sampdoria, and Perugia. (Saadi, while on the rosters of these teams, only ever got the most limited playing opportunities. He became more of a team mascot who enjoyed fraternizing with the players and showering them with gifts.) In Syria, Hafez al-Assad's son Bassel was groomed as a symbol of the country's youth before he died in a car racing accident; in Egypt, Mubarak's sons Gamal and Ala'a were designated youth leaders. The official strategy was twofold: establish new, softer layers of patronage and loyalties among the youth, while dissuading them from politics and directing them toward soccer and other sports.

When Egypt faced Algeria in a 2009 playoff game to secure qualification for the 2010 World Cup, the state television channel made Gamal and Ala'a Mubarak the face of national soccer by constantly zooming in on their booth. Although Egypt lost, it did not prevent the brothers from exploiting an opportunity to promote themselves. They went on to direct the nation's anger against Algeria, accusing Algerians of misbehavior and harassment, while they defended Egypt's "lost honor." That this rhetoric was deployed during an election season was highly convenient for the regime.

Recruiting Passionate Souls

The Muslim Brotherhood was among the first to establish student affiliates in universities in Egypt, Tunisia, Algeria, Jordan, Kuwait, Morocco, and elsewhere, particularly after these countries became independent. Young Arabs from across the region who studied in Egyptian universities and Islamic educational and religious centers went back to their countries inspired by the thinking of the Brotherhood. Likewise, Egyptian scholars close to the Brotherhood or other Salafist groups participated in "Arabization" and general education programs in the Arab world, notably in North Africa, where they spread the new thinking among the youth.

The heavy-handed crackdown on the Brotherhood in the 1950s, after which its charismatic leader Sayid Qutb was executed and others were jailed, bought the regime some time. But soon Qutb was turned into the symbol of a new, more extreme Islamist movement that emerged during the 1970s. With the advent of President Anwar al-Sadat in 1970, the regime turned a blind eye to the rise of the Islamists in the hope of further weakening the nationalist and leftist opposition, who were popular in the universities and society at large, and who opposed his overture to Israel and alliance with the United States. Al-Sadat pursued his nationalist and leftist opposition with the same vengeance that his predecessor, Gamal Abdel Nasser, had toward the Islamists following their failed attempt on his life. However, al-Sadat was not so lucky.

Young, impatient Egyptian Islamists who gave up on the Brotherhood's traditionally passive approach to dealing with the regime went on to found "Islamic Groups" whose *raison d'être* was the use of violence in the defense of Islam. They targeted female and minority students for assault, and carried out attacks throughout the country. They also took on the political elites, and al-Sadat topped their list. He was assassinated when a sleeper cell broke away from an annual military parade as it approached the presidential stand and opened fire. Hosni Mubarak, who was sitting close to al-Sadat escaped death, but the assassination cost Egypt dearly.

The new Mubarak regime that took over, like those of its counterparts in Algeria, Syria, Iraq, Tunisia, Libya, Saudi Arabia, and other Arab states, accelerated the crackdown on Islamist groups during the 1980s and '90s, whether they were violent or not. With many of their leaders and foot soldiers imprisoned, the radical movements began to recruit aggressively among the more educated, daring, and passionate youth.

The Islamists took refuge in the health and cultural clubs of Islamic educational institutions and in the mosques where they were more likely to find new recruits. Satellite networks specializing in Islamic education and Quranic studies mushroomed alongside Web sites and chat groups that sought to recruit the young to their ranks.

While the Salafists avoided politics from the 1980s until about 2010, occupying themselves instead with social and religious issues, they have since emerged as an extreme political force, with the support of Saudi Arabia—a force that is proving to be more fundamentalist and destabilizing than the Brotherhood. The Salafists, who centered their mission around the implementation of Shari'a as they believed it was at the time of the Prophet, were conveniently (for the United States and Saudi Arabia) vehemently anti-Shia, anti-Iran, anti-nationalist, and anti-communist.

Indeed, the first cross-regional recruitment of youth for an "Islamic cause" was the result of Saudi-U.S. intelligence coordination against the Soviets in Afghanistan in the early 1980s. They created the Arab Afghans who went on to establish al-Qaeda soon after the Soviets were defeated, and after that they fought more wars in Bosnia, Chechnya, and Iraq. But most of them returned to their own Arab countries in the late 1980s and joined local Salafist groups. The result was the growth of social conservatism and political extremism across the region, from Algeria to Yemen, which led to greater instability and violence prior to September 11, 2011.

Preaching the American Dream

As Washington's intelligence services and armed forces responded to the 9/11 attacks by "taking the war to the enemy" in the form of military intervention, occupation, assassinations, torture, proxy, and all-out wars, U.S. government agencies in tandem with multinationals, especially those in the communication and entertainment industry, tried to win Arab hearts and minds through "soft power." The strategy emphasized entertainment, consumerism, and Western-style freedoms as an antidote to extremism.

The Bush administration financed and guided the establishment of Radio Sawa for Arab pop music and news, *Hi Magazine*, and even an Arabic television channel. Apart from these propaganda outfits, the United States also financed various youth initiatives and nongovernmental organizations (NGOs) working with the young.

And more quietly, the United States promoted the hedonistic Dubai-model of liberalization, consumerism, and entertainment as the way forward for the Arab world. Dubai was also a hub for

Western companies and satellite networks dedicated to entertainment, including offshoots of TV networks specializing in showbiz news and sports. This was meant to balance or defuse the proliferating Islamic media outlets that were making inroads among the young.

The United States also expanded its educational exchanges with the Arab world through scholarship programs and the establishment of branches of American universities in the region with special emphasis on liberal arts. The proliferation of English (and French) at the expense of Arabic as the principal language in private and some public schools has reached new levels over the past decade.

THE CLASS OF 2011

Courage

The tragic deaths of two young men, Mohamed Bouazizi of Sidi Bouzid and Khaled Said of Alexandria, became the rallying cry for the Tunisian and Egyptian revolutions. While the two never met, millions of people united in their memory, denounced their deaths, and held those responsible accountable—whether they were the thuggish "law enforcers" or national leaders who had stripped the people of all hope and dignity.

The self-immolation of Bouazizi was the endpoint of decades of political and economic repression that have inhibited and impoverished people in the Arab world, deepened fear and despair, curtailed innovation, and blocked progress.

As for Said, on June 6, 2010, he happened to be in an Internet café on Boubaset Street in the Sidi Gaber neighborhood of Alexandria, doing what many of his generation do nowadays: connecting. Two plain-clothed policemen approached him and

then twisted his hands behind his back as they asked for his identification. When the twenty-eight-year-old Egyptian inquired as
to the reason they needed identification, they held him down,
smacked his head across the marble wall, and began kicking and
beating him. When Said started bleeding, they took him outside
to a nearby alley and continued to hit his head across an iron
staircase, kicking more furiously as he screamed, "I am going to
die." When, finally, he stopped moving and shouting, they continued the beating, accusing Said of pretending to be dead. Finally
realizing that he was, in fact, dead, they called their superior, and
according to an eyewitness, told him, "(Basha) master, we have a
situation here." An ambulance arrived to take the clearly bruised
body away. Photographs of Said's battered and deformed face that
were later posted on the Internet show a fractured skull, dislo-
cated jaw, broken nose, and numerous other signs of trauma. Predictably, the police said he had died after swallowing a bag of
marijuana, even though nine witnesses came forward to describe
the terrible beating. His mother said he had been uploading
videos to the Internet, implicating policemen in drug pushing.
The case of Said is one of absolute political repression—an internal military occupation justified on the grounds of national security needs, managed mostly through emergency laws, and
justified by foreign threats.[2]

Contempt

What then are we to learn from Said's killing? First, that the public
and fatal beating of an unarmed citizen is unacceptable in today's
world. Second, if you must act illegally and inhumanely, it is best
not to do it at an Internet café in front of young bloggers, as word
is bound to get out in a big way. Third, the arrogance of power
breeds stupidity, and vice versa.

Like their counterparts in most Arab countries, the brutal Egyptian internal security services reckoned they would get away with this killing as they did with countless others. The value of an Egyptian or an Arab life was of no value for those at the helm, nor was justice.

The indifference of the Egyptian regime to human life mirrored its dictator, Mubarak: a president who had no charisma, no ideas, no ambition, no passions, and absolutely nothing to be remembered for. He lived in the shadows of his predecessors: Nasser, a popular president whom the cameras loved; and al-Sadat, who loved the limelight, but was extremely unpopular. Mubarak reportedly became vice president because Sadat (and his wife, Jihan) reckoned that, as a military man, he was so colorless and bland that he would never pose a threat. Sadat's assassination in 1981 brought Mubarak to the fore, and for the next thirty years he would leave behind no accomplishment beyond cutting ribbons. As he grew old, Mubarak became increasingly indifferent to the plight of his people as their rights eroded and was apathetic to the eclipse of his country's status in the region. When more than a thousand Egyptians died in a 2006 ferry disaster, Mubarak and his family showed no sensitivity. But when Mubarak's grandson Mohammad died, the nation was expected to mourn the president's loss.

As the careless Egyptian regime and its enforcers stagnated, a new generation of Arabs had emerged, rooted in a long and courageous struggle. Scared by a new socio-political reality, and transformed by the information revolution, they turned their peaceful and, at times, virtual protests into something like people power. Like Said before him, Bouazizi's humiliation and death generated a national outcry after it was transmitted by activists and Arab satellite television throughout Tunisia and the rest of the Arab world.

The reaction against these actions opened up a space for spontaneous, heartfelt protest, which demolished President Ben Ali's twenty-four-year-old dictatorship and produced a domino effect across the Arab world.

The Tunisian regime's myopic responses and vacuous promises in the days after Bouazizi set himself on fire further inflamed passions. Ben Ali told Bouazizi's family he would secure medical treatment for their son but didn't deliver. Instead, he treated protestors gathered in Sidi Bouzid, 200 km southwest of the capital Tunis, with tear gas and arrests. And when repressive measures failed to deter more and bigger demonstrations, Ben Ali made a speech promising to spend billions of dinars for development and the creation of new jobs while vowing to crackdown on the protesters. Increasingly, the protests turned political, demanding the removal of Ben Ali, who had been elected for the fifth time with a purported 89 percent of the vote. People no longer believed the president, nor his claim that he would one day vacate the presidency.

Ben Ali, a security man who came to power amid socioeconomic tension in the mid-1980s, had often exploited the desire for change to strengthen his grip. His early speeches and constitutional amendments made in 1989, and again in 1997 and 2002, promised a "state of law" and prosperity, but in reality established a powerful "closed presidency" in full control of the nation and a weakened government authority that paved the way for years of despotism and the rolling back of human rights.

Tunisia's liberalization was highly praised by Ben Ali's Western allies who deemed it "an economic miracle." However, Tunisian scholar Dr. Aisha al-Tayeb begs to differ: "That myth, while seemingly convincing at first, quickly lost its allure when contrasted with a different local reality and daily life . . . [that] would exhibit itself through stories of deprivation, extreme poverty, long-term unemployment, stories of the 'boats of death' and the drowning of young men seeking to illegally enter Europe, the spread of companies selling emigration dreams to those seeking work and quick wealth."[3]

That didn't stop the Ben Ali regime from exploiting Western support to enhance its image. But the lies were destined to go to ruin sooner or later. After all, as the old saying goes, you can fool some of the people some of the time, but you can't fool all of the people all of the time. Eventually, they are bound to stand up and fight for their rights, as Said and Bouazizi did when they died for the right to work with dignity and to express opinion without fear. Little did their peers know that their solidarity and struggle would bring down dictatorships, and, in the process, their generation would transform their nations and the region. If they truly knew what their elders had learnt the hard way about the ruthlessness of their uncanny regimes, they might have reconsidered their actions. Sometimes inexperience is a blessing.

THE YOUTH WAY

Within a few days of Mohamed Bouazizi's death in January 2011 in Tunisia, the solidarity protest held by street vendors, local unionists, and civil society activists had turned into major national demonstrations, the repercussions of which would soon be felt throughout the region and the world. As the strong internal security services failed to quell the protest, the regime tried to bring in the military, which had previously been dragged into a bloody crackdown on peaceful labor protests in January 1978, and again in January 1984. However, this time the military refused to carry out the regime's orders. In the south of the country, where two army units were deployed to protect national installations and financial institutions, officers threatened to shoot the internal security men who took aim at peaceful protestors. At that point, the military was clearly not about to destroy the country to save a presidency. Ben Ali had no choice but to escape or face the consequences. Warned of an assassination attempt on his life, he took the cowardly path, or was tricked, under the pretext of escorting his family, to flee the country to Saudi Arabia, leaving a dumbstruck population rejoicing at the end of his despotic regime.

The Tunisian revolution against a dictator who had ruled over an entire generation became an inspiration for neighboring Egyptians who believed they could do the same. Armed with laptops and mobile phones and united by youthful energy and a passion for justice, their revolution soon spread like brushfire. Like Tunisia's, the Egyptian revolution, while shocking, was not surprising, considering the legacy of civic and political struggle in that country. The Egyptians were in touch with their counterparts in Tunisia via social media and kept abreast of the evolution of their revolution via Arab satellite television. Three days prior to the big January 25 demonstration, activists led "warm-up" demonstrations where they raised loaves of bread and Tunisian flags in a clear nod to the Jasmine Revolution.

They prepared, organized, and motivated their popular base on the Internet and, more importantly, on the street. One group was in charge of Tahrir Square at the center of Cairo, where the big demonstration was to take place. Another group showed people where the water and blankets were, to aid the march and the overnight sit-in; others arranged first aid. An upbeat spirit took over as fear receded. The young leaders received from their Tunisian comrades a manual on how to deal with armored vehicles, tear gas bombs, electric batons, police cordons, and so on. It was suggested they start their demonstrations at night, as the security forces would be exhausted.

Thanks to the information revolution, the Arab youth were able to think for themselves, freely exchange ideas, and see clearly beyond their rulers' deception, vengeful jihadist violence, or cynical Western calculations. The online world had become their refuge. Despite countless confrontations, severe repression, and total polarization between dictators and Islamists, only a few sided with the autocrats or joined violent jihadi movements. They overwhelmingly rejected U.S. wars and policies in the region.

The majority of young Islamists preferred peaceful jihad in order to achieve a better life. Young members of the Muslim Brotherhood, male and female, were the first to join their counterparts from various social and political trends in leading the Arab upheaval without their elders' permission or using the names of their affiliates. They collectively rejected the choice between thuggish dictators and cynical foreign powers, between repressive patriarchies and imported paternalism, between surrender and suicide. The Arab youth had opted for a third choice: freedom. Freedom of expression, freedom from fear, from want, from military intervention, and from war—those were their slogans from the very outset.

Humble Beginnings

Unlike the opposition parties, the youth activists didn't impose ideology or empty slogans on their peers. Instead, they started with everyday needs such as jobs, clean running water, electricity, and freedom of assembly. They connected these basic demands in people's minds with the need for better governance. What seemed to be an unconventional social appeal turned into an effective political strategy that didn't ask people to adopt ideological or religious beliefs in order to assemble and protest against administrative inefficiencies, incompetence, and injustice.

Like their counterparts in other Arab countries, Egyptian and Tunisian youth demanded specific socioeconomic rights that people related to. For example, they explained to people in poor Cairo neighborhoods that they faced cuts in electricity because their government sold Egypt's gas to Israelis on the cheap. In this way, they connected immediate needs with the regime's servitude to Israel. Only after they gained momentum and picked up widespread support from major unions, syndicates, and opposition groups did they raise the level of their demands to political reform and, ultimately, regime change.

In Yemen, Libya, Bahrain, and Syria, where regimes responded violently, the protesters remained on task under duress, and peaceful despite violent repression. Indeed, the youths' leadership generally helped maintain the civic and democratic nature of the revolution, restraining those who were eager to arm the protestors, seek foreign intervention, or ask for tribal, clan, or ethnic support.

The Arab men and women who spearheaded the uprisings did not behave like desperate souls or hooligans in search of chaos, destruction, or revenge. They came out by the millions, but never became mob-like. They were disciplined, civil, and well-organized. Leading by example, they cleaned the streets after their demonstrations, cared for the injured, and protected the defenseless. Never has the region, indeed the world, witnessed such youthful elegance. Their behavior was humane and exemplary by any standard, teaching regimes and their allies a lesson in the politics of power. This is particularly important in the context of Islamic history, as I will discuss later, because revolution was generally discouraged, fearing the chaos of a post-revolutionary state would be far worse than living with autocracy.

Cool Revolutionaries

The spontaneity and improvisation made the protests poetic, artistic, and liberating. The areas around the square at the center of Cairo were transformed into a "city state" or rather a "Tahrir state"—with its own permanent residents, rules and rituals, security arrangements, and slogans for change.

It was like a Greek drama—switching between tragedy, comedy, and satire. One fleeting moment could bring death and injury, as snipers shot and the military advanced; another could bring relief and irony as the youth danced, prayed, and sang. The situation was not so different in public squares elsewhere—from Alexandria and Taiz to Manama, Tunis, and Hama. The "Egyptian drama" never repeated itself. With each passing day, a new narrative was improvised and played out, a spectacle that dazzled as the world watched, applauded, and cheered with excitement. It was reality imitating fiction—and surpassing it.

The handwritten signs revealed the spirit and psychology of those clamoring for change:

"Please leave, my arm is hurting"

"You leave, I go"

"Leave already, I miss my wife"

"Leave, I want to shower"

"Leave, my shoulders hurt" (little boy sitting on shoulders)

"What are you? . . . a glue?"

"Leaving is the solution" (a play on words of "Islam is the solution")

"Mubarak challenges boredom"

"Mubarak, you're over draft"

"My wife can't deliver; the baby doesn't want to see you"

"Freedom of speech for all, including douche bags"

"The end of the Pharaoh"

"Sorry for the disturbance, we're building Egypt"

"Game over"

"NO, YOU CAN'T!" (an inversion of Obama's "Yes, we can!" campaign slogan)

A sign in Hebrew said **"GO,"** subtitled, **"in case it's the only language you understand."** And probably the strongest came in the form of a sign with new media sites spelling out **"Egypt."**

An extremely cute kitten, being held by a man, had a collar around its neck with a sign reading **"No Mubarak."**

Dance, music, and theater were present throughout Tahrir and other revolutionary squares. Countless comedies played out as more people poured in, many of them artists, performers, and musicians. But some of the best examples found their inspiration in the imaginative, ironic, and humorous Egyptian culture. In one such sketch (Irhal yah hmar or "Leave, you mule"), a man takes on the role of a first-grade teacher to lead his audience, a chorus of people who clamored around him repeating the basics of the revolution uninhibited and unrehearsed. Holding a ruler, he would say, "Leave, you mule," and the chorus would bray along. They would repeat the same in English, French, and Hebrew, and the improvisation would continue.

So ironic and humorous were the revolutionaries that their whole attitude, and that of the regime, seemed like a parody. Undeterred by the threats of the authorities and their infamous security services, they continued critiquing the regime's power with so much bite that it was clear the fear barrier had been broken, with ease replacing tension and confidence replacing doubt. The regime sensed this and retaliated by hiring thugs to ride camels and horses into the crowded square, trampling everyone and everything in their way, in what came to be known as the "Battle of the Camel"—a reference to the first recorded war among Muslims between the followers and family of the Prophet.

Why would the regime make such an ill-prepared and humiliating show of force, hire thugs, and exhibit such poor judgment in reacting to the uprising? It turned out that the regime had tried and failed miserably to mount counterprotests by recruiting from the ranks of its bureaucracy and from the large companies associated with the ruling party. Only the hooligans came out on horses and camels, hardly the image the regime needed to project as the world's cameras were fixed on Tahrir Square. The liberating images of the young revolutionaries and the desperate acts of the aging dictatorship went on to dominate the airwaves and the Internet, inspiring millions around the region and the world; this moment was the revolution's turning point.

SCORING BIG

The youthfulness, authenticity, and popularity of the revolution were most pronounced in the active participation of the followers of Egypt's major soccer clubs: Cairo's Al-Ahli Ultras, Zamalek

White Knights, and even the Ismaili Yellow Dragons. The youth movement was able to incorporate the thousands of fans into its show of force in Tahrir and other public squares, with crowds sometimes reaching as many as fifteen thousand. The fact that the followers of competing clubs like Al-Ahli and Zamalek—clubs that had a history of violent rivalry—could coordinate their defiance against the regime was in itself as revolutionary as the uprising.

The passions and tensions that separate Egyptian fans of different soccer clubs go beyond the typical rivalry of, say, Barcelona and Real Madrid, or Liverpool and Manchester United. In Egypt, soccer is political. There are sociopolitical differences between the fans, with Al-Ahli and Al-Wahdat traditionally representing many of the poorer and less fortunate.

Soccer fans tend to be viewed with suspicion by the police and internal security services. The regimes continuously play fans against one another or try to bribe players and fans in order to pacify them. Indeed, stadiums, like mosques, have generally been seen with suspicion by the regimes, as their subversive atmosphere can act as a refuge for those wanting to vent their frustration and anger toward the establishment.

The coordination between the red-shirted Al-Ahli and white-shirted Zamalek fans against the regime underlined the popular nature of the Egyptian revolution. Psychologically, its effect was greater than the coordination between say Islamists and nationalists, or leftists and liberals. Remember, these passionate and vociferous fans are blindly tribal and loyal, and they can whistle, scream, shout, and confront police like no other section of society. In fact, it was the fearless and well-organized Ultras that broke the fear barrier as the regime intensified its bloody crackdown on the protests.

As I mentioned earlier, the dictatorships have long understood the importance of sports for youth and tried to hijack or domesticate these clubs and their fans in favor of the regimes. When playing "foreign teams," the ruling class has tried to make it appear as though the home team and the dictatorship are one and the same. But as it became clear that soccer fans were part and parcel of the movement for political change, the regimes acted with caution and venom. For example, the national leagues in Algeria, Tunisia, and Libya were shut down, just as soccer was suspended in Iran during the Green Revolution for fear that matches would turn stadiums into anti-regime forums. However, the closures worsened people's fury. Instead of being contained within stadiums, the people spread into streets and public squares.

As crowds took to the streets in the early days of the revolution, the Ultras chanted: "Regime! Be very scared of us. We are coming tonight with intent. The supporters of Al-Ahli will fire everything up. God almighty will make us victorious. Go, hooligans!" And this was the PG-rated version.

It was expected that the security forces would concentrate their violent crackdown on these brave souls and arrest as many of them as possible. Their subsequent ill-treatment provoked widespread condemnation by the political organizers of the protest movement with the April 6 group and Revolution Youth Coalition issuing statements in their defense as "heroes of the revolution." Eventually, the soccer fans gave the protest movement its oomph, just as the revolution provided the fans with venues to channel their social frustration. In the process, soccer was made sacred by the revolution as many of its fans were injured or killed by the security forces. Immediately after the fall of Mubarak, matches between rival clubs ended with hugs, regardless of the results.

SOCIAL MEDIA FOR SOCIAL JUSTICE

In the wake of Khaled Said's death at the hands of the Egyptian internal security service, a Facebook group entitled "We are all

Khaled Said" was created and maintained by geeks and bloggers. It soon became a rallying cry for a popular movement intent on bringing those responsible to justice, be they security men or political leaders. At the beginning of 2011, there were twenty-seven million Arabs on Facebook, including six million Egyptians, comprising more than 5 percent of the population. Within a few months, two million more Egyptians joined, underlining the centrality of the medium to the changes in the country. Indeed, the countries witnessing upheavals were also the same nations witnessing the greatest increases in social media membership.[4]

More than sixty million people in the Arab world are online. In a poll conducted in nine Arab countries, 60 percent of the youth said they had access to a desktop computer and a comparable number had e-mail access. Likewise, among Arab youth, four in five own a mobile phone and a quarter of these phones are Web-enabled.[5] Despite their digital access, one in two people surveyed (probably in urban areas) said they also read a newspaper daily. The numbers rise with every passing day. The fact that two-thirds of the young spend most of their leisure time in front of a TV means they could also see the alternative to their miserable lives, real and fictional. All of which also explains why more than two-thirds claimed that global citizenship was very or somewhat important to them.[6]

The Arab youth increasingly comprised a modern, transnational tribe that bypassed borders, religion, and social strata. As a distinctly modern social construct, the youth transcended traditional hierarchy in favor of open and pluralistic characteristics. Thanks in no small part to the information revolution and its twin byproducts "new media" and "social media," Arab youth have developed their own social and cultural codes and jargon. They shared opinions and experiences freely, and in the process established a diverse Arab community that was creative and innovative.

It is true that much of their time online was spent on entertainment and socializing, but even that has contributed to shaping a distinct national identity among the young. Even the banal act of voting for the best talent on a satellite television show through text messaging became the embodiment of free choice, for it was a vote that counted, unlike rigged general elections carried out by the ruling class.

Yemeni activist and 2011 Nobel Peace Prize co-winner Tawakkol Karman describes the use of social media:

> The revolution in Yemen began immediately after the fall of Ben Ali in Tunisia on 14 January. As I always do when arranging a demonstration I posted a message on Facebook, calling on people to celebrate the Tunisian uprising on 16 January. The following day a group of students from Sana'a University asked me to attend a vigil in front of the Tunisian embassy. The crowd was shouting: "Heroes! We are with you in the line of fire against the evil rulers!" We were treated roughly by the security forces, and we chanted: "If, one day, a people desire to live, then destiny will answer their call," and "The night must come to an end"—the mantra of the revolutionaries in Tunisia. The demonstration was astonishing; thousands turned up, and Sana'a witnessed its first peaceful demonstration for the overthrow of the regime. "Go before you are driven out!" we cried.[7]

By no means has this been a unique case. In fact it's been the norm in spreading the word among young bloggers and activists in various Arab countries.

MAKING AND
EMPOWERING INDIVIDUALISM

The new media has had an important cultural, even sociological, role to play in patriarchal Arab societies. It helped young people break free from social constraints, it propelled them into uncharted territory, and it helped them mold a certain type of individualism. They began to enjoy an uninhibited space where they could share information and experiences, join chat rooms, and participate with one another.

Theirs is a newfound egalitarianism that contradicts the intrinsically hierarchal and inhibiting sociopolitical system. Paternalism was replaced with collegial relations; censorship was replaced by free expression. Internet citizens were not judged according to gender, ethnicity, age, or class, but on individual contributions, ability, and wit. Indeed, identities could be invented or tailored to fit personal taste or fantasy.

With no fear of retribution, Arab citizens set out to express themselves as free souls, as sovereign members of a community of individuals that is as real as the world they inhabit. They choose on the basis of free will, devoid of social and political pressures—joining, subscribing, sharing, reading, saving, deleting, working, investing, playing, as well as making friends, starting romances, joining global activism, speaking foreign languages, and communicating across borders with no limits and with no Big Brother watching over their shoulders.

They have taken routes beyond the neighborhood alleys, have listened to music not played on local radio, have watched films not aired on local television, and have developed an imagination that went beyond the realm of the acceptable or the possible. It was only a matter of time until the free spirit that ruled the online world spilled over into the real world, putting technology at the service of people and moving the emerging diversity and consensus from the digital public space into the metropolitan square.

GEEKS AND DICTATORS

For the last decade, bloggers and other citizen-journalists have gained prominence in the Arab world in relation to traditional state media and Western-dominated global media. They aimed at providing uncensored information and expanding the realm of public debate. Slowly but surely, a fusion of social media and satellite networks provided a revolutionary alternative to the dominant state and Western outlets. The improvised and occasionally misleading reporting can be traced to the second Palestinian Intifada in 2000, through the 2003 invasion and occupation of Iraq, the 2005 Hariri assassination, the 2005 Egyptian election, and the Israeli wars in Lebanon and Gaza in 2006 and 2008.

The use of cell phone images, videos, and documents to provide an alternative view of the occupation of Iraq opened the floodgates of information in its later years through Twitter, blogs, Facebook, and other multimedia forums. Some of the most dramatic footage was provided by U.S. soldiers in Abu Ghraib. In Israel's assessment of its wars in Lebanon in 2006 and Gaza in 2008, the military admitted its failure in the information war in the former, but boasted of learning lessons and applying them successfully two years later. The Palestinians, who kept feeding the Arab media with images and information, disagree.

At any rate, the popularization of technology introduced new tools of empowerment and motivation that went beyond standing armies and armored vehicles. An activist or an average protester could demonstrate during the day, circulate video clips in the evening as citizen journalists, and watch themselves at night making a difference. Armed with smart phones and laptops, protestors fought on two fronts at the same time: the global information front and the domestic political front. This was citizen-journalism at its best.

Like the Tunisian youth, young Egyptians were more than ready when they started "revolutionary dissidence," kicking off what amounted to a countdown toward the end of the regime. Not only were Egyptian bloggers very politically active, but they also comprised the largest blogging force in the Arab world, occupying a third of the regional blogosphere.[8]

Young Egyptians had prepared multiphased plans and backups that anticipated the security forces responses. For instance, they calculated how long and how far from a police station they needed to demonstrate in order to avoid arrest; how to maneuver in a way that would destabilize the security forces; how to secure multiple entries and exits; and how to devise a division of labor that would ensure that requirements from first aid to blankets were secure for the long January nights. All of that was to be coordinated and implemented online and on modest street corners. And no function was as important as spreading the word in real time in order to guarantee a maximum, orderly show of peaceful people force. This was a reenactment of events in Tunisia. The events were soon duplicated, with less intensity though, in Yemen, Bahrain, Libya, and Syria where YouTube video clips destroyed the regime's propaganda, showing the regime's thugs attacking peaceful protestors.

Cyber Warfare

New media has been essential for social and political organization. But just as it earned the admiration and interest of the people, it also drew the contempt of dictators determined to monopolize the flow of information. Tech-savvy youth became a threat, bloggers were seen as dissidents, and hackers were considered insurgents who brought down firewalls and broke fear barriers.

The circulation among Tunisian youth of the WikiLeaks documents that revealed Ben Ali's corruption drew the attention of the Ben Ali regime, especially the damning information and reports about the crimes and excessiveness of the ruling family that were written by U.S. diplomats, some of the regime's closest friends. Despite its despotism and nepotism, the United States saw the regime as an important regional ally and client, information that infuriated Tunisians trapped between a dictator and his cynical Western patrons.

Unable to control the spread of the leaks that were evidently blocked by the Tunisian media, government security services accelerated their assault on the Internet, stealing passwords, hacking accounts, spying on activists, and blocking access to some of the more vocal opposition figures, journalists, and so on. Sofiene Chourabi, a journalist for *Al-Tariq al-Jadid* magazine and an outspoken blogger, was one of many harassed by authorities. He told Al Jazeera news network that his personal account on Facebook, which included around forty-two hundred friends, was hacked, and a few days later he was locked out of it completely.

As Tunisian and Egyptian governments started to treat these bloggers as political dissidents, online activists began to see themselves as such and started to act the part. Blogging was no longer a mere hobby indulged from the safety of homes but a political act that came with possible retribution. None of this was new for the Tunisian government, which for years blocked YouTube and Facebook.

These digital crackdowns were by no means specific to the Tunisian regime. As the Internet skeptic Evgeny Morozov argues in his book *The Net Delusion*, governments, like the youth, have also learned how to use the Internet in their favor.[9] From Belarus to Israel, governments have used the Internet to spy on dissidents, paralyze their movements, and build firewalls to block information, connectivity, and organization. Indeed, some U.S. lawmakers and political leaders argued that hackers and distributors of government electronic records, as in the case of WikiLeaks, should be treated as terrorists.

During Iran's 2008 "Green Revolution," which followed that country's rigged elections, the government used the Internet against the opposition, either shutting down certain services or breaking into networks of dissident bloggers and making mass arrests. Similarly, the Egyptian regime tried to shut down the Internet for a few days, but soon discovered that it was also obliged to take down the cell phone service used to send out videos and tweets through alternative networks. This, in turn, paralyzed the economy and hurt the country's international standing. With the outbreak of the Syrian revolution on March 15, 2011, the regime tried to learn the lessons of Egypt and Tunisia by forcing young people on the streets to give out their social network names and passwords in order to check for any anti-government sentiments.

Tunisia's besieged bloggers were helped by the hacker-collective known as Anonymous, whose global activists launched "OpTunisia" to overthrow the Tunisian censor regime and, in the process, succeeded in taking down at least eight Web sites, including those of the president, prime minister, the ministry of industry, the ministry of foreign affairs, and the stock exchange. By attacking these sites from outside the country, hackers were able to avoid the risk of arrest.

The information revolution and the popularization of technology have helped level the battlefield between dissidents and dictators, while opening it up to the rest of the world to the disadvantage of rulers that obsess about national boundaries and sovereignty. The Syrian regime attempted to black out all information from the cities and towns invaded by its forces but failed to stop the footage made available through cell phones, which played a major role in weakening the Assad regime. Ironically, it was the Assad family, which monopolizes the cell phone market through the president's cousin Rami Makhlouf, that ensured most Syrians had a cell phone in hand during the protests.

MEDIA CLICHÉS

Shortly after the beginning of the Arab revolution, the media began to fixate on the role of social media, ignoring other social and political factors. While important, there is no need to sensationalize the role social media played, treating it as if it were a silver bullet.

Namedropping social media networks became a cliché that reduced the totality of the transformation into revolutionary software. Though both the 2008 Iranian revolution and 2011 Egyptian revolution used new media to their advantage, only the latter succeeded in toppling the regime, while the Green Revolution failed. Why? Because of the many other factors that come to bear. Facebook doesn't organize, people do. Twitter won't govern, people will.

Western media's constant referencing of the "youth" in the abstract, all the while ignoring other components of the revolution, became a cliché intended to fascinate and entertain, not inform. Indeed, packaging youth with Western technology became a media construct devoid of all social and political components. So while the young did encompass the majority of the population, women, the unemployed, blue- and white-collar labor, the middle and upper classes, and activists were all pushed into a generational pigeonhole. Such categorization, while fascinating, doesn't say enough about the forces behind the revolution and how they would manage the future.

Regrettably, the fascinating David versus Goliath story of the people taking on oppressive regimes was translated by the Western media into a Hollywood narrative.

Enter the "Google Executive"

U.S. officials and media executives inflated the role of a Google employee who was designated as the "hero" and brain behind the people-power demonstrations. Wael Ghonim was a young Egyptian blogger, writing under a pseudonym, who was arrested on suspicion of anti-government activity. Along with others, he helped mount the "We are all Khaled Said" Facebook page. When the authorities released him, long after the demonstrations and sit-ins were underway, he was allowed to appear on television where he was emotional, sobbing, and denying responsibility for the death of young Egyptians. The appearance backfired as the youth movement shrugged off the government's coercive tactics. But the emotional "executive" continued to sob his way to Tahrir Square where he joined a massive rally that took him in as one of its own. Ghonim, like his peers, deserves praise. He has earned his place in modern Egyptian history, but U.S. president Barack Obama's special citation of the "Google executive" gave him, or more implicitly Google, too much credit.

In a rather flimsy attempt to highlight Google's role, aides to U.S. secretary of state Hillary Clinton suggested to Al Jazeera a town-hall gathering between Clinton and Egyptian bloggers and activists to be aired on the network. They were specific about how they would like it to be produced, including choosing the names of the guests and the order in which they would appear in the program. Topping the U.S. list was the Google executive, Ghonim. Alas, the town-hall program never aired because Al Jazeera responded with its own journalistic prerogatives to balance the program by putting "the town" back in the hall.

We understood that the revolutions would not have been possible without the active participation of a wide network of mobilized labor, civil society organizations, opposition parties, neighborhood associations, those attending Friday prayers, soccer fans, tribes, extended families, and entire communities. However, many have embraced an overly simplistic explanation regarding the events, finding it easier to give credit to a handful of Web sites than to study the more complicated Arab reality from which the youth emerged. And we overemphasize the importance of online activity at the risk of downplaying the sacrifice of the all-too-often invisible activists, intellectuals, union members, and artists who died unknown and unrecognized.

Satellite media, which has been present in the Arab world for the last two decades and covered the revolution extensively, has also had a great influence on public awareness, communication, and the mobilization of millions across the region.

Throughout history, youth have stood at the forefront of popular upheavals and revolutions, where their active participation has been indispensable, helped by one form of connectivity or another. Since the days of word-of-mouth and pigeon-post, communication and connectivity have been prerequisites for change. People mount revolutions the way they do business, and the way they live their lives.

In his important work, *History of the Arabs*, Philip Hitti traces how the "Arab awakening" at the turn of the twentieth century evolved thanks to the fresh participation of the relatively young, along with the help of the printing press, and the networks of trains that brought new blood into metropolitan areas. While it has become fashionable to talk about the role of the youth movement, often in simplistic and clichéd terms, the younger generation has had their influence on the course of the revolution. Some of these representations might be false, but the resulting euphoria is real and affects reality no less.[10]

The youth have sparked a revolution not only in the public squares, but also in the minds and hearts of those long subdued by repression, broken by oppression, domesticated with proverbial carrots, or deterred by sticks. But if these old worriers were down, they weren't out. In no time, people of all types and age were awakened by the calls for change and encouraged by the will of the youth to go all the way.

INVISIBLE COMMUNITY ORGANIZERS

"The young people instigated the spark, but the protests straddled all strata of society, all ages; it was a people's revolution."

—AHMED MAHER IBRAHIM,
EGYPTIAN YOUTH LEADER

Watching the young people who occupied Tahrir Square, in Cairo, I saw many familiar faces. One particular white-haired, hot-blooded spokesman stood out. Several years earlier, while I was on a book tour in Egypt, George Ishaq hosted me at his Cairo community center. A charismatic community and political organizer, he emerged as a leader of Egypt's democracy movement. Ishaq, along with seven other militants, cofounded and later directed the Egyptian Movement for Change (EMC)—also known as Kefaya—which played a central role in organizing the protests leading to the revolution.

The center's large auditorium was filled with an unlikely mix of students, trade unionists, Christian nuns, and Islamic scholars, as well as human rights activists and intellectuals. The group included men and women of all ages; the same kind of mixture that later took over Liberation Square in Cairo. They came to hear about the situation in Israel-Palestine, and the atmosphere was unmistakably sympathetic to the Palestinian cause. Many of the Christians and Muslims present were active in the popular committees that were set up in solidarity and support for the Palestinian people under occupation following their second Intifada in 2000.

Later that evening, a number of attendees were invited to Ishaq's home where we continued the discussion about what needed to be done for the cause of freedom in Palestine. Ishaq was as enthusiastic and animated as a person could be at the end of a long and exhausting day. I witnessed firsthand this industrious community leader playing host to, and engaging with, neighborhood organizers, human rights militants, and opposition leaders, including the outlawed Islamist leaders of the Muslim Brotherhood. It took optimism, audacity, and a special brand of Egyptian humor to maintain hope.

One of the many jokes that night was that President Hosni Mubarak's son Ala'a was about to buy apartments in two Cairo neighborhoods, Zamalek and Ma'adi. "So what's wrong with that?" asked the president. "Well, Ala'a wanted the apartments to connect!" Another joke hit Mubarak personally: The history of presidential succession in Egypt? Nasser searched for a dumb, unthreatening vice president and found Sadat. Sadat, in turn, looked long and hard for someone less smart than he, and found Mubarak. Two decades later, Mubarak was still looking for a less intelligent vice president! Finally, my favorite joke of the night went something like this: the interior minister asks Hosni

Mubarak to write a farewell letter to the Egyptian people. Mubarak replies: "Why? Where are they going?"

George Ishaq knew soon after the rigged November parliamentary elections that Egypt's time had come and that Tahrir Square had to be the goal. "If the Egyptian street does not move, there will not be any change," he told Al Jazeera in late 2010. During their long days and nights at the "liberated" square, I've watched and spoken to other community organizers taking center stage as representatives of a wide coalition of demonstrators: Kefaya, the April 6 movement, the left-leaning Freedom and Justice Movement, the Coalition for Change, the committee for the support of Barad'ie, and many others. These are the tireless coalition builders who've worked with labor unions and opposition parties, old and new, including the Muslim Brotherhood, to bring about political change in Egypt.

My Friend
Mohammad El-Sayed Said

One particular coalition builder who was absent from George Ishaq's gathering that night was the late Mohammad El-Sayed Said. A brilliant thinker and a dedicated community organizer, Said laid down the theoretical foundations for today's civic activism in the Arab world, insisting on human rights, the rule of law, and the independence of religious institutions as pillars of democracy in the region. He helped to found the Cairo Institute of Human Rights Studies and the Egyptian Organization for Human Rights.

When President Mubarak invited a number of journalists for a chat at the presidential palace a few years ago, Said tagged along. During the session, Said approached the much-feared president in front of opinion makers with a paper that included a list of demands for democratization and human rights. Mubarak shunned the journalists and rejected Said's paper and gesture. He would, of course, pay for his arrogance.

Said's investigative reports systematically presented damning proof of the regime's violations. As the English-language newspaper *Al-Ahram Weekly* pointed out in its obituary of Said, "He wrote a much-acclaimed report about the punishment of dissidents by torture, for which he was punished by being arrested and tortured."[11]

Years of such ill-treatment at the hands of Mubarak's regime took a heavy toll on Said's health. He died in 2009 after a two-year struggle with cancer and was much missed in Tahrir Square. You could say, an Arab community organizer is like a Chicago community organizer, but with greater responsibilities, higher risks, and fewer rewards.[12]

As Said showed me during several visits to Egypt over the past two decades, a network was slowly forming of bold community organizers who were bypassing the stale, established opposition parties to mobilize the young and the disaffected against Mubarak's regime. Just the mention of Said's name to Egyptian civic leaders, young and old, brought out smiles and tears in reaction. Thanks to their hard work, the network spread throughout Cairo and other Egyptian cities. The contrast between Said's and Ishaq's visions for Egypt and that of the deposed Mubarak and his Western backers couldn't be starker.

Like Mohammad El-Sayed Said, the new youth leaders that emerged from Tahrir Square sought a united, humane, prosperous, truly democratic Egypt for all of its citizens. The professional pundits who were parachuted into Egypt by the international media have come with their prefabricated conclusions about the youth and what it takes to ensure regional stability. But the Saids of Egypt and the Arab world have shown that we don't have to sign up for a world of extremes, a world where Osama bin Laden and Ariel Sharon are the only possible choices for leadership.

Mohammad El-Sayed Said understood long before many others that technology is indispensable for democratic struggle. His 1997 book, *Progress Initiative*, called for Egypt's transformation with the help of modern technologies, and Internet communities have long been a part of the opposition networks he helped form. I remember sharing a panel with this pan-Arab intellectual at the Human Rights Studies Center in Cairo a few years ago where Said explained the connection between the struggle for freedom and democracy at home in Egypt and in Palestine. For many Arabs, their solidarity with Palestine underlined their condemnation of all repression—whether carried out by Israel or by their own regimes. Alas, while it was mostly permissible, even encouraged, to manifest their support for Palestinian rights, the Arabs were not as free to defend their own rights. In a way, Palestine became not only an example of injustice, but also a proxy that represented the injustice many other Arabs lived under.

Mohammad and George represent countless community organizers, civil society activists, and human rights advocates. Some organized in middle-class associations with limited room to maneuver, others through media outlets and marginal political associations. During these largely unreported years, courageous public intellectuals, many of whom were imprisoned or tortured, also played a role in fermenting the revolution.

The story of the 2003 Cairo literary festival illustrates the courage of these people. At the final ceremony, a well-known dissident and novelist Son'allah Ibrahim was granted the Arab Novel Award, an honor bestowed by the Egyptian Ministry of Culture, which includes a significant cash prize. The novelist attended the ceremony to the surprise of many and was granted a podium to deliver his appreciation. Instead, he denounced the complicity of

Arab regimes with the foreign policies of Israel and the United States and had the following to say about his country: "We no longer have any theater, cinema, scientific research, education. Instead, we have festivals and the lies of television. . . . Corruption and robbery are everywhere, but whoever speaks out is interrogated, beaten, and tortured." He then went on to reject the prize, "for it was awarded by a government that, in my opinion, lacks the credibility to bestow it."[13]

THE RISE OF LABOR

"How could syndicate action have a meaning with the guarantee of basic freedoms that all men aspire for? How is it possible to realize social and economic achievements for a people that don't enjoy democracy?"

—FARHAT HACHED,
TUNISIAN LABOR LEADER, 1949

Farhat Hached, who became the head of the powerful labor federation the Union Générale Tunisienne du Travail (UGTT), was one of the many labor, community, and political organizers who struggled for civil justice and democracy, a struggle that went on for almost a century before the Jasmine Revolution took root at the end of 2010. As a result of his vocal support for Tunisian independence from France, Hached was assassinated in 1952. The French-backed death squad, the Red Hand, killed him after he became a key political player in the nationalist movement.[14]

During the so-called Arab Spring, the youth-cheering media preferred to concentrate on the apparently nonideological young middle classes, generally, while neglecting the vital role played by the Egyptian and Tunisian labor unionists and activists in 2011 and the likes of Hached, decades earlier. Tunisian and Egyptian workers have a long history of clashes with the authorities and the military in the 1970s and '80s, the result of which is that labor unions and middle-class syndicates in both countries evolved quite sophisticated, highly networked, and democratically organized membership and leadership structures—regime-controlled syndicates and unions notwithstanding.

The connectivity and coordination among many of these movements existed well before the introduction of electronic media, producing connections that ran so deep, the 1952 assassination of Hached in Tunis provoked bloody clashes in Morocco's Casablanca in solidarity with their Tunisian counterparts.[15]

The Tunisians who took to the streets in December 2010 could draw upon a huge reservoir of experience, cumulative struggle, and a well-developed capacity to organize from even before Tunisia gained independence in 1956. The liberation struggle centered on resisting colonialism and combating autocracy, which often led to imprisonment, death, and exile. But in the decades after independence, political and social struggles continued to intersect. As recently as 2008, two years before Bouazizi's death triggered a regional and national outcry, protests flared over wages and work conditions in the mining regions of Qafsa and then in the far south near the borders with Libya. While the revolution marked a break with the past, it was also a byproduct of a long history of social and political struggle in the Arab world.

What started as a youth protest in Tunisia was soon joined by labor unions and banned opposition groups, from Islamists to Communists, turning their demonstrations into a national uprising. This protest spread to the major coastal cities of Sfax, Sousse, and Bizerte, and then to the greater Tunis region, starting in poor neighborhoods and moving on to the center of the capital, crippling the regime's capacity to respond adequately.

Ali al-Bouazizi, who was first on the scene of Mohamed Bouazizi's act of self-immolation, testified that the Tunisian revolution was the culmination of twenty-three years of struggle:

> One of [Muhamed] al-Bouazizi's relatives called me and said that he had set himself on fire, and I began, along with a number of other strugglers within the party, to coordinate with civil society and rights and legal activists. I was the first to gather photos of [the self-immolation of] Muhamed al-Bouazizi and I distributed them to get the issue into the media, and the uprising in Sidi Bouzid was launched with the twin demands of freedom and dignity. It was the culmination of movements and struggles that lasted for the last 23 years, during which the Nahda Party, the Labor Party, the Communist Party, and many strugglers made hefty sacrifices.

Al-Bouazizi went on to describe how the revolt in Sidi Bouzid was organized:

> I was active in the Democratic Progressive Party, and we formed a core group in the university around the notion that the regime of Zine al-Abideen had weakened and was witnessing its last days. We attempted to attract as many youth as possible in order to garner political concessions from the regime. We held a sit-in for the release of a political prisoner, and we demanded a legislative pardon even though the police scattered us by force. We were then arrested. Ben Ali's regime would arrest us under public rights regulations, such as cases of "begging" and inability to pay, which were often falsified against us in cafes and restaurants. . . . Six students from the university were arrested, and our objective was to have the province rise up with its demands, to break the wall of fear

and to lift the veil of media secrecy. Peasants joined the protests in the Riqab region after their lands were confiscated due to their inability to pay their loans."[16]

Within weeks, the Tunisians transformed popular outrage into a revolution that unseated the Ben Ali regime. They took the much-feared internal security forces by surprise, and exposed the weakness of the political parties that continued to play catch up until Ben Ali's departure. The domesticated political leaders had long coexisted with the regime and clearly didn't believe the youth could transform a modest protest into a sweeping revolution that would inspire other Arabs, near and far.

Tunisians overcame a major psychological barrier in Tunisia as well and arguably opened the way toward a "Tunisization" of the Arab imagination—the ability to imagine life after dictatorship. This is especially important, considering that Ben Ali's efficiency in security affairs was the envy of his authoritarian Arab counterparts. With 130,000 internal security personal, or thirteen for every one thousand Tunisians, the intelligence chief and commander-in-chief mastered policing the people and their national army in a way that didn't allow for major outbursts that could embarrass Western patrons.

Mahallah Unites Egypt

Like Tunisia and other Arab countries, Egypt's economic liberalization came with massive opportunities for corruption and cronyism for the ruling elite and yet at the same time exposed ordinary workers and farmers to the volatility of international markets. These ordinary citizens were also at the mercy of loan sharks due to poor state protection and a lack of social services. From the early 1990s to the late 2010s, the government stripped farmers of protective laws, cut their subsidies, and went on a privatization spree. Because union leaders were installed by the regimes through rigged elections, workers were forced by circumstance to defy their leaders and go on frequent strikes, starting in 1977 when people flooded the streets during the infamous "food riots."

Between 1998 and 2004, there were more than one thousand cases of collective worker action throughout Egypt. The number of such actions jumped from four hundred in 1995 and 1996 to more than six hundred in 2007. The turning point, however, came on April 6, 2006, when more than twenty thousand workers went on strike in Mahallah, a major center for textile production. In December 2006 and September 2007, civil servants and white-collar labor groups joined the movement. Their demands were straightforward: the dissolution of their trade union committee, which workers claimed was fraudulent, a minimum monthly wage of LE1200 (U.S.$200), improved contract agreements, their long-overdue bonuses, and opportunities for promotion.[17]

During the April 2006 Mahallah textile factory protests, men and women of all ages joined hands to demand higher wages and months' worth of back pay owed to them to enable them to "live, eat, and marry," as one female worker put it. Their motto was simple: "We want to get paid." The workers got support from tech-savvy youth, who went on to form the national April 6th movement that began to be the vanguard of similar protests throughout the country.

Kareem el-Beheiry was one such youth. The twenty-year-old became Mahallah's first blogger and a living example of how young Egyptian workers were forged in the struggle for justice. His initiation began after he took part in his first labor strike in December 2006 when he "didn't know what a strike was." Watching women crying because "they couldn't feed their kids," he started filming the agony of everyday Egyptian workers. Because of his filming, labor leader Jihad Taman initially suspected that he was a security agent, but he soon took him under his wing and from there he became the blogger for the unofficial union. That labor strike broke down a barrier of fear among Egyptian labor activists. By the time of the next strike, in September of 2007, el-Beheiry and his fellow strikers were chanting against the World Bank's role in the "colonization" of Egypt and calling for the downfall of President Hosni Mubarak.

In April 2008, food prices hit a new high and Mahallah was once again the site of dissent. The workers were helped by a group of youth activists from Cairo and other metropolitan areas. For instance, a Facebook page created by a twenty-seven-year-old woman, Israa Abd el-Fattah, encouraged people to support the strike in Mahallah. She was arrested soon after, but by then some seventy thousand people were supporting her page. The beating of a woman and her daughter by security officers ignited workers' anger, escalating clashes, with scenes reminiscent of the Palestinian Intifada playing out on Egypt's streets. Soon strikes, sit-ins, and protests were springing up all over the country. Anger only increased as security forces made a habit of beating activists in public and torturing many behind closed doors. During the strike, state security agents arrested and tortured el-Beheiry, along with many other labor activists. He was released seventy-three days later. In 2009, the government transferred el-Beheiry to Cairo, and in 2010 he was fired.

Al-Masry Al-Youm newspaper summarized what has happened since that day in April 2008:

> Police cars and train tracks were set ablaze with the intention of sending a message: Under this regime, life has become unbearable. In May 2008, a 10,000 person sit-in of real-estate tax collectors caused the government to give in to demands

for a 300 percent wage increase. On April 21, 2009, thousands of tax collectors gathered at the Ministry of Manpower and Immigration, forcing Minister Aisha Abdel Hady to recognize their independent union, the first in Egypt since 1957. At the end of 2009 more and more sit-ins moved to the sidewalks of downtown Cairo. When workers' calls for government interference—particularly in recently privatized factories—went unheeded, they moved to the gates of parliament. [On] February 20, 2011, protesters held placards reading "Shoot us."[18]

The participation of the workers and the unemployed had transformed a youth protest into a national upheaval that couldn't be defeated. The entry of the working-class families into the political and revolutionary fray transformed it into a mass movement, transferring the focus from the economic to the political until it became a rallying cry that demanded the ultimate change: "The people want to bring down the regime."

"WHERE ARE THE MEN?"

On December 7, 2006, some three thousand women left their work stations at a Mahallah textile factory and walked toward the men's working area chanting: "Where are the men? Here are the women." They summoned the male workers to action leaving them no other option but to join. Some ten thousand men and women walked out to the square chanting and calling for their rights and promised bonuses. Despite heavy police deployment to the area, the demonstration wouldn't fizzle away. And the reason, according to men's testimonies, was the "women's refusal to leave." When management mediators tried to offer explanations and throw them some "bones," the women threatened to rip them apart. Only after long debates did the women agree to leave late at night in order to show up the following morning for more of the same. According to the testimonies of men, the women were far more militant than the men, even though they were exposed to far greater pressures and threats. Almost one-quarter of Egyptian households are headed by women, with a similar rate of unemployment to men.[19]

Like their Egyptian counterparts, the struggle for women's equality has been long and arduous. In societies where women are discouraged from raising their voice in public, these young women have spoken in the freedom squares of the Arab world. Their visible presence has been one of the most striking and liberating scenes of the Arab revolution. Along with their fellow young revolutionaries, they have reinvented the Arab landscape in unprecedented ways. Nowhere has the Arab woman been as respected as an equal partner, and indeed as a courageous leader, as in Tahrir, Pearl, November 17, and other public squares that became the nerve centers of the Arab revolution. There was no harassment, no ridicule, no intimidation, only appreciation for their courage and determination.

These young women are the latest generation of feminist activists. The previous generation was particularly steadfast in pursuing awareness campaigns through feminist and social networks and other nongovernmental organizations, using anything at their disposal—from religious texts to international humanitarian law.

I met with two Egyptian activists, Nawal Sa'dawi and Rabab Abdulhadi, who had camped at Tahrir Square until the ouster of President Mubarak. They represent two generations of women revolutionaries that believed the struggle for women's rights was an integral part of the broader struggle for democracy and human rights. Nawal prefers the term "liberation of women" rather than feminism to describe their activism. They also see Egypt's domestic and foreign failures as two sides of the same coin. Sa'dawi struggled for women's equality during the Nasser and Sadat regimes and was jailed by the Mubarak regime for her views on questions relating to women's liberation in Egypt. A doctor and novelist, she believes that women's rights must be central to the new Egypt. But it will be Abdul Hadi's generation that must keep their struggle alive during these uncertain times.

Elsewhere, as in Tunisia, women have made even greater progress, since their equality was formally guaranteed by law in the 1970s. However, for those in Yemen, women have come some distance, but they still have a very long way to go. Tawakkol Karman is a thirty-two-year-old political activist who became the symbol of Yemeni women fighting for change. For her, along with her peers at Women Journalists Without Chains (WJWC), the struggle started long before 2011. For the last decade they have struggled not only to change their own status but that of the country as a whole. And regime loyalists have filled their journey with consistent harassment and death threats. A week after the revolution, Tawakkol became a rallying cause for the protestors after security forces detained her. She was chained as if she were a dangerous criminal, but the public pressure on the government was so intense that she was released less than two days later. After her release she wrote optimistically but with a sense of realism about the future of her country:

A new Yemen awaits us, with a better future for all. We are not blind to reality, but the fact is that the revolution has created social tranquility across the country as the people put their differences to one side and tackle the main issue together—no mean feat, given that there are an estimated 70m weapons in Yemen (21 million Yemenis on an average own three guns per person).[20]

Karman, married and a mother of three, went on to win the 2011 Nobel Peace Prize, along with two other women, for their defense of human rights. This young activist who belonged to the Al-Islah party—an offshoot of the Muslim Brotherhood—was harshly criticized by her conservative "brothers" in the movement for being outspoken and exposed in the public eye. But Karman made it clear that she believed equality as demanded by the revolution must begin with gender equality, and called for a civic and democratic, not Islamic, state.

Double and Triple Victims

Arab women are victimized as citizens and as females in the male-dominated society. Just as dictatorships abuse the majority of their nations, so do patriarchal societies abuse half of their members. Arguably there's a strong correlation between the state repression of citizens and men's repression of women as humiliated men take it out on their families in a failed, albeit subconscious, attempt to recover personal dignity. Working women have been exploited in three ways: on the job, at home, and by the political system. Nonetheless, at least employment offers them limited financial protection, something the jobless are forced to do without.

The generally macho state security services were particularly annoyed by women activists in Tahrir Square and tried to humiliate them repeatedly and publicly. Their harassment took an ugly turn when, during the revolution, security agents insisted on checking the virginity of eighteen women who were allegedly arrested so that they couldn't claim they had been sexually harassed. Their crime: peaceful protest. Although state security spokesmen denied any such examinations took place, a security chief told a Western journalist from CNN that such degrading treatment of women was a necessary precautionary measure to deter girls from making allegations of rape against officers, as if a woman who was not a virgin could not be raped.

"These girls were not like your daughters or mine," the Egyptian official told the journalist. "These camped out in tents with male protesters in Tahrir Square, and we found . . . molotov cocktails and [drugs]."[21]

After Amnesty International researched these allegations, it warned that "Women and girls must be able to express their views on the future of Egypt and protest against the government without being detained, tortured, or subjected to profoundly degrading and discriminatory treatment." In a different report, the group estimated that female genital mutilation is carried out on more than 70 percent of Egyptian girls.[22]

Interestingly, young women who face greater challenges in male-dominated Arab societies tend to do better than their male counterparts. Despite, or perhaps because of, the patriarchal nature of Arab society and sociocultural pressures, they seem more motivated to study and work harder in order to pursue a future in the workplace.[23]

3 | Rude Awakening

THE BAD AND THE UGLY

By the summer of 2011, the pattern of the Arab revolutions was following a familiar pattern. With their backs to the wall, the Arab world's dictators refused to see the writing behind them. Instead, they threatened their own citizens with terrible retribution and brought their wrath to bear when their warnings weren't heeded. When that, too, failed, the dictators made it clear that if pushed to the brink, they would take their countries down with them.

This led to a terrible waste of human life, national resources, and the breakdown of state institutions. It was as if the dictators were behaving like crime families rather than as national leaders. It also left a legacy of pain, hatred, and revenge, prolonging the transition to a better form of governance. The longer it took for a regime to fall, the more difficult it was to heal and rebuild.

The contrast between the relatively swift and peaceful pre–February 11 revolutions in Egypt and Tunisia, and the more complicated and far more violent revolutions that followed wasn't lost on anyone, nor was the difference among the regimes' reactions.

The Arab revolutions shared a common sociopolitical agenda, but their trajectories were different because of the political circumstances on the ground in each country. How the protestors mobilized mattered in each case, as did the way the regimes reacted to the protests. Equally important was how each of these regimes came into historical being. Those in the Mashreq (the countries to the east of Egypt) were carved out by imperial powers, those in the Gulf gained their independence peacefully, and the Maghreb (the countries west of Egypt, in north Africa) gained freedom through a long resistance struggle. Some of the regimes were totalitarian and others authoritarian, some were semi-developed and others terribly underdeveloped, some enjoyed a relatively harmonious civic nationalism, while others suffered from strong tribal, clan, and ethnic fault lines. Some regimes were rich with per capita annual income as high as $100,000, while others had a per capita income as low as $1,500.

In contrast to their Arab peers, Egypt and Tunisia have had strong middle and working classes, durable national institutions, and a cohesive modern identity within a long-established nation-state backed by thousands of years of collectively shared history. While Egypt and Tunisia both had cohesive national identities, this characteristic was missing from the other Arab states as they embarked on their revolutions. This explains in part why the Mubarak and Ben Ali regimes were kept relatively separate from the military and state, and how the military succeeded in breaking away from the dictators' grip and sided with the revolutions once they passed the threshold. This also allowed for the relatively peaceful, albeit slower and less radical, transformation of the revolutions, where the generals' power and privileges remained intact after the ousting of Mubarak and Ben Ali.

The fall of the two dictatorships within a few weeks is exceptional by any standard. But the persistence of their militaries in public life poured cold water on the revolutions. The generals of the old regime continued to hold onto emergency laws and military trials several months after the success of the revolutions. They were expected to pose more challenges to democratic change in the short and intermediate run.

The Supreme Council of the Armed Forces (SCAF) that took over from the president moved quickly to dissolve both houses of Egypt's parliament, the People's Assembly and the Shura Council, the week Mubarak was ousted. The revolutionaries raided the infamous State Security Intelligence (SSI)—the chief enforcer of Mubarak's repressive policies—before it was dissolved by the SCAF, following decades of allegations about widespread use of torture. A constitutional referendum was held in March of 2011, less than two months after the fall of the regime. Nearly 80 percent of the Egyptian people voted to overhaul the political system. And for the first time their votes counted. The NDP-infested student unions were purged and more than seventeen hundred local councils across the country were dismissed. And on April 16, the Supreme Administrative Court ordered that the National Democratic Party be dismantled. No surprise, perhaps, but not one prominent figure spoke out in defense of this sham organization.

Meanwhile, some of the old NDP officials and their backers—some of the most powerful people in the country—joined the ranks of common criminals. Mubarak and much of his inner circle had been arrested. Mubarak's two sons Gamal and Ala'a, Prime Minister Ahmed Nazif, People's Assembly Speaker Fathi Sorour, Shura Council Speaker Safwat el-Sherif, Interior Minister Habib el-Adly, Tourism Minister Zuhair Garranah, and Housing Minister Ahmed el-Maghrabi were put on trial. Steel tycoon Ahmed Ezz, as well as Hussein Salem, a major shareholder in the East Mediterranean Gas Company who allegedly sold gas to Israel at below-market prices, had both been arrested on charges of squandering public funds. ex-finance minister Youssef Boutros-Ghali, who fled to London, was convicted and sentenced in absentia to thirty years in jail. (Reportedly, he was acquitted on the corruption charges in early July 2011.) Adly, viewed as a key organizer of the counter-revolutionary violence that left more than eight hundred people dead, was sentenced to twelve years in prison for corruption.

On the same day the SCAF dissolved parliament, it suspended the constitution and later selected a committee to write Egypt's interim constitution—or simply amend parts of it, notably those articles relating to the parliamentary and presidential elections. The process was marred by lack of public debate; many of the young revolutionaries argued the committee's make-up wasn't satisfactory and didn't go far enough. Its chairman—seventy-seven-year-old Judge Tarek el-Bishry, who was a major critic of Mubarak—had Islamist ties. The committee also included a Coptic judge and a member of the Muslim Brotherhood, but there were no women. The committee's limited mandate also left important issues—such as the greatly criticized presidential powers—which will remain intact until a new draft constitution is written by a committee appointed by the elected assembly. The military made public its final draft only three weeks before it went up for national vote, though the vote was considered orderly and transparent, and the interim constitution was quickly approved by public referendum. Among other things, it opened up political participation, reinvigorated the judiciary, and restrained some executive power, but it fell short of overhauling the system. The interim constitution required that a one-hundred-member committee write a permanent constitution within six months of the new parliament taking office.

On the down side, the military regime didn't lift the emergency law that was first instituted during the 1967 war with Israel and was reintroduced in 1981 after the assassination of Anwar Sadat. Despite the regime's commitment on February 11, 2011, to "end the state of emergency as soon as the current circumstances are over," the country continued to live under the emergency law through the spring, and it was not until the end of the summer that the SCAF spoke about lifting it. Under the law, security forces could violently break up public demonstrations, search property, arrest civilians without a warrant, and detain whomever they wished indefinitely. They could refer anyone to special emergency courts whose decisions only Mubarak could overturn. The revolutionary movement believed that the military police had arrested up to ten thousand civilians during, and in the period leading up to, the revolution. Many were subject to ad-hoc military trials without legal representation and given suspended sentences, while others were shipped off to prison.

To add further insult to the revolutionaries, the SCAF-appointed interior ministry replaced the State Security Agency with a new National Security Force with arguably no more than cosmetic changes to its original mandate, which did little to reform the central security forces. The state's riot police, which disappeared during the revolution, now returned with a vengeance to violently confront demonstrations. Their involvement in breaking up a demonstration in the summer of 2011 left more than one thousand people injured. Only one policeman, Mohamed Abdel Moneim, was tried and sentenced for killing protesters during the revolution, but he remained at large.

The situation wasn't all that different in Tunisia. In both cases, once the dictators had been driven out, the military took over, suspending the revolution in time until elections could be held at the end of the year.

Tunisia's relatively peaceful move toward instituting the goals of the revolution was made possible, thanks to the military's support of the protestors. But it's slow, frustrating, and at times reactionary posture served only to defuse the revolutionary process. After Ben Ali declared a state of emergency, fired his government, dissolved parliament, and fled the country—all in one night—Tunisia's constitutional court, the highest legal authority on constitutional affairs, ruled that Speaker of Parliament Foued Mebazaa would be interim president. He was sworn in the following day, on January 15, 2011. Supported by Tunisia's military, which had tried hard to slow down the revolution and prevent any further escalation, Mebazaa asked Mohamed Ghannouchi to form a coalition government. The fact that Ghannouchi had served as prime minister for the previous twelve years, and that his new government included many of Ben Ali's lackeys, didn't go well with the revolutionaries. The protest movement continued, though, demanding the dissolution of the government and putting Ben Ali's cronies on trial. The resignations of Mebazaa, Ghannouchi, and other ministers from Ben Ali's ruling party, the Constitutional Democratic Rally (RCD), were hardly enough to satisfy the angry opposition. Government reshuffling and promises of responding better to people's demands were also ignored.

But when Tunisia's military leader, General Rachid Ammar proclaimed, "Our revolution is your revolution," he had, for all practical purposes, ended *l'ancien régime*'s chances to rebound and retake power. "The army will protect the revolution," he said to demonstrators nearby his headquarters, leaving the regime's security forces little choice but to abandon their plans to hold on to power. It was the military's refusal to fire on civilians that had led to Ben Ali's final exit, and it was its insistence on moving beyond Ben Ali that paved the way toward a new coalition government headed by the eighty-four-year-old former Bourguiba minister Beji Caid Essebsi. Ben Ali's ruling party, the RCD, was finally dissolved by court order in March of 2011.

In April, Tunisia's electoral commission adopted a gender parity law that required each party to run an equal number of male and female candidates in the October 23, 2011, elections. But the situation remained far from satisfactory as most leading candidates in the fall elections were men. A curfew was imposed amid fresh street protests in May that year, and more protests followed in the summer as the government fell short of people's expectations. After violence rocked the center and southwest of Tunisia, and three towns were placed under curfew in late summer, Prime Minister Caid Essebsi pledged the "strict imposition of the state of emergency" decreed after the fall of Ben Ali—a state of emergency that was prolonged by successive decrees until after the elections. Essebsi's government banned "all demonstrations, all strikes, and all meetings that could affect the security of the country." He insisted, "The minister of the interior has the right to place under house arrest any person known for activities affecting internal security."[1]

In retrospect, the events that led to and followed the fall of Mubarak and Ben Ali were as much military coups as they were the culmination of revolutionary pressures. The highly publicized Egyptian and Tunisian military appearances following the revolution, and the at times less-than-merited praise by the revolutionaries, allowed the generals to slow the pace of the revolutions and take the steam out of the pressure for the radical change their nations hoped for.

But Arab youth elsewhere were ecstatic about the quick victories in Tunisia and Egypt, and they wanted more of the same. Like a virus, the will for change spread to every corner of the Arab world.

THE REVOLUTIONARY CONTAGION

Smelling the Jasmine

Soon after Tunisian and Egyptian youth began their protests, young Libyan activist leaders traveled to Egypt to absorb the revolutionary atmosphere. In Syria there were large solidarity marches; likewise in Bahrain and Jordan, where the youth began challenging the monarchy. Farther down the Red Sea, in Yemen, young men and women led big crowds to the public squares in protest. Three-quarters of all Yemenis were born under Saleh and knew no other leader since the 1990s. For these eighteen million Yemenis, political change was long due. They began to organize at Sana'a University Square, which was renamed Change Square, calling for better education, employment opportunities, and an end to poverty and illiteracy.

The young Libyans, Yemenis, Syrians, and Bahrainis learned valuable lessons about civil disobedience and peaceful protest from their counterparts in Egypt and Tunisia and soon turned shows of solidarity into mass protests across their own governments. Their slogans, chants, signs, and humor, as well as their courage, mirrored Tahrir and November 7 squares. Within the protest movement in Syria, Bahrain, and Yemen, women took on a prominent role, becoming leading spokespersons and coordinators of revolutionary activity. Even when there was resistance to the prominent role they were playing, they marched on.

No one, for example, could stop Syria's Dr. Fida Horani, the daughter of one of the Ba'ath founders, Akram Horani. The elected head of the Damascus Declaration (a 2005 manifesto that united three major opposition groups), Dr. Horani had already served time in jail. Alongside her were human rights activists Razan Zaitouneh, Suhair al-Atassi, and countless others. Many others have fought for freedom and democracy in Syria: community organizers, nongovernmental organization leaders and members, labor unions, and members from professional associations. Others have been activists and opposition figures such as author Michel Kilo, filmmaker Omar Amiralay, businessman Riyadh Seif, economist Aref Dalila, poet Faraj Beirakdar, and authors Yassin Haj Saleh, Fayez Sara, Ali al-Abdallah, Walid al-Bunni, and Dr. Yasser Eiti. Like the Egyptian George Ishaq and Mohammad El-Sayed Said, these revolutionaries' long and bitter dealings with the regime have gone unnoticed by the outside world, but they were not lost on a new generation of Syrians and Arabs.

In Syria and, to a greater degree, Libya, where the regimes had destroyed political life by banning or domesticating opposition parties and destroying civil society, protests were organized rapidly from the bottom up in neighborhoods, villages, towns, and regions. These coordination committees or revolutionary councils started to put together and plan their efforts. Slowly but surely, they nominated spokespersons to articulate a guiding vision and rally popular support internally while seeking international solidarity. The segmented, polycentric network of revolutionary groups, often referred to as SPIN, allowed them to function in relative autonomy. The absence of a hierarchy allowed for greater mobility and adaptation to the facts on the ground in each town and protected the revolutions from one quick and catastrophic blow the regimes hoped to inflict in order to decapitate them.

Allergic to Jasmine

While the protestors proved to be nimble and inventive, the Arab dictators, on the other hand, lacked imagination. A clever promotion on Al Jazeera news network featured the grand statements made by Ben Ali, Hosni Mubarak, and Muammar Gaddafi since the earliest days of the popular uprising and juxtaposed them against each other to show a similar pattern of deception in their reactions. All three started by underlining their legitimacy as servants of the state and its people. When calls for reform intensified, the dictators underlined how they sought no glory or position and were more than happy to move on once they could secure "responsible alternatives." Soon after, the regimes began to escalate the use of force even as they repeated slogans about the greatness of their nations. Indeed, all the autocrats, including those of Yemen, Bahrain, and Syria, responded to people's demands for serious reforms with severe repression. When that didn't work, they changed course and offered empty appeasement that was hardly convincing. This change was no more than a delay in tactics, but even if their motives had been sincere, it was too late.

The regimes continued to ignore the inevitable, insisting that their countries were different and immune to revolutionary change. The Egyptian regime quickly dismissed the comparison to Tunisia as "an invention of silly television" in the words of Ahmed Aboul Gheit, its foreign minister, words he spoke a mere three weeks before the government was ousted.

Gaddafi berated the Tunisians for getting rid of Ben Ali, while boasting of the stability and vitality of Libya's people's democracy. A few weeks later, opposition groups swept through most of Libya; within six months he was toppled.

The Yemeni regime followed the same path as its neighbors. It mocked the hundreds of students who first assembled in the university esplanade as childish imitators only to see them take over the streets and public squares of the capital Sana'a and spread their protest to seventeen of the nation's nineteen regions. The regime dispatched its party's loyalists to the streets and public squares to project its own power. However, the regime's reliance on live ammunition and their use of excessive force soon backfired.

Bashar al-Assad ridiculed any comparison between Syria and the "sell out regimes" and boasted of his regime's popular nationalistic credentials. Assad told the *Wall Street Journal*, "Syria is stable. Why? Because you have to be very closely linked to the beliefs of the people. This is the core issue. When there is divergence . . . you will have this vacuum that creates disturbances."[2]

The Syrian autocrat didn't think his people were ready for democracy, and if change did come, it would be short lived—in other words, a chimera. Regardless of the alternatives, Syrians weren't buying into Assad's stale Ba'athist nationalism, an ideology that served as a mere slogan or an alibi to justify dictatorship in the name of the people.

When the region's various dictators finally realized they had no choice but to face up to their peoples' demands for justice, some regimes hoped to buy more time to weather the storm, while others used force to calm the storm and restore old times.

Buying Time

The Saudi monarchy was unhappy with the change in Egypt and Tunisia and distressed by the way in which the West gave up on Mubarak and Ben Ali. King Abdullah characterized the protesters on the streets of Egypt as intruders, who "in the name of freedom of expression, have infiltrated the brotherly people of Egypt, to destabilize its security and stability and they have been exploited to spew out their hatred in destruction, intimidation, burning, looting, and inciting a malicious sedition."[3] The Wahhabite kingdom stood against popular participation of any sort in the running of state affairs, and rejected on principle the toppling of a Muslim leader through revolution or its equivalent.

The rich authoritarian regimes showered their people with money, in order to prevent revolutionary change. The monarchies of Kuwait and Saudi Arabia doled out billions of dollars directly to their people and made huge contributions to Bahrain, Jordan, and Oman to contain potential upheaval.

A week after the ousting of President Mubarak, Saudi Arabia's King Abdullah made $130 billion available for royal grants, public sector salary increases, and other immediate spending, and made bombastic promises about housing and investments without announcing any reforms. Although an increasing number of Saudis sought constitutional reforms and the younger generation of royals wants to play a greater role in ruling the kingdom, the monarch and his advisers seemed adamant on maintaining their own pace and calendar regardless. By the end of the summer, Saudi Arabian women were allowed for the first time to participate in municipal elections and cast votes for the Shura (Consultative) Council picked by the king.

In Morocco, King Mohammad VI sought to contain the brewing dissatisfaction by rushing to cede certain powers to elected institutions through a referendum on new constitutional reforms. The people voted for it, but clearly they wanted much more. And so did King Abdullah of Jordan, who approved by royal decree new constitutional reforms in an attempt to release some steam from the mounting popular dissatisfaction. The reforms fell short of the opposition's expectations, which demanded more powers for the parliament and less for the monarch in such issues as appointing a prime minister or dissolving parliament.

TINY KINGDOM, BIG GRIEVANCE

In Bahrain, one of the poorest of the Gulf States, money and promises failed to restrain the people's anger. Bahrainis demanded their rights and a stronger power-sharing arrangement with the regime they had grown to distrust. The island-kingdom has been ruled by the Khalifa family for the last sixty years, divided between father, Isa bin Salman (1961–1991), and son, Hamad, who succeeded him as the Emir and changed the tiny country into a kingdom for no obvious reasons other than power and prestige. The Khalifas belong to the ruling Sunni minority that had for a long time relegated the Shia majority to second-class status. Tensions between the monarchy and the majority have at times flared, particularly since the 1979 Islamic revolution in Shia-majority Iran. Indeed, the spread of the Arab revolution after Tunisia and Egypt was complicated by regional and international power equations, starting with a proxy war between Saudi Arabia and Iran over the future of Bahrain.

Historically, the Bahraini majority has been quite diverse, including secular nationalists, leftists, and Ba'athists. Like other victimized Arab majorities, Bahrainis have had civic and political grievances of their own, unrelated to religious, ideological, or geopolitical considerations. They protested the dictatorship of the absolute monarchy and demanded democratic and economic rights like those demanded in other Arab countries. The speed at which the protest movement expanded served only to increase the urgency of their demands.

It started with hundreds of Bahrainis demonstrating on February 4, 2011, in support of their peers in Egypt. Within ten days, mass protests erupted across the island, with February 14 marking the beginning of the Bahraini revolution, a revolution that was supported by various political associations and encouraged by the fall of the Egyptian dictator. Subsequent days brought intense crackdowns by the security forces. However, the demonstrations continued to grow as the opposition centered on Pearl Square in Manama, making their mark in the wake of Tahrir

Square. Young men and women led the protest, supported by people of all ages and backgrounds. The turning point came in the middle of March when it became clear that the monarchy was going to lose to the people, and opposition members of parliament walked out in protest against the regime's unwillingness to initiate constitutional reforms.

King Hamad Bin Khalifa invoked martial law and asked for military assistance from Saudi Arabia and the Gulf countries, which was answered within days, as Riyadh and the United Arab Emirates dispatched forces under the auspices of the Gulf Regional Council (GCC) to help quell the protest movement. The ensuing crackdown and the gross violations of human rights were condemned by international human rights organizations. The attack on the Sulaymaniyah Hospital in the city, which involved the abuse of doctors, nurses, and patients, exposed the horrors of a regime eager to finish off the protest movement at any cost.

It was astonishing to hear during the brutal crackdown that the regime was primarily worried, not about the loss of human life or the unravelling of Bahrain, but by the cancellation of the Formula One car race hosted by the kingdom every winter. Like their Arab counterparts, the younger generation of Bahrain's ruling family had ostentatious hobbies, which gave a new meaning to the axiom "men are boys with more expensive toys." Eventually, a rescheduled race in March was also canceled as instability continued on the island, sending a clear message to the world about the gravity of the situation in the kingdom.

However, the heavy-handed, regional military approach succeeded in quelling these peaceful, public protests. The crown prince was entrusted to start a national dialogue to bridge differences. The main opposition group, Al Wifaq, expressed interest if talks would lead to change, not to a stalemate. However, the regime's own divisions and lack of seriousness coupled with pressure from Saudi

Arabia, drowned dialogue, and the regime continued its crackdown through arrests, torture, and dismissals from jobs.

Meanwhile, the Saudi and Iranian exploitation of Bahraini tensions to preserve and advance their own interests continued to polarize the kingdom. These rival theocracies opportunistically recast a struggle essentially about equality and democracy into a Sunni-versus-Shia conflict. For sure, Bahrain was not without sectarian tensions, especially since the Sunni minority had kept the Shia majority at an arm's length from power. It is also true that not many Sunnis rallied with the protest movement. But by trumpeting the cause of Bahrain's Shia, Iran undermined the civic nature of the Bahraini struggle.

By the end of the summer, the protests resumed with tens of thousands demonstrating to underline their continued commitment for constitutional reforms and more equitable power-sharing in the country. They also boycotted the partial September 2011 parliamentary elections, which were held to fill the seats vacated by protesting Al Wifaq members when the upheaval began. Ali Salman, the general secretary of Al Wifaq, insisted: "The situation is a tinderbox, and anything could ignite it at any moment. . . . If we can't succeed in bringing democracy to this country, then our country is headed toward violence. Is it in a year or two years? I don't know. But that's the reality."[4]

IMPERIOUS REPUBLICS
FLEDGLING REVOLUTIONS

The Supremacy of Violence

None of the Arab regimes were willing to give up power voluntarily, but some resisted more violently than others, depending on circumstances and their capacity to preempt or prevent change. In Yemen, Libya, and Syria, the power structure was less amenable to change. Ruling families, clans, tribes, and ethnicity had direct and total domination of the army and state institutions, making a military breakaway from the regimes improbable. They were also complicated by regional and international interference, a point upon which I will later elaborate. Not only has this delayed the toppling of these regimes, but it has also led to prolonged bloodshed with great cost to life and property. The dictators' own militias, Special Forces, and Republican Guards were better equipped, trained, and financed than their own national armies, which gave the dictators greater staying power. The personnel of these militias were recruited on the basis of ethnic or clan identification with the regime. They would fight for the status quo until death. And they had the necessary experience in repression.

But instead of containing the upheavals, the dictators ended up emboldening the new protest movements and their supporters. They failed to learn the lessons from the fall of their counterparts. With their long and bloody history of repression of public protests, the security forces of the various regimes were unaccustomed and even indifferent to riot control. They rushed to use excessive force and live ammunition and dispatched tanks to major cities. Worse, they demonized their own people to justify their bloody crackdown, referring to them as rats, germs, spies, terrorists, a fifth column, and foreign agents. They also blamed Islamists, foreign powers, and foreign media outlets, specifically Al Jazeera news network, for instigating violence. Realizing that their fight was primarily against time, the regimes tried to avoid increasing public and international pressure, which could weaken their hold on power or strip them of whatever remaining legitimacy they had as sovereign state actors that are shielded from international intervention.

LIBYAN TRAGEDY

The Libyan leader, Muammar Gaddafi, was as eccentric as his regime had been callous. Although he paid more attention to foreign policy, Gaddafi left a dreadful mark on his people after four decades of repression. When he took power through a military coup in 1969, Gaddafi was only twenty-seven years old and a great admirer of the pan-Arab and socialist ideals of Egypt's Gamal Abdel Nasser. The latter's death a year later had for all practical purposes left Gaddafi politically orphaned.

Gaddafi hustled to build Arab unity but failed dismally at each and every occasion to establish an "Arab federation," "Arab union," or "Islamic Arab republic" with his counterparts, near and far. After these failures, he turned his attention to domestic affairs in the mid-1970s by declaring a "cultural revolution" and the formation of "People's Committees" or subsidized regime loyalists in schools, hospitals, workplaces, and administrative districts. Within four years, he changed his mind and this time declared a "people's revolution," changing the country's official name from the Libyan Arab Republic to the Great Socialist People's Libyan Arab Jamahiriyah. He set up the "Revolutionary Committees" that answered to the regime, implemented its dictates, and defended its policies—through fear tactics if necessary—and in the process ushered in political chaos, administrative nightmares, and eventually economic stagnation.

Libya, a country of nearly six million, could never satisfy Gaddafi's megalomania. He went on to intervene militarily in neighboring Chad and became active in African affairs during the Cold War, a move that earned him wrath from the United States. A tit for tat ensued, with the United States downing Libyan planes and bombing Gaddafi's headquarters in the 1980s, in response to him reportedly masterminding the bombing of French and

American airliners, as well as a discothèque in Berlin. Tensions continued to define his relations with the West through the post–Cold War period, until a major shift in Libya's foreign policy took place after the September 11 attacks and the U.S. invasion of Afghanistan and Iraq. He came clean with his nuclear program and began a normalization of relations with Western powers after paying a few billion dollars in compensation for the families of the victims of the bombing of Pan Am flight 103 over Lockerbie, Scotland.

In no time, the "rehabilitated" Gaddafi was embraced by Western leaders and the Gaddafi family was hosted in Western capitals with open arms. Soon after, Libya became the head of the African Union, which it had helped found a decade earlier, the Arab League, and was elected to the U.N. Human Rights Council, and the UN Security Council. Libya's improved status on the world stage led the megalomaniacal Gaddafi to crown himself Africa's "king of kings."[5]

Western leaders laughed at his appearance, Arab leaders laughed at his jokes, and Africans laughed at his jabs against the former colonial North, but the Libyans weren't laughing. Gaddafi's despotic regime continued to repress, terrorize, and torture his opposition.

Breaking the Fear Barrier

As soon as the popular uprising erupted in Libya, notably in Benghazi and the eastern parts of the country, Gaddafi tried to frame it as a criminal activity carried out by hallucinating drug addicts and their pushers. But as soon as the desire for change turned into reality and the revolutionaries swept through a number of cities and took over state institutions, Gaddafi began to speak of serious threats faced by the republic from "thugs and rats." Later, he threatened to punish the foreign-instigated "armed gangs" whom he accused of kidnapping and threatening national security.

When Libya gained international attention in the wake of the dramatic changes in Tunisia and Egypt, Gaddafi changed his tune once again. Playing on Western fears of al-Qaeda, he said his regime was confronted by the "terrorist organization" and its Libyan Islamist affiliates. He warned of an escalation that would threaten stability of the Mediterranean and affect the security of all its surrounding nations, including Israel. The mention of Israel raised eyebrows among those who long trusted his nationalistic rhetoric.

As more and more officials, diplomats, and military personnel began to defect in favor of the revolution, Gaddafi warned of betrayal by traitors and the existence of a fifth column. The regime's failure to stem the defiance of Libyans and their aspiration for change prompted "Gaddafi junior," Saif al-Islam, to threaten civil war and "rivers of blood." The Gaddafis preempted Arab and international condemnation of the regime's use of excessive force by taking a righteous path, boasting of their "great republican" fight against reactionary Arabs whom they cursed and mocked at the Arab League.

Libya could have gone down the Tunisian or Egyptian path of change after its militaries conceded the need for regime change. But the Gaddafi dynasty would not have it, instead threatening to take down the whole country. The powerful, clan-led militias, financed and groomed to defend the regime's "country estate," sided with their paymasters. The Gaddafis continued to put on a brave face by projecting images of pro-Gaddafi demonstrations in Tripoli to offset the images of anti-Gaddafi ones in the East.

Slowly but surely, many members of the Libyan regime and military began to defect and the country rallied around two visions: a majority that demanded free and democratic Libya and a heavily armed minority that wanted to maintain Gaddafi's despotic rule. The split took on a territorial divide in the early phase of the fighting, with the opposition taking control of the east and Gaddafi loyalists controlling the western part of the country.

The bombastic tone of the ruling family gave Western powers the pretext to legitimize "international intervention to protect Libyan civilians." The U.N. Security Council promptly adopted Resolution 1970, which slapped the regime with tough sanctions. It then adopted Resolution 1973, which authorized the use of all means necessary to protect civilians, short of boots on the ground. Russia, China, Germany, and Brazil abstained from the vote over fears of a repeat of the military campaign against Iraq and the subsequent chaos that ensued.

However, the leading Western powers, which all looked so powerless as revolutions swept through Tunisia and Egypt, grew worried as the region began to slip from their dominion. They were eager to play a role in this key oil rich Mediterranean country set strategically at the heart of North Africa.

The battle over Libya took a turn for the worse as Western-led intervention got underway and NATO began to impose a no-fly zone by bombing facilities all over the country. The military intervention of former colonial powers, coupled with the ensuing civilian casualties, further complicated the situation and set a dangerous precedent in the region. Soon after its intervention in Libya, NATO considered the "humanitarian intervention" under the pretext of "the Right to Protect" a success, which some Western commentators considered a prototype of more interventions to come. A repeat in the likes of Syria, for example, could have disastrous consequences on the country and the region.

In response, Gaddafi resorted to one of his favorite tactics: framing the conflict as a populist Muslim battle against the oppressive Christian West. He rushed, once again, to condemn this new "crusade" against Islam and rally national and religious sentiment against the "Western-led military assault." Thousands died by the time Gaddafi was ousted at the end of the summer of 2011. Some in the National Transitional Council —the resistance movement in Libya—say about fifty thousand had died, and thousands more were injured and displaced. However, these figures were suspicious.[6] As the Transitional Council took over the capital and the dust began to settle in the country's urban centers, it became clear that the opposition had also been responsible some brutal acts of their own during the same summer months.

YEMEN UNHAPPY

A soldier and canny operator, Yemen's President Ali Abdullah Saleh is a street-smart politician. Since his power grab in 1978, he has had one main concern: how to maintain the primacy and longevity of his regime. For more than a decade, he secured and strengthened his power at the helm of North Yemen by manipulating the country's tribal makeup through a system of patronage. In 1990, he expanded his authority to the People's Democratic Republic of Yemen, the Marxist South Yemen, by signing on to a union between the two states over which he presided. When the southern leaders discovered that their union was going to be similar to the German union, where the west overwhelmed the east, they tried to secede. But Saleh wouldn't have it and dispatched his military to take full control of Aden, the former capital of the south, in 1994. Unification by military fiat gave the autocratic president more influence. What began as an attempt to establish a unified democracy in the post–Cold War era, soon turned into a dictatorship. The president consolidated his power by boxing in his potential adversaries, playing off northern-led Islamists against socialist, secular southerners.

However, Saleh couldn't stabilize the country. The political and security tensions in the south continued, while socioeconomic conditions deteriorated in the country. It exposed the failures of the regime and its dependency on foreign economic and military aid. Renewed confrontations against the Houthi minority in the north in 2009 led to direct Saudi military interference on the side of the government and exposed the weakness of a regime incapable of imposing order on its own territory. The precarious military instability exacerbated an already unstable situation in Yemen where, according to the interior minister, there are sixty million guns, a figure that is perhaps exaggerated, but worrying nonetheless.[7]

Little wonder that Yemen, a country of twenty-two million, has been at the bottom end of the Arab human development index. Half of the population is illiterate and lives under the poverty line. One-third is unemployed—a high percentage of which are young people. Despite having the capacity to produce around 450,000 barrels of oil per day, Yemen has long teetered on the edge of social and political unrest. The regime's corruption and waste led to continuous economic woes, a faltering currency, and oil production plummeting to two-thirds of the country's capacity.

None of that seemed to worry Yemen's Arab neighbors or the larger global community until al-Qaeda made Yemen its center of operations for the Arabian Peninsula. The group's attacks against British interests and the USS *Cole* in 2000 paved the way after the 9/11 attacks for new cooperation with the United States on all security fronts. In January 2010, a year before Yemenis descended on the streets to begin their revolution, Western powers convened in London, along with Saudi Arabia and other Arab autocracies, to find new ways to support the thirty-two-year-old dictatorship as an ally in "the global war on terror." Saleh knew all too well that he was secure in his position, and he was more than ready to exploit it to solidify his power. He was also ready to deceive not only the West, but his own people as well. He reportedly told his American counterparts to let him take credit for U.S. drone attacks against suspected al-Qaeda targets in his country, demonstrating that he was willing to conspire with a foreign power to bomb and cheat his own country.

Youthful Euphoria

Long referred to as "The Happy Yemen" in Arab folklore and history, the country isn't so happy anymore. Yemen's incredible natural beauty has been brutalized by several decades of conflict. A generally easy-going people, thanks to their daily dose of qat, a mild, druglike stimulant, Yemenis have been dealing with depression on all fronts. Worse, the pent-up tensions in the country threatened to turn it into another Somalia.

However, contrary to fearful warnings about the alternative to Saleh's centralized rule, Yemenis didn't disintegrate into civil war, and al-Qaeda hardly made inroads in the country. Nor did the nation splinter into separate warring regions. Instead, Yemenis of all backgrounds have followed in the footsteps of Tunisia and Egypt. In January 2011, students and youth protested under the slogan "We want to get an education. We want to put an end to unemployment, poverty, and illiteracy" and chanted "Peaceful! Peaceful!"

In a country where every man is armed, peace is easier said than done. The youth set up checkpoints at the entry to the university square and searched protestors for weapons. Most came unarmed to join the peaceful revolution; peaceful at any cost, said one human rights activist after getting a vicious beating. They denied the regime the pretext to use heavy weapons against the protesters. Saleh nonetheless unleashed his thugs to gun down protestors.

The more violence the regime used, the more the protest movement swelled and spread. Young men and women joined and led the protests with a steadfast spirit never seen before. Yemenis not only shocked the regime, but they also surprised themselves. The high level of civility, passion, clarity of vision, and persistence in the demand for democratic change has underlined the promise of a new beginning for the burdened nation.

The Yemeni youth have focused their peaceful civil disobedience on regime change, but in reality they were eager to overhaul the whole sociopolitical structure in the country. Not only were their slogans directed against Saleh, but also the political parties and personalities that had long appeased or schmoozed with the regime for narrow, factional interests or personal gains. The youthful protest was revolutionary in its spirit, and the crackdown failed to deter the protests from spreading to the other major cities of Taiz and Aden.

As in Egypt and Tunisia, the success of protests led to better organization and less improvisation among the youth. Three important groups became visible:

1. The Supreme Council for the Youth Revolution, the face of the protest movement, which included civil society and young political activists.
2. The Supreme Coordination, which included many of the Islah Party's youth wing, along with many independent activists. As with Egypt's young Islamic brothers, who were the first to join the revolution, the young Islahists were far ahead of their elders.

3. The Revolutionary Coordination Council for Change, consisting of liberal, left-leaning civil society activists.

The success of the youth in sustaining and widening the protest movement was the result of focusing only on the fall of the ruling family, ending corruption, and demanding parliamentary elections.

Bigger and More Problematic

The escalation of violence by the Yemeni regime began to tip the balance and led to mass defections from the establishment to the opposition. Five generals, including Ali Muhsen al-Ahmar from the president's tribe, defected to the opposition, causing a split in the army, and encouraged the defection of many high-level government officials. The mounting support for change among most of the political parties, tribes, and Islamist groups weakened Saleh. By the end of the summer, the opposition claimed they were in control of most parts of the country, excluding the capital Sana'a, which remained under the control of Saleh's forces.

However, once a section of the old elite, many of whom had previously worked for Saleh, joined the opposition forces, the democracy movement began to show signs of stress. What began as a clear-cut fight between youth and an autocratic regime was soon overshadowed by an inter-elite conflict. The clearest danger came in the form of an armed showdown between the tribes affiliated with the opposition and the regime's special forces or the Republican Guards.

Likewise, attempts by Gulf States to mediate between Saleh and a coalition of opposition parties in order to reach a compromise that would remove Saleh but allow the regime to remain intact posed a problem for the young revolutionaries in freedom square. Saleh accepted the initiative in the summer but didn't sign off on it until the end of November 2011. The initiative, however, wasn't ironclad, nor was Riyadh serious about replacing Saleh or his regime in favor of the revolution.

The Saudis backed a transition managed by a coalition that included the old regime, especially the Congress Party, which controls four-fifths of the legislature, as well as other symbols of the old rule. They wanted to ensure that any future government in Yemen didn't pose a challenge to its regional power, and certainly wouldn't contest the border agreement signed with President Saleh that left Saudi Arabia with rich oil regions it annexed after their war in 1934.

And like Bahrain, the Saudis dominated the debate over Yemen. Even Washington felt compelled to follow in Riyadh's footsteps. Saudi Arabia had long nurtured a system of patronage inside Yemen through the transfer of billions of dollars and the establishment of mosques and Salafi religious schools. When asked what happened if the Gulf initiative failed, U.S. undersecretary of state Jeffrey Feltman insisted that the United States was behind the Gulf/Saudi role. Indeed, U.S. policy toward the Arabian Peninsula was basically outsourced to Saudi Arabia.

Meanwhile, various components of the revolution, including the Islamists, leftists, and nationalists had reached a "salvation accord" that envisioned a democratic state and agreed to replace the presidential system with a parliamentary system. The accord also offered to support the youth in Change Square, who, all along, remained indifferent to all attempts at dialogue and reconciliation with the ruling regime. Saleh's response was categorical, as he dispatched his forces in the beginning of June to arrest or kill major opposition figures, notably attacking the headquarters of Sheikh Hamid al-Ahmar. They failed. Within two days, a suicide bombing targeting the president killed five and forced Saleh to seek four months of medical treatment in Saudi Arabia.

The course of the revolution in Yemen was very similar to that in Egypt and Tunisia. It started with demands for limited political and economic reforms, but escalated soon after into calls for regime change after a major security crackdown. What started as a youth movement was soon joined by political elites and tribal and military factions. However, unlike the relatively peaceful ousting of Ben Ali and Mubarak, Salah proved to be a much tougher opponent. His son Ahmad al-Ahmar, the head of the Republican Guards, along with his brothers and cousins, who hold leadership positions in the military, dragged the country into a bloody morass, just as Gaddafi had done in Libya.

Saleh was unrelenting. He blackmailed his American sponsors, threatening in a *Washington Post/Time* magazine interview in September 2011 that his fall would empower al-Qaeda. The same week, Saleh leaned on a government-financed religious council of scholars to issue a decree against the revolutionaries, many of whom were themselves Islamists. The council complied, declaring that it was "sinful" to protest against the state and proclaiming that the security forces were "fighting for the sake of God." The statement of the so-called religious scholars declared in their Fatwa, "What happens at demonstrations and sit-ins in residential areas and public roads is ungodly."

SYRIA, THE FEARLESS AND FEARSOME

Like their Arab brethren, Syrian political and human rights activists have had long and bitter encounters with the repressive regime. But as Syrian youth followed in the footsteps of their peers elsewhere, the transformation has been complicated by the tough resistance put up by the Assad regime.

Soon after his controversial accession to power in 2000, Bashar al-Assad called for a national dialogue to usher in democracy. The opposition began to prepare proposals for a transition toward a more pluralistic polity, and the subsequent exchanges came to be known as the "Damascus Spring." However, it proved to be short-lived, as it became increasingly clear that the regime was buying the young president time to strengthen his grip on power.

It's not clear why Assad was seen as a promising young leader, wanting and willing to institute reform and put an end to his father's dictatorship. At any rate, he showed himself as a leader incapable or unwilling to put the interests of his country ahead of those of the party, or the interests of the party and regime ahead of those of his clan.

Michel Kilo, an author and one of the human rights activists who joined the Damascus Spring dialogue and who was later jailed for his efforts, reflected that while the opposition movement was stopped in its tracks before it was able to broaden its circle of supporters, the country's educated middle class had been awakened. "Once the spark ignites the younger generation, we can withdraw. . . . At least we have paved the way."[8] They certainly did.

When a street vendor was attacked by a policeman in the middle of February, it provoked street protests in the capital, calling for the humiliation to stop. Within three weeks, the situation deteriorated in Dera'a, one of the impoverished districts of the country, a neighborhood similar to that of Tunisia's Sidi Bouzid, which triggered that country's revolution. After several children were arrested for writing graffiti that called for the end of the regime, the neighbors and clans protested to the local authorities. The local officials only humiliated the families, and the regime fired live ammunition at those gathered to protest in front of the regime's headquarters, which further inflamed passions and triggered large protests demanding an end to the humiliation.

Assad's belated attempt to appease the "nationalist people" of Dera'a fell on deaf ears as he had only words to offer them. It was too late: The Syrians had already joined the Arab revolutions. On March 20, protestors set fire to the ruling Ba'ath Party headquarters in Dera'a while chanting: "No, no to emergency law. We are a people infatuated with freedom!"

Wrong Conclusions

President Assad had the advantage of time. He had the opportunity to learn from the experiences of his Arab counterparts and to affect serious reform by breaking the Ba'ath hold on power and calling for elections. Instead, in the most surreal but truly Ba'athist way to deal with people's anger, Assad ordered the formation of a committee to raise living standards as if that would change anything. Worse, his long-promised speech on March 30, 2011, was extremely disappointing and insulting to those who patiently awaited similar promises over the last decade. The president boasted of having eradicated corruption and nepotism, gave flimsy excuses for not reforming since he took power a decade earlier, and promised to set up special committees to study any legitimate demands. His second speech a couple of weeks later was more humble in tone but brought too little. He admitted there was a gap separating the regime and people, tried to justify it, and offered more of the same vague promises to look into people's grievances. In the words of one opposition activist, the president spoke repeatedly of dignity but didn't recognize the regime's own violation of people's dignity. Just as Assad lifted the "state of emergency," he increased the regime's crackdown across the country to levels not seen before. His excuses for not following through with promised reforms over the previous decade included al-Qaeda's 9/11 attacks, the U.S. invasion of Iraq, the fallout from the assassination of the Lebanese prime minister Rafiq Hariri, the subsequent Syrian withdrawal from the country, the 2006 Israeli invasion of Lebanon, and Israel's 2008 invasion of the Gaza Strip. But what reform, if any, did the Syrian dictator have in mind?

Responding to a *Wall Street Journal* reporter about the sort of changes Assad envisioned, Assad made it clear how unclear the whole issue was in his mind:

> As for the internal, it is about doing something that is changing; to change the society, and we have to keep up with this change, as a state and as institutions. You have to upgrade yourself with the upgrading of the society. There must be something to have this balance. This is the most important headline . . . internally, there must be a different kind of changes: political, economic and administrative. These are the changes that we need. But at the same time you have to upgrade the society and this does not mean to upgrade it technically by upgrading qualifications. It means to open up the minds. Actually, societies during the last three decades, especially since the eighties have become more closed due to an increase in close-mindedness that led to extremism. This current will lead to repercussions of less creativity, less development, and less openness. You cannot reform your society or institution without opening your mind. So the core issue is how to open the mind, the whole society, and this means everybody in society including everyone. I am not talking about the state or average or common people. I am talking about everybody; because when you close your mind as an official you cannot upgrade and vice versa.[9]

No wonder, the regime went on to set one up panel or committee after another to study the need for change. The president was either utterly confused or deliberately confusing. But the Syrians knew all too well not to take this seriously. They remembered how it took only a few minutes in parliament to change the constitution to allow the young son to run for president in a referendum that won him a ridiculous 97 percent of the vote in 2000 and again in 2007. The regime never seemed to have any problems passing new laws when Assad wanted it. But when the people demanded change, suddenly there were bureaucratic obstacles invented to kill or slow down the process.

Fortunately, the Syrian revolutionaries had learned the right lessons from their fellow Arabs and would not be fooled by empty promises. Assad, on the other hand, had drawn the wrong conclusions from his fellow dictators. People went on the offensive, peacefully, and he took defensive action violently. The more force he used, the less effective it became. The regime dispatched tanks and other heavy weaponry to the urban areas and deployed snipers and armed thugs to take on protestors to no avail. Assad also drew the wrong conclusion from Western and Arab governments who supported reform within the existing system, for fear of chaos. He took their diplomatic encouragement for him to spearhead change as a political weakness, resulting from lack of collective will to apply pressure or impose tough sanctions. Turkey was especially supportive of reform under Assad in the beginning and attempted to mediate between him and the Turkey-based leadership of the Syrian Muslim Brotherhood. When that didn't work, Turkey turned against the regime with a vengeance.

Nor did the Syrian regime heed the call by prominent intellectuals and opposition figures for a national pact to establish a democratic, civilian, and modern state in Syria, based on national unity and the rejection of violence and sectarian divisions. Their agenda for political reform along "patriotic" lines included the following: the abrogation of the state of emergency and its replacement by a new emergency law solely for situations of war and natural disasters; the release of all political prisoners; the cancellation of Article 8 of the Constitution (which states that the "Ba'ath Party leads the state and society"); the amendment of the Constitution within a maximum period of six months; a change of the electoral law to include new political parties on condition that they do not accept foreign funding; new parliamentary elections; in-depth reform of the judicial system; a ban on all intelligence services from interfering in civilian affairs, except for national security issues; the end of any state control over the press; the launch of immediate economic measures to end corruption; nationalization of the two mobile phone companies; and the delivery of passports to all Syrians with no restrictions, except in cases of high treason.

While these basic reforms were all legitimate, it was abundantly clear that Assad rejected them for fear of losing his grip on power. So while he theoretically annulled the emergency laws that had governed the country for almost five decades, his security forces escalated their crackdown on peaceful protests. They accused the revolutionaries of betrayal and collaboration with foreign powers, and of carrying armed insurgency against the state. With a history of armed crackdown on its opposition, the Syrian regime made it clear that it won't be taught any lessons by outsiders. Instead, it was bent on teaching the Syrians another lesson they wouldn't forget!

Clearly, Assad had concluded that Mubarak and Ben Ali were too quick to quit, and Gaddafi and Saleh were too late to respond. The Syrian regime emulated Bahrain by preempting further escalation of popular upheaval through nationwide arrests and military deployment to the country's civilian hotspots in the south, middle, and north of the country. Within a few days, they killed hundreds, and within six months the crackdown left almost three thousand dead and tens of thousands arrested, as many fled the country to neighboring Turkey and Lebanon. Syrians hoped change in their country would look neither like "the insanity of Iraq or the chaos of Lebanon." And those in the relatively stable and more well-off cities of Damascus and Aleppo hesitated to join the revolution months into the protests. Their affluent communities and relatively prosperous middle classes had more to lose and were concerned that violence and instability would destroy their commercial interests for years to come. Damascus was especially fortified by the regime's Republican Guards to scare and preempt any major revolt. Like in the case Tripoli and Sana'a, the regime's forces tightly secured the capitals.[10]

However, the disproportionate use of force did little to quell the spirit of the uprising. After all, Syria isn't a tiny kingdom. Instead, the escalation emboldened an increasingly fearless population that had broken the fear barrier in the likes of Homs, Hama, Latakiyah, Deir al-Zour, Dera'a, and other towns and villages in the north and south. By the time the regime's Republican Guards started to shell various cities in the northwest and bomb Latakiyah from the sea, it was as if they were invading Syria. And the Syrians responded by calling for the "execution of the president."

Cell phone pictures documented the atrocities and humiliation faced by protestors chanting "Silmiya, silmiya" (peaceful, peaceful). In one widely viewed film, political cartoonist Ali Ferzat could be seen with broken fingers and a bruised face after he defended the protestors' peaceful demonstration. And only a few weeks later, a young woman was reportedly beheaded, mutilated, and sent back to her parents in the city of Homs as a lesson for all to learn.

But, as in Libya and Yemen, it became clear that the Syrian regime's use of force wasn't working. Once violence failed to deter people from turning out in large numbers, and once soldiers started defecting (or deserting), the regime's capacity to silence its critics crumbled. The regime's violent escalation pushed an increasing number of soldiers to defect, while at the same time a growing number of citizens began to carry and use arms against the military. In the process, hate killings and tensions increased between the Sunni majority and the Alawite-based regime, threatening the breakout of sectarian violence throughout the country.

Fearing a sectarian spill-over to an already instable region, the Arab League made proposals to the Assad regime that allowed for serious reform on the basis of dialogue with the opposition under the auspices of the League, which began with the withdrawal of its military forces from the cities and the release of all political prisoners. After much hesitation, the weakened regime accepted the initiative, perhaps to buy itself more time, but it had become increasingly clear that the struggle between the regime and its opponents had become a zero-sum clash where only the demise of, not reforming, the regime could end the escalation. Eventually, the Arab League suspended Syria's attendance and called on its member states to withdraw their ambassadors from Damascus, slapping the Assad regime on the wrist and the face.

ARAB POWERS VS. PEOPLE POWER

It wasn't just internal factors that complicated things in these states. Regional and international interference were also at play. Egypt and Tunisia may have provided the inspiration for the protests in other Arab states, but they were too preoccupied with their own post-revolutionary challenges to assist others in their own revolts. Other states weren't as passive or neutral. Algeria's generals weren't enthusiastic about the changes in its neighborhood, particularly where Islamists were playing a leading role in the revolutions. The North African country had already had its civil war in the 1990s, leaving tens of thousands of dead after the Islamist movement won the first round of parliamentary elections. Despite early protests in Algeria, the country wasn't ready for another bloody showdown. Meanwhile, critics of the Algerian regime accused it of aiding Gaddafi. (In fact, soon after the ousting of Gaddafi from Libya, some of his family members and associates fled to Algeria.) Sudan, which had gone through two major conflicts in the south and in Darfur, was also not eager for more political conflict as its border dispute intensified with South Sudan following its independence. Sudan's president Omar Al Bashir continued to exploit the tensions with his new southern neighbor to win nationalist support and deflect criticism away from his despotic rule.

The Shia-led Iraqi government wasn't thrilled by the Syrian revolution. Baghdad was particularly fearful that the conflict might spill across the border or that unfriendly Syrian Sunni fundamentalists might take control. The fact that the Syrian regime was an ally of its supporters in Tehran also aided Iraqi indifference. And a similar situation evolved in Lebanon where the Hezbollah and its governing coalition partners continued to support their Syrian ally, President Assad, and expressed concern about deepening sectarianism and the weakening of their front against Israel.

But the greatest complication to the Arab revolutions came from Saudi Arabia. If it was too late to reverse the changes in North Africa, the Saudis reckoned it wasn't so in Bahrain, where the protest movement was geographically too close for comfort to be allowed to take the upper hand. The Saudis defied regional and international pressures by moving swiftly to contain the Bahraini protest movement. Ruling over an antsy Shia minority of its own with a history of political agitation, the Saudi monarchy was adamant on preventing the upheaval from spreading. It warned against the ayatollahs of Iran exploiting the situation to form a fifth column among the Gulf Arabs.

But it was the regional pretext for its military intervention in Bahrain that further complicated the situation there. Saudi-Iranian rivalry had turned the just cause of a victimized people into a proxy conflict with each side accusing the other of interfering in Bahrain's internal affairs. Recent WikiLeaks information about the Saudis urging the United States to "cut the snake's head," in reference to the Iranian regime, didn't help calm the anger of the ayatollahs.

Like the Iranian ayatollahs, the Saudi monarchy is hostile to the nationalist, leftist, and even Islamist Arab trends that were an integral part of the Arab revolutions. After the Gulf Cooperating Council's Peninsula Shield Force's incursion into Bahrain, which helped the Saudi monarchy establish its authority under the pretext of "security is not negotiable in the Gulf region," Saudis turned their attention to Yemen.

The Wahhabite kingdom has long projected its influence in neighboring Yemen, first against the republicans who toppled the conservative imam in northern Yemen in 1962, and later against the Marxist regime that took power in southern Yemen after the British colonialists evacuated Aden in 1967. Riyadh has spent billions of dollars to buy tribal and political support in its troubled neighbor. It also helped support the Salafi movement in Yemen as part of its overall campaign to strengthen Wahhabite influence against the rise of nationalist and leftist ideologies throughout the Arab world, beginning in the early 1980s. These were the same Salafists that Saleh used to neutralize his opposition, according to a report from the U.S. embassy in

Sana'a on April 21, 2009—a report that was later made public by WikiLeaks.

When Saleh began to face more regional and international isolation as a result of his bloody crackdown on the peaceful revolution, Riyadh stepped in to prevent the total collapse of the regime. It was proposed that Saleh step down in favor of his vice president to pave the way for elections. However, as the proposals fell short of ousting the regime, it was rejected by the revolutionary youth. After an explosion led to the injury of Saleh, it was Saudi Arabia that hosted Saleh for four months of treatment.

Riyadh also expressed its support to the Assad regime, despite past strategic and political differences, most notably over Lebanon. But there were also limits to Saudi support of the Yemeni and Syrian leaders in light of the crackdown and escalation of violence. The only regime change in the region that Riyadh enthusiastically supported was that of Libya's Gaddafi, for whom it harbored a long-running hatred.

The bottom line was that the Wahhabite Saudi monarchy was hostile to the revolutionary changes in the Arab region from its beginning. Being one of the most conservative and theocracies in modern times, it worried that the contagious spirit of liberty would come to haunt it at home. Potential changes in Syria and Egypt and a preoccupation with its own internal affairs rendered the Saudi monarchy ever more vulnerable and prompted Riyadh to look elsewhere for support. For many years, agreement among Saudi Arabia, Egypt, and Syria provided a triangle of stability at the center of the Arab world that could confront major challenges or provide a balance against other regional powers. With the triangle displaced, Saudi Arabia was left exposed, even more than before. It was no surprise, then, that Riyadh spearheaded the GCC's offer to Jordan and Morocco to join their Gulf Council, in an attempt to unite all the Arab monarchies against Arab or international pressure to democratize. Saudi Arabia has established a "united league of Arab monarchies" to strengthen its regional position and preempt the revolutionary contagion from breaching its stronghold.

The all too visible and vocal role of Saudi Arabia and other conservative Gulf countries in the changes sweeping through the Arab world were quite confusing and indeed shocking to many. For example, they played an important role in extracting Arab League support for an international role in Libya and later participated in the international effort to enforce a no-fly-zone, while at the same time making sure the international community kept out of Bahrain. Likewise, Riyadh's support for an Arab league role in the Syria initiative, its insistence on an exclusively Gulf role in Yemen, and military intervention in support of the monarchy in Bahrain was not revolutionary by any standard; indeed, it was a double or triple-standard.

4 | Regional Power vs. People Power

The Arabs have long suffered from dictatorship, and they have also suffered from the interference of regional and global powers whose interests in the area have been in stabilizing these dictatorships, playing one power off another, and ignoring the will or the hopes of the Arab masses. Furthermore, the Arab-Israeli wars, the Iran-Iraq war, and the U.S.-led Gulf war have all taken a terrible toll on the Arab world, touching each and every individual. The failure of the pan-Arab project of the 1950s and '60s, Egypt's abdication of its leadership role since the late 1970s have left the region less united and more easily exposed to foreign interference. It was no accident that Iran, Turkey, and Israel have tried to fill this void and project their own influence. This has been especially true in the wake of the revolutions.

Considering their geographic proximity, strategic interests, and shared cultural and economic ties with the Arab world, Ankara and Tehran have shown an almost proprietary interest in the transformation taking place in their neighborhood. Backed by different pan-Islamic visions, Turkish and Iranian policies have had far-reaching implications.

With no love lost for Mubarak or Ben Ali, Iran's and Turkey's leaders rushed to support for the revolutions in Tunisia and Egypt in the hopes of taking advantage of the new political openings. They have presented themselves as pan-Islamic allies and prospective models for Arab revolutionaries, especially for the Islamists among them.

IN THE SUMMER OF 2011 I met Ahmet Davutoglu, the Turkish foreign minister, in Istanbul. He is architect of the so-called neo-Ottoman doctrine that has become the guiding inspiration of his country's policy toward the Arab and Muslim world. "Of course, our focus will be Egypt," he said. "Why? Because we want Egyptian process as a success. If there is a success in Egyptian process of transition, I am sure that will be a good example for other countries. All, global powers, regional powers, must help Egypt and Tunisia to make this transition a success."

For their part, Iran's ayatollahs rushed to take credit for the transformations sweeping the Arab region. "Today, as a result of the gifts of the Islamic revolution in Iran, freedom-loving Islamic peoples such as the peoples of Tunisia, Egypt, and nearby Arab countries are standing up to their oppressive governments," said Ayatollah Mohammad-Taghi Mesbah-Yazdi, a leading cleric.[1] The Iranian regime underlined what it saw as similarities between the Arab revolutions against its secular leaders and the 1979 Islamic revolution against the shah. Predictably, the regime also rejected any comparison or similarities with the 2009 Green Revolution, underlining the difference between its own Islamic government and the secular regimes of Ben Ali and Mubarak. (The Iranian regime argued that the Islamic Republic enjoyed an open and competitive electoral process that was unlike any other among Arab dictatorships and that its dual system of Islam and republicanism satisfied the aspiration of Iranians. Those who protested in the aftermath of the elections were accused of being either sore losers or working for foreign powers.) For sure, there were many structural, ideological, and political differences between the Arab and Iranian revolts, but both were incited by political repression and economic depression. Iran's Green Revolution was brutally repressed by the security forces and the Basij militia, while the Egyptian revolution succeeded, thanks to the military's complicity.

CONTRAST AND CONTRADICTION

Turkey and Iran's ties with the Arabs go back centuries.[2] Both countries will inevitably have a huge influence on the Arab region as it remakes itself over the immediate and long term. Both were ruled by secular, totalitarian regimes over much of the twentieth century—dictatorships that inspired anti-government revolts that were dominated by Islamic movements, through revolution in Iran and with the ballot box in Turkey.

Arab relations with Iran first started deteriorating after the 1979 Islamic revolution. This was exacerbated by eight horrific years of war between Iran and Iraq in the 1980s. During the same period, Turkey's relations with the Arabs chilled, as Turkey sought the warm, diplomatic embrace of Israel. However, from 2000 to 2011 Tehran and Ankara have taken advantage of the Arab malaise and championed pan-Islamic and Arab causes in Palestine, Iraq, and Lebanon. In the period preceding the Arab revolution, President Mahmoud Ahmadinejad of Iran and Prime Minister Recep Tayyip Erdogan of Turkey worked hard to win Arab hearts and minds. (Turkish trade with Arab countries rocketed from $7 billion in 2002 to $37 billion in 2008.)

Iran's opposition to the U.S. invasion of Iraq in 2003 and its support for Lebanese and Palestinian resistance groups earned it high praise among ordinary Arabs. President Ahmadinejad's populist slogans against Western and Israeli aggression had an enthusiastic audience among Arabs as he championed, along with Syria's Assad, the "radical camp" that opposed foreign designs for the region. Ahmadinejad's defiance of the West on the nuclear question also impressed Arabs who felt humiliated by their own leaders' acquiescence to Western diktats.

Turkey's governing AK Party—the Justice and Development Party—took similar interest in pan-Islamic causes. It refused to join the U.S.-led invasion of Iraq, even though Turkey is a NATO member, opposed Israeli policies in the occupied territories, and championed the cause of Palestinians, including those in Lebanon and the Hamas-controlled Gaza Strip. Ankara's support took a dramatic twist on the afternoon of January 29, 2009, at the Davos World Economic Forum, when Turkey's prime minister Erdogan stormed off the stage that he was sharing with Israeli president Shimon Peres when he was not given enough time to respond to Peres's verbose justification of Israel's brutal twenty-two-day war on the Gaza Strip. Upon Erdogan's return home, he was given a hero's welcome, and his stock went up in the Arab world. Relations with Israel deteriorated significantly in May the following year when Israeli forces stormed the Turkish vessel *Mavi Marmara* as the ship tried to break Israel's blockade of Gaza to deliver food and humanitarian aid to Palestinians living under siege. Eight Turkish nationals and one Turkish American were killed in the attack. Turkey was furious when Israel refused to apologize and severed diplomatic and military relations with its erstwhile ally.

However, despite the pan-Islamic vision Iran and Turkey share and recent rapprochement between them, one cannot emphasize enough the gulf between the their respective systems and their approach toward the Arab world. It is not a matter of Iran being vehemently Shia and Turkey being moderately Sunni; it is a matter of style. Ahmadinejad's populist rhetoric has inflamed the perception of a "clash of civilizations," while Erdogan has cosponsored a "dialogue of civilizations" with Spain. Although there are sharp contrasts in style, both countries conflate civilization with religion and show a similarly narrow understanding of human civilization.

TURKEY HAS INSPIRED COOPERATION and coordination, while Tehran has orchestrated confrontation and conflict, especially with the West. Likewise, the two countries espouse two very different systems of governance. Although Iran has an elected parliament and president, the authority of the people is tamed by the authority of religion as interpreted by the supreme leader, the Grand Ayatollah. Turkey, on the other hand, is a secular state with a democratic system of government, where for the last decade Islamists have been granted the right to govern as long as they respected the secular nature of the republic.

Iran and Turkey reflect two faces of the new pan-Islamic revival, with Ahmadenijad and Erdogan touting their own models for emulation in the Arab and larger Islamic worlds. Interestingly, the Arab revolutionaries haven't expressed much interest in pursuing the Iranian model. Again, it is not because Iran stands for Shiaism while the Arab Islamist opposition is Sunni, with the exception of Bahrain. Rather, the revolutionaries seem to like the Turkish model more. Today's Turkey provides a striking example of a compromise between the religious and the secular. This will become more important in Arab nations with strong secular sentiments and substantial ethnic and religious minorities.

Bridging the Islamist-secular divide isn't the only thing that makes Turkey interesting. Its impressive economic transformation, along with the diminished role played by the military in managing the economic and political affairs of the country, has been attractive to the young revolutionaries of the Arab world. Erdogan emerged at a time when Turkey was embroiled in a battle over who ruled Turkey. Grassroots civic movements and business groups agitated for greater openness, while the entrenched institutions of the Kemalist state resisted. Edrogan made his mark as a highly popular mayor of Istanbul before taking power in Ankara. Three successive landslide national election victories have solidified his position as the democratic visionary of post-Kemalist Turkey. The guiding principle of Erdogan and his AK Party has been fighting corruption, spreading wealth and opportunity, and closing the distance between the traditionally hierarchical state and the people. As one AKP leader stated, "The state was up here and the people down there."[3] Erdogan changed that, fostering a new, inclusive polity that embraced tradition and modernity in a distinctly Turkish way.

Turkey became an inspiration for so many Arabs because of its independent foreign policy. As a proud regional power, Turkey refused to be boxed in by either the West or the East, looking toward both as it determined its future.

TAKING A STAND

Tehran, however, remained indifferent to Libya throughout its ordeal. It was also steadfast in its support for its ally Bashar al-Assad, who stood by the Iranian regime during the Green Revolution two years earlier. Only after thousands of Syrians had been killed did Iran urge reform, all the while making it clear it rejected any foreign intervention in its neighbors' internal affairs.

Although it justified its support for the Syrian regime on its anti-Israel and anti-American credentials, there was a strong suspicion that Iran's posture was being guided by its sectarianism. Iran supported the Shias of Bahrain and Lebanon against their rulers, but supported Syria's Alawite regime against its Sunni majority.

Initially, Turkey watched with trepidation at the uprisings in Libya and Syria. At the outset, it opposed Western intervention and supported dialogue and reconciliation. But as the Libyan and Syrian regimes persisted with their bloody crackdown against civilians, Erdogan threw his support behind the revolutionaries and in the process put Turkey on a diplomatic rollercoaster. To a cheering crowd in Cairo, he said, "Democracy and freedom is a basic right as bread and water for you."[4]

Attempting to improve relations with its neighbors and establish a constructive role in the wider region, the new Turkey seemed to provide a viable alternative in the absence of collective Arab leadership. After decades of strained relations between the military and civilian parties, which resulted in four coup d'états, the new Turkish state had gone through a major transformation that created a space for Islamic parties. Turkey's newfound equilibrium has helped it attain improved developmental, human, and minority rights standards—a sharp contrast with the Islamic Republic of Iran.

The successful tenure of the Islamist-leaning AK Party under Erdogan probably set the bar too high for the failed Arab leaders. Turkey didn't only provide a successful political alternative to failed Arab dictators, but more importantly it provided a new template for the relationship between religion, state, and governance in the Islamic world. For decades, the post-colonial Arab republics have been torn by tensions and conflict between regimes and Islamist parties. Suddenly Turkey provided a workable formula for the coexistence of Islam *and* state in a democratic framework. While polarization between military-backed secular regimes and mostly banned Islamist parties paralyzed the political processes and development in most Arab countries, Turkey has evolved into a stable regional powerhouse with its own geopolitical interests centered around its pan Islamic project.

Turkey's troika of nationalism, Islam, and good governance will be vital to the evolution of the modern Arab state, as well as the Arab revolution. As I discuss later the question of Islam, nationalism, and democracy has been answered in different ways in the wider Muslim world while the role of Islam or Islamists in Arab politics and state affairs has remained problematic. Clearly, the Islamist and the secular trends in the Arab world will have to come up with an historic compromise or a social contract of sorts in the transitional period while they define the nature of their constitutions in accordance with the needs and circumstances of their countries.

5 | The West: Interests over Values

"I was afraid for my people, Jake. No more."
—NEYTIRI OF THE MA'VI PEOPLE, *AVATAR*

Arabs in the Age of Empires

Since the breakup of the Ottoman Empire, Western military and political interference has had a role in all major transformations in the Arab world and the region in general. After European colonialism redrew the fault lines and contours of the new Middle East and North African regions, the Cold War reshaped the region with the United States at the helm of interregional and even domestic affairs of most Arab countries. The United States, guided by imperial security doctrines, put itself center stage as the most powerful player in the Middle East.

Since 9/11, the U.S. presence in the region reached a new summit, deepening regional divisions that threatened a further breakup of the Arab world and its states, as witnessed in Sudan, Palestine, Iraq, Lebanon, and Somalia. During this period, Washington toppled regimes, made destabilizing alliances with the worst human rights offenders, monopolized regional diplomatic processes, intervened in the domestic affairs of sovereign states, invaded unfriendly nations, and deployed the world's greatest military in the name of U.S. national security.

In turn, Arab leaders were forced to devise policies that put U.S. reactions first. Historically, those who dared oppose Washington's dictates paid heavily for it, either directly or by proxy. From Egypt's Nasser to Iraq's Hussein through Arafat in Palestine, all were defeated, sanctioned, or isolated. Most other dictators courted the West and selectively adopted the U.S.'s neoliberal dictates while rejecting its democratic model.

By contrast, the Arab people rejected the U.S.'s imperialist agenda—seen as another form of regional dictatorship—but admired its constitutional democracy and even the humble, middle-class notion of the "American dream." More importantly, Arabs rooted for political and strategic independence and tended to unite around pan-Arab issues such as that of Palestine and Iraq. However, the voice of the invisible Arab masses was always silenced by the ruling elites.

By the end of 2010, the Arab world looked evermore stagnant, leaderless, polarized, and downtrodden. While it was clear where the blame lay, Arab dictators continued to outdo one another in appeasing the United States, as the latter folded them into its regional order. And the United States—after having looked at the region through the prisms of the "war on terror," Israel, and oil— was completely oblivious to changes on the ground. However, that did not prevent Washington and its Western allies from claiming credit for the peaceful Arab revolutions.

Manufacturing a Modern Day "Lawrence of Arabia"

The West has boasted of inspiring, supporting, and fighting for the success of the Arab revolutions. It was striking how some pundits credited President George W. Bush's "democracy agenda," which his supporters claimed planted the seeds of change after he made the cause of democracy in the Middle East a U.S. national security priority and vowed that the United States would do what it takes for the cause of liberty. According to Bush's national security advisor and secretary of state Condoleezza Rice, the demise of repressive dictators in Tunisia, Egypt, and elsewhere during the Arab Spring stemmed, in part, from Bush's "freedom agenda." Rice claimed, "The change in the conversation about the Middle East, where people now routinely talk about democratization, is something that I'm very grateful for, and I think we had a role in that."[1] Bush's vice president Dick Cheney went further in an interview with Fox News by connecting the invasion of Iraq with the Arab Spring: "I think that what happened in Iraq, the fact that we brought democracy, if you will, and freedom to Iraq, has had a ripple effect on some of those other countries."[2]

Fellow neoconservative columnist Charles Krauthammer argued, "Today, everyone and his cousin support the 'freedom agenda.' Of course, yesterday it was just George W. Bush, Tony Blair, and a band of neocons with unusual hypnotic powers who dared challenge the received wisdom of Arab exceptionalism."[3] More of the same was expressed by commentators such as CNN's Fareed Zakariya, who said: "But give President George W. Bush his due. He saw the problem, and he believed that Arabs were not genetically incapable of democracy, and he put America's moral might behind the great cause of Arab reform."[4] This was echoed by the *Economist* in an article titled "Was George Bush right? As Egypt erupts, his Arab 'freedom agenda' is suddenly looking a little cleverer":

> The Americans leant on Egypt to hold more open elections in 2005, and in 2006 they talked an astonished Israel into letting Hamas contest Palestinian elections in the occupied territories.

Even the Saudis were prevailed on to hold some (men only) local elections. All this was based on the post 9/11 neoconservative conclusion that the root cause of terrorism was the absence of Arab democracy.[5]

Clearly, the facts were irrelevant in this case. The Egyptian elections of 2005 and 2006 were rigged. The majority of the elected Hamas parliament members ended up in jail, and its government was toppled with the complicity of the Bush administration. The elections in Saudi Arabia were merely municipal and totally apolitical. The implementation of the "democracy agenda" was carried on the backs of tanks and aircraft carriers that destroyed Iraq, tore up its national fabric, inflamed hatreds, and ultimately, exacerbated anti-Americanism, while weakening the secular, liberal trend in the region and causing the death of at least one hundred thousand Iraqis.

Neither did it matter to America's democratic credentials that during a 2004 visit by Ben Ali to the White House, Bush praised his guest as an ally in the war on terrorism, and praised Tunisia's reforms on "press freedom" and for holding "free and competitive elections." It was no secret President Bush was inspired by Russian immigrant Natan Sharansky, the author of *The Case for Democracy: The Power of Freedom to Overcome Tyranny and Terror*. Sharansky served as a minister in the right-wing Ariel Sharon coalition government. The fine romance between Bush and Sharansky was widely covered in the Arab media, and so were Sharansky's positions. He advocated what the late Israeli academic Baruch Kimmerling termed as Sharon's "politicide"—political genocide—the total destruction of the elected Palestinian authority and its institutions. Sharansky also opposed Bush's own roadmap for peace and credited the Israeli military with exposing the Palestinians to "Israeli democracy." Of course, when you factored in that Bush sincerely believed that Sharon was a "man of peace," it all started to make sense. The Bush administration might have spoken of democratization, but in reality the Washington supported autocrats from Tunisia to Saudi Arabia under the guise of the same "national security" agenda.

Duplicitous Arab leaders expressed their loyalty and provided implicit and explicit support for Bush's policies in Iraq, Afghanistan, and Palestine in the context of its global "war on terror" in return for the United States not pressuring those countries to democratize. The failure of the "freedom agenda" to bring about freedom by way of war empowered the region's autocrats, who exploited the carte blanche offered by the U.S.'s war to crack down on their own political opposition. The Bush administration's post-9/11 strategy of "taking the war to the enemy" plunged the region into awful bloodshed and—as the neoconservatives put it—a "constructive chaos" whose victims have been liberal and secular democrats, first and foremost. Perhaps the only inspiring thing to come out of Bush's (democratic) war and occupation of Iraq was the symbolic but powerful action by an Iraqi journalist who threw his shoes at the president during his last press conference in Baghdad.

Bush made massive policy blunders; his successor, President Barack Obama, however, has lacked any discernible policy. Many pundits credited Obama's "non-interference strategy" and his "inspiring oratory" with the rise of youthful democratic movements. Some even cited Obama's own journey from a black community organizer to president of the world's only superpower as inspirational to a whole new generation of Arabs! President Obama's three major speeches directed at the Arab and Muslim worlds were viewed as a departure from the Bush era, as well as an affirmation that Washington was ready to open a new chapter with the Arab and Muslim worlds on the basis of "mutual interest and mutual respect." The Obama administration even leaked to the U.S. press corps how it was in the midst of putting the final touches on its official democracy agenda for the Arab world.

Actually, the Obama administration has been engaging in pragmatic policies toward Arab autocrats in the hope of ensuring more regional cooperation. The president's visit to Egypt only six months before the revolution erupted was seen by Hossam el-Hamalawy, a prolific young blogger, as "a clear endorsement of President Hosni Mubarak, the ailing 81-year-old dictator who has ruled with martial law, secret police, and torture chambers. No words that Mr. Obama will say can change this perception that Americans are supporting a dictator with their more than $1 billion in annual aid."[6]

The pragmatic president, who visited Riyadh before Cairo, characterized Mubarak as a "stalwart ally" and commended the "wisdom and graciousness" of the Saudi monarch. This wasn't lost on the Arab world. The Obama administration had, in fact, decided to reduce budgets marked for NGOs in the Arab world, foregoing even the appearance of supporting democracy in the region. Obama's overtures to the Arab world came at a time when he was expanding the war in Afghanistan into Pakistan, extending the use of drone attacks on the likes of Yemen, even as he failed to pressure Israel into freezing its creeping settlement into the occupied Palestinian territories. By the time the Arab Spring began, Obama's popularity was at its lowest among people in the region who had seen him as a promising statesman. At the outbreak of the Arab revolution, his administration made pathetic efforts to appear to be on the side of the Arab masses by selectively leaking reports to the media that were said to be a blueprint for democratization in the Arab world.

Of course, there was always room for the American lone star, a hidden hero. The *New York Times* unearthed Gene Sharp, an eighty-five-year-old professor, from his modest Boston home to credit him for the Egyptian revolution. Sharp had authored a three-volume work called *The Politics of Nonviolent Action* based on his doctoral thesis, which he'd been preaching at special seminars. I remember reading his work as a student during the first Palestinian uprising in the late 1980s and finding it interesting. But crediting Sharp with such sweeping change in Egypt was particularly insulting to Arab intelligence, especially since the Arabs who filled the streets of the Arab world never heard of the American's playbook. One commentator criticized the *New York Times* for inventing a "new Lawrence of Arabia." Yet the newspaper persisted, publishing a follow-up article underlining the role of the American professor who, paradoxically, sounded less enthusiastic than the paper about his role.

That is not to say Arab Non-Governmental Organizations and human rights groups did *not* receive American or European financial help or even training in legal, civic, and human rights action. Indeed, as Sa'ad Eddeen Ibrahim, the head of the Cairo-based Ibn Khaldun Center for Studies and Research, told me, American experts gave seminars and workshops at his center to Egyptian youth and other human rights activists, but these sessions were limited in scope and duration. Simply put, these contributions might have had added value but shouldn't be credited with the uprisings. Strangely, the bombastic U.S. and European claims of instigating the Arab revolutions have awakened more than a few Arabs to the possibility of "an invisible Western hand"; some go as far as detecting a Western conspiracy behind the Arab uprisings. One can only hope they will be able to express their views in their own homelands without fear of prosecution, as outrageous or as revealing as they might be.

DICTATOR-FRIENDLY EUROPE

The United States wasn't alone, though, in its ambivalence toward the Arab dictators. European powers were perhaps even more so. Europe's accommodation and embrace of Arab dictators had little to do with so-called European values and had more to do with classic European expediency and neocolonial paternalism. In 2008, French president Nicolas Sarkozy commended Ben Ali for the improved "sphere of liberties" at a time when human rights abuses were rampant in Tunisia. In one instance the same year, at least two hundred people were prosecuted after protests in the southern mining town of Redhayef, according to Human Rights Watch.[7] Tunisian human rights groups rejected Sarkozy's utterance as a betrayal of all that France stood for, in theory at least. But France was Tunisia's leading trade partner and its fourth largest foreign investor. When certain European officials did criticize Ben Ali's human rights record, they simultaneously praised his economic performance.

That European business and Arab policy have always been happy bedfellows was made clear when British prime minister Tony Blair brought Gaddafi out from the diplomatic cold in 2003. Blair appointed MI6 counterterrorism chief Mark Allen to lead secret talks with Libya. The deal they thrashed out paved the way for normalization of relations with Gaddafi that allowed for lucrative deals to follow for British, Italian, and American oil companies. In exchange, Gaddafi paid $10 million each to the families of the 270 people who perished in the bombing of Pan Am Flight 103 over Lockerbie in Scotland. Gaddafi also renounced his nuclear development program. Allen, who would be knighted shortly after, went on to advise British Petroleum, negotiating oil deals in Libya. BP, not the British government, dictated policy when problems emerged between the two countries, particularly over the status of the Libyan convicted and imprisoned for the Lockerbie bombing,

Abdelbaset al-Megrahi. His continued imprisonment was complicating a $900 million deal BP was trying to make with Libya. Jack Straw, the foreign minister at the time, admitted it was BP calling the shots. "Yes, a very big part. . . . I'm unapologetic about that."

Nobody embraced the Libyan dictator like the former Italian prime minister Silvio Berlusconi. Gaddafi pitched his tent in the gardens of Rome's most prestigious villa, and their relationship was cemented by the Green Stream natural gas pipeline that allowed Libya to overtake Saudi Arabia as Europe's third-largest energy supplier. Berlusconi bragged that his greatest foreign policy achievement was the friendship treaty he signed with Gaddafi.

In a rather frank admission, foreign minister Franco Frattini told me, "All the Western countries used to accommodate themselves on partnerships of convenience instead of partnerships of coexistence and sharing values . . . including President Sarkozy receiving Gaddafi with all the honors to the Élysée in Paris. . . . This was the mistake made by the West." The same was underlined by the head of the Italian senate: "Spain has Morocco, France has Tunisia. We have Libya, and others are more prominent in Egypt." The only reprimand for this farcical policy came from an unlikely quarter. NATO secretary general Anders Fogh Rasmussen told me in the summer of 2011, "Personally I do believe that political leaders should be very careful in picking and choosing political friends and partners and always take into consideration our obligation to protect human rights and basic political liberties."

BALLYHOOING DEMOCRACY, PROMOTING BUSINESS

The United States and Europe advanced similar imperial visions for the Middle East in the post–Cold War era. The United States hoped for "A New Middle East" around the vision of Shimon

Peres (who, incidentally, wrote a book titled the same) that foresaw a leading role for the Jewish state of 5 million in a region of 250 million Arabs. Because the United States remained hostage to Israel's continued occupation of Arab lands, this new Middle East never got off the ground. It soon became evident that President Clinton's post–Cold War doctrine of "promoting democracy and opening markets" would be reduced to the latter. With the launch of the Euro-Mediterranean Partnership in 1995 in Barcelona, Europe aimed to create a security and prosperity zone that attempted to lock in Arab countries into an enduring multilateral partnership with Europe. When that failed, Sarkozy tried to repackage it in the framework of the "Union for the Mediterranean" in 2008 by taking human rights issues off the table. In both cases geopolitics overrode human rights, and economics triumphed democracy as Western powers closely embraced Israel and the Arab dictatorships.

Following the 9/11 attacks, American and European geopolitical priorities took precedence. The Arab and Muslim world were told to take sides. This, of course, was not the first or last time they were given an ultimatum. Since the United States took over from colonial European powers as the imperial power in the region, the peoples of the region were asked to choose between Washington and its choice of regional villain every decade or so: Egypt's Nasser in the early 1960s, Arafat of Palestine in the early '70s, Iran's Ayatollah in early '80s followed by Iraq's Saddam Hussein in the '90s, and then Al Qaeda's bin Laden in 2001.

Ultimatums and false choices, however, are never a substitute for policy. Despite having been deeply involved in the region for decades, the United States has never had an Arab policy. As a people, Arabs have been completely absent from the U.S./Western agenda. Western leaders have obsessed over their economic interests and Israel's security, leaving the Arabs at the receiving end of their aggression. They have dismissed Arab unity as a threatening fantasy and Islam as fertile ground for dangerous ideas. Arabs have been valued not for their embrace of freedom or respect for human rights, but rather in terms of their proximity to U.S. interests. A subservient ally and energy-providing partner made for a good Arab regime, regardless of its despotic and theocratic rule. In short, Western leaders have talked in slogans and clichés about democracy and Islam, but have always been as indifferent to the people of the region as their dictators. The general impression in the region goes as follows: "The West sees the Arabs as anything but Arabs, and Muslim as no more than Muslims."

Democracy has always been officially advanced as a U.S. national interest; prêt-à-porter, from the shelves of the U.S. State Department, the U.S. Agency for International Development (USAID) and its attendant NGOs, to be built on the ashes of national sovereignty. However, democracy advanced by strategic imperatives and prostituted by war soon proved to be a farce, as we saw during the elections in Iraq and Afghanistan. Worse, on more than a few occasions, they've regretted their overzealous public relations ploy. Washington and its allies rejected the election results in the case of the Islamic Front's victory in Algeria or Hamas's victory in Palestine, as well as when Hezbollah was able to establish a coalition government in Lebanon. Eventually, they were also disappointed by the results in Iraq and Afghanistan.

In reality, the Arabs could hardly trust U.S. rhetoric on democracy, knowing all too well that truly representative governments would oppose the U.S.-Israel axis. Countless U.S.-commissioned polls underlined Arab antagonism to Washington's designs on their region. Almost 80 percent of the Arabs polled believed U.S. military intervention increased terrorism and decreased the chances for peace, while almost 70 percent doubted its sincerity in spreading democracy and reckoned it was motivated by an ambition for regional domination, while also preserving Israel's. Paranoia? Imagine, if you like, if a coalition of Muslim nations were to invade and occupy Canada and Mexico, Americans in all likelihood would be furious.[8]

Caught in the Headlights

While people across the world marveled at the Tunisian "revolution" that toppled Ben Ali's authoritarian regime, Western governments remained conspicuously indifferent, or at best ambivalent. The same hesitation was repeated in Egypt. What a dramatic contrast this was with the West's swift and enthusiastic support of the Iranian "uprising" two years earlier! Secretary of State Hillary Clinton's observation that the United States didn't take sides during nationwide confrontations in Tunisia and Egypt was illustrative of habitual Western hypocrisy, in comparison with its sharp statements on Iran. Western leaders only began to take clearer positions and make coherent statements in favor of the orderly and peaceful transfer of power only after it became clear that their close allies were on their way out.

When it was obvious that the uprisings were revolutions that signaled a clean break with the past, the United States dithered. It saw multiple risks and not opportunities to be grabbed, defended, and nourished. President Obama stuttered, "The United States has a close partnership with Egypt. . . . President Mubarak has been very helpful. . . . We cooperate on many issues, including working together to advance a more peaceful region . . . (and) . . . those protesting in the streets have a responsibility to express themselves peacefully" and "What's needed right now are concrete steps that advance the rights of the Egyptian people: a meaningful dialogue between the government and its citizens."[9] Vice

President Joe Biden insisted, "Mubarak is not a dictator."[10] White House press secretary Robert Gibbs remarked, "We are not picking between those on the streets and those on the government," as he created a moral equivalence between the dictators and the dictated.[11] When the U.S. government finally caught on with the uprisings that were sweeping through the Arab States, the Obama administration decided to cherry pick, supporting change in Libya and Syria but staying quiet on Bahrain and Yemen.

European leaders figured no better. They acted lethargically as democratic revolutions swept through Tunisia and Egypt, and the extent of Europe's links with Arab dictators became clearer. The French prime minister François Fillon had recently visited the Egyptian city Sharm el-Sheik on board an Egyptian plane, and he and his foreign minister, Michèle Alliot-Marie, went on frequent vacations as Ben Ali's guest. Although French president Sarkozy sacked the latter for her close ties to the Tunisian regime, he didn't exactly stray from the herd in his embrace of Arab autocrats. And Italian prime minister Silvio Berlusconi recused himself from all European deliberations on Libya and was reluctant to join any effort against Gaddafi.

As soon as the United States and its allies realized that the uprisings weren't going to subside but were gaining momentum instead, and that maintaining Mubarak, Ben Ali, and company was going to be too costly and too embarrassing, they immediately shifted their emphasis to the Arab militaries in the hope of salvaging what remained of their strategic leverage and influence in the region. After decades of strategic cooperation, Washington, London, and Paris were all too privy to the inner working of the Arab militaries and had close allies among the generals. Indeed, when the Egyptian uprising took off in the end of January 2011, Lieutenant General Sami Anan, chief of staff of Egypt's armed forces, was in Washington for pre-scheduled, weeklong talks. With $1.3 billion in U.S. military aid and several hundred million in economic aid, there was much to discuss. The revolutionary escalation in Egypt meant there was also much to agree on in terms of the way forward. Like the Tunisian military, which also has had close relations with Western capitals and refused to intervene to safeguard the Ben Ali regime, the Egyptian military decided not to intervene on behalf Mubarak. The Egyptian president's attempts to pressure the U.S.-supported military chiefs to confront the demonstrators failed, just as his attempts to remove them led to his own ouster.

Operation Cleanse Your Sins

Following its sluggish response to Tunisia and Egypt and the exposure of its close ties with Arab dictators, the West saw a great opportunity in Libya. Like a beast flailing, the Gaddafi regime was desperate to stop the revolution from succeeding. Here was a relatively rich, oil-producing nation conveniently located on Europe's southern flanks between Egypt and Tunisia and ripe for regime change. It didn't have the regional complications that characterized Yemen. In short, this was the easiest location for the United States and Europe to wriggle their way into the Arab Spring. They obtained U.N. Security Council sanctions against the Gaddafi regime with Resolution 1970 and later obtained a more potent and loosely formulated Resolution 1973 that allowed them to act militarily with little restraint. Within hours, NATO powers intervened under the pretext of protecting civilians from Gaddafi's wrath "by all means necessary."

Predictably, Western media—both liberal and conservative—cheered French and British courage, as well as U.S. leadership for preventing "genocide." Much of the Arab satellite media was embedded exclusively with anti-Gaddafi forces and also covered it favorably. But the massive sacrifice of the Libyan resistance mattered little for those promoting Sarkozy, United Kingdom prime minister David Cameron, and Obama. This was the West "prepared to fight for its values against barbarism," according to the *New York Times*, "the best hope for a 21st century less cruel than the 20th century."[12] It was amazing how short the media's memory was, how easily people selectively recalled history.

It soon turned out that most of the pretexts for war were either exaggerated or invented to justify the Western military intervention. The U.N. resolution and the subsequent NATO bombardment were based on the exaggerated urgency of saving Benghazi from "genocide" following Gaddafi's menace. But Gaddafi had always been theatrical with his statements. When his forces did capture other cities, they reportedly carried out many offenses against the population but not outrageous atrocities or genocide. There was also disinformation regarding Gaddafi's early bombing of Tripoli from air, the use of mass rape as a weapon, and the shipping of African mercenaries by planes—all to justify the no-fly zone. The controversial and emotive notion of "the right to protect" was exploited to justify Western military intervention on a humanitarian basis. Libya began to look increasingly like Iraq. A sensation of déjà vu was palpable as the number of dead following the Western imposed no-fly-zone climbed from one thousand or so to an estimated thirty thousand. In other words, the intervention to protect led to the death of so many, but NATO considered it a success, a "NATO Spring" of sorts.[13]

The militarization of the Arab Spring in Libya didn't bode well for it or other Arab nations such as Syria and Yemen. Western exploitation of the Libyan escalation had also tarnished the Arab revolution with more of the same foreign intervention that had long been detested by the Arabs for being selective and motivated by cynicism. So, yes to the intervention in Libya as it was on the side of the people and against a dictator who had out-lived his usefulness to the West; but no to intervention to support people power in Bahrain, because it was contrary to Saudi inter-ests. The intervention also encouraged a reinvigorated NATO to speak of the Libyan operation as a prototype of operations to come.

There is one last aspect of this debacle that has continued to irritate me. And if it sounds like a conspiracy, it is not. In late 2010, France and Britain decided to stage a war game titled Oper-ation Southern Mistral.[14] It would involve thousands of military personnel and hardware from both countries. The scenario envi-sioned the two longtime military rivals joining forces for a bomb-ing campaign against an imaginary southern dictator. The simulated war was condoned by a fictitious U.N. Security Council resolution and was scheduled to begin on March 21 of 2011. Well, the actual bombing of Libya began on March 19. This is surely a coincidence. But it does highlight the French and British mind-sets and why no serious diplomatic effort got off the ground. The bombers were already on the runway.

Identity Card

Write down:
I am Arab
my I.D number, 50,000
my children, eight
and the ninth due next summer
—Does that anger you?

Write down:
Arab.
I work with my struggling friends in a quarry
and my children are eight.
I chip a loaf of bread for them,
clothes and notebooks
from the rocks.
I will not beg for a handout at your door
nor humble myself
on your threshold
—Does that anger you?

Write down:
Arab.
a name with no friendly diminutive.
A patient man, in a country
brimming with anger.
My roots have gripped this soil
since time began,
before the opening of ages
before the cypress and the olive,
before the grasses flourished.

My father came from a line of plowmen,
and my grandfather was a peasant
who taught me about the sun's glory
before teaching me to read.
My home is a watchman's shack
Made of reeds and sticks
—Does my condition anger you?

There is no gentle name,
write down:
Arab.
The color of my hair, jet black—
eyes, brown—
trademarks,
a headband over a keffiyeh
and a hand whose touch grates
rough as a rock.
My address is a weaponless village
with nameless streets.
All its men are in the field and quarry
—Does that anger you?

Write down, then
at the top of Page One:
I do not hate
and do not steal
but starve me, and I will eat
my assailant's flesh.
Beware of my hunger
And of my anger.

—Mahmoud Darwish,
    translated by John Mikhail Asfour

6 | Arabism and Identity

The strong pan-Arab and Islamist influences on the Arab revolutions will have a lasting effect on governance in the region. These intellectual currents have developed over the last century in the context of the region's geopolitics. Contrary to conventional wisdom, pan-Arabism and Islamism are not fixed dogmas, nor should they be seen merely as cultural identities or political ideologies. Nationalism, Islamism, and governance are hybrid concepts likely to further develop with time and in the context of sociopolitical change.

But since the first revolutionary protests in Tunisia, all of the popular uprisings have taken place only in Arab countries. They have not spread to the non-Arabic nations of northern Africa or the Middle East. Arabs share the same history, culture, geography, and language. They also share the same political grammar after years of occupation, oppression, and humiliation. Arab society has its own built-in sociological constructs regarding freedom, resistance, unity, justice, and so on. That's why it is not by chance that they used a similar revolutionary vocabulary with comparable objectives. It was only a matter of time for the Tunisian and the Egyptian revolutions to produce a domino effect throughout the Arab world. Beyond the local community and union organizers, the young Arab revolutionaries had also been inspired by decades of nationalist and Islamist cross-regional resistance to foreign intervention and occupation.

Historically, the Arab national identity was not born out of economic transformation and integration, or statehood. It evolved through political awareness anchored in their resistance against foreign intervention. And by resistance, I am not referring to the means applied, such as civil disobedience, armed struggle, or outright terrorism. In speaking of resistance, I am referring to a social and political culture that struggles against any injustice, one that transcends geography, class, race, and religion. In a sense, today's upheavals and revolutions are the natural, albeit belated, continuation of the resistance to colonialism and foreign occupation—two aspects of the same journey to freedom.

The anti-colonial resistance led to collective self-determination in sovereign independent (or dependent) states, and the ongoing civic revolutionary resistance to dictatorship aimed to attain self-determination of Arabs as individual free citizens in their homelands. Indeed, today's Arab generations are finishing the job their grandparents started several decades ago by extending the liberation of the land to its people, and in the process, recovering their personal and national dignity. That's why today's revolutions are the culmination and embodiment of the social and national consciousness that rejects the repressive Arab state order and favors democratic change. Those rushing to count the losses and gains and to judge the casualties of each passing Friday are missing the point about the historic transformations sweeping through the region. Regardless of barriers and setbacks, the genie has now left the proverbial bottle. This break with the past may not necessarily bring about positive and/or immediate change, but the decisive break has been made.

Needless to say, not all Arabs are Muslims, and not all Muslims are Arabs. Indeed, Arabs are a minority in the Muslim world, and 10 percent of the Arab world isn't Muslim, particularly in its eastern part where significant Christian minorities and others ethnicities have resided since before the rise of Islam in the seventh century. But Arabic is the language of the Quran, and Islam is a formative factor in the making of the Arab nation and the "Arab mind"—all of which binds Arabism and Islam historically and culturally. Any attempt at understanding the revolutions of the Arab world without factoring in the influence of nationalism and Islamism is futile.

But as I stressed earlier, there is no point or logic to discussing some form of textual or "museumized" Islam, as Muslims have evolved in multiple directions over the last century. Since the seventh century, when Caliph Omar Ibn al-Khattab said, "No one has the right to enslave people after their mothers delivered them free," Muslims have been divided over how best to live as free people. (Judging from the last thirteen centuries, Ibn al-Khattab's wisdom rang a bit hollow on more than a few occasions.) The Islamists' world views have continuously contrasted and evolved, ranging from the twentieth century's leading Islamic reformer-thinker Mohamed Abdo (who reflected after his return from a European tour that he saw Islam on the continent but met no Muslims, and he encountered Muslims at home but saw no Islam) to Osama bin Laden's call to the establishment of a caliphate and incitement to kill Christians and Jews.

Be that as it may, the evolution of the Islamist movements in the Arab world has been influenced mainly by the nationalist agenda, whether positively or otherwise. When secular nationalism was uprooted, deformed, or tamed by cynical foreign powers and powerful dictators during the past few decades, Arabs found refuge in their mosques, at times literally, to escape brutal violence. In the absence of legal, political, or any other earthly protection, divine intervention was more than welcome for the Arabs. But beyond the basic personal piety or need by some to "return to God," two distinct, politically oriented Islamic movements have emerged over the last few decades: a fundamentalist Islamic movement with predominantly social agendas, and an Islamist movement with political/nationalist agendas, which at times have merged, but have also been quite separate from each other. These movements gained currency with the retreat and/or failure of secular pan-Arab movements to bring about unity or good governance and prosperity in their own birthplaces, namely Egypt, Syria, and Iraq.

Interestingly, any hostility to pan-Arabism by certain Islamist movements have been met with popular skepticism, while Islamists who embraced pan-Arab causes like the Muslim Brotherhood or the jihadists benefited a great deal, at times to the disadvantage of these causes.

PALESTINIZING THE ARAB STRUGGLE FOR FREEDOM

Liberal, western commentators who reported from Tahrir Square have noted that the Arab revolutionaries didn't burn Israeli flags or rail against the United States. Rather they reported that the protestors rooted for socioeconomic change and political freedoms. You could almost detect a sense of relief in their writing as they described to their readers and viewers how this was not an Islamist, nor a nationalist revolution but a "friendly revolution" inspired by Western software and soft power. In reality, however, there are greater nationalist and Islamist influences than meets the liberal eye, and these influences were not necessarily in the alarmist fashion described by Western conservative skeptics.

The protests against Israel in the late summer and the September demonstrations and attack on the Israeli embassy in Cairo in 2011 made clear where the revolution stood on the question of Israel/Palestine. Most of those involved in grooming, leading, and organizing the protests that resulted in the Egyptian revolution came from the ranks or the offshoots of the "Popular Committees" that were established to support the second Palestinian Intifada in 2000—a time when the Egyptian regime persisted in its complicity with the United States and Israel. Their support for their Palestinian co-nationalists under occupation was a true act of solidarity and struggle for an Arab cause. The Palestinians have long inspired the greater Arab public through their struggle for liberation, and most particularly since their first peaceful uprising in 1987, and their second uprising in 2000 against Israel's dictatorship.

When the invasion of Iraq occurred in 2003, the Popular Committees organized against the U.S. war, using the less-advanced online tools of the time, such as Yahoo groups and chat rooms.

In 2004, the establishment of the popular Egyptian movement for Change, Kefaya (Enough), culminated in a serious turnaround in Egyptian politics as the cross-party movement concentrated its mission on rejecting any notion of succession under Mubarak and democratizing the regime. In its founding manifesto, Kefaya's liberal, Islamist, leftist, and nationalist coalition partners underlined its two grand missions as follows: the first objective underlined the struggle against the Israeli and U.S. invasion and occupation of Arab lands, and the second outlined its democratic struggle against the dictatorship.

The socioeconomic emphasis came at a later stage in 2008 when the April 6 youth movement sprung from Kefaya and its constituents. Their actions gave them national prominence and ensured the participation of the labor movement. The unity of youth and workers—two revolutionary components of the Egyptian and Arab society—transformed a metropolitan youth action into a full-scale national protest.

Largely unreported, these movements organized countless sit-ins, strikes, and public appearances against all forms of aggression directed at the Arab world, which then helped them build a solid base for the pro-democracy movement. They embraced various social and political tools to spread their program and when Mohammad el-Baradei appeared on the Egyptian political scene after he retired from the International Atomic Energy Agency, Kefaya and other grassroots groups supported him in his efforts to stand for democracy. As a credible international figure, they hoped he would make a dent and popularize their cause inside and outside of the country. It was no fluke that George Ishaq, the community and political organizer, spearheaded the campaign for el-Baradei, which earned him more than 250,000 Facebook supporters. These nationalist influences applied to most other activists from Morocco to Bahrain.

ARAB INSPIRATION

Squeezed between the likes of Ben Ali and Bush, Arab youth looked for inspiration from its collective national symbols. Thanks to satellite TV, every Arab was able to follow in real time the recent dramatic events in the region's conflict zones. Young Arabs were particularly mesmerized by three relatively young leaders: the secular Palestinian democrat Marwan Barghouti, the resistance leader Hassan Nasrallah, and the leader of global jihad Osama bin Laden. They symbolized the struggle against totalitarianism and subservience to U.S. and Israeli dictates—two of the most powerful factors that fomented popular Arab anger. In the end, very few supported or followed in bin Laden's footsteps, while countless others have subscribed to Barghouti and Nasrallah's struggle for liberation.

Barghouti was among the leaders of the peaceful Intifada in 1987, and later of the second Intifada in 2000. I came to know him when he was a student leader at Bir Zeit University and later as a leader of the nonviolent uprising against Israeli occupation, a few days before Israeli soldiers captured him for his role in the Intifada. It was clear to me that despite a decade of imprisonment and deportation, he remained a believer in reconciliation and stood against the killing of innocent civilians. In the 1990s he advocated freedom, democracy, and reconciliation, and became a member of the first freely elected Palestinian legislature and emerged as a vocal critic of corruption and nepotism. Soon after the failure of the Middle East peace process in 2000, Barghouti led the struggle against the entrenched Israeli occupation. A charismatic and courageous leader, Barghouti inspired his generation. His vision of liberty, democracy, and justice seemed diametrically opposed to those of Israeli and Arab leaders.

The Israeli judges who condemned Barghouti to life imprisonment in May 2004 admitted that he had not participated in any violent acts and that he had opposed attacks against Israeli civilians inside the Green Line "on principle." From his prison cell, Barghouti vehemently rejected all charges against him under Israel's anti-terrorism act. When he was sentenced to life imprisonment, Barghouti was the same age as South Africa's Nelson Mandela when he was convicted on charges of terrorism in June 1964—forty-six.

Sheikh Hassan Nasrallah championed the cause of liberating Lebanon from Israeli occupation and built a formidable resistance force in South Lebanon with the help of Iran and Syria. In the process, he improved the status of the Shia in Lebanon, who despite their larger demographics were historically relegated to the margins of the establishment. Although he got his spiritual guidance from the Iranian city of Qum, Nasrallah preached national harmony and Arab solidarity. He was particularly in his element when issuing threats to the "Zionist enemy" and its American backer. Nasrallah's Hezbollah was credited with the unilateral withdrawal of Israel from south Lebanon in 2000. Arabs considered him a bigger hero outside his own country where sectarian divisions influenced politics.

Hezbollah's resistance to Israel's 2006 invasion, which was a response to an attack on its border post, made Nasrallah a pan-Arab champion admired by the young from all walks of life. Nasrallah demonstrated that it was possible to defy Israel and in the process raised Arab hopes after repeated defeats on the battlefield. His widely watched, fiery, and defiant speeches from his secret bunker made him ever more popular, especially when Arab dictators were incapable of accomplishing much for their people.

ARABS RECONSTITUTED—
IT'S THE LANGUAGE, STUPID

Pan-Arab sentiment was best echoed by one of the most popular songs in the second part of the twentieth century, written by an Egyptian poet with the refrain "The land speaks Arabic, the land speaks Arabic, the land. . . . " At the outset of the twenty-first century, this still resonates, this time through the new Arab satellite media that has given the Arab street its voice and linked its various liberation squares.

If it wasn't for satellite television, it's doubtful that Egyptians would have been able to watch and live through the upheaval of their co-nationalists in Tunisia, or for Syrians, Yemenis, Bahrainis, Libyans, and other Arabs to live one another's experiences or incite and inspire one another. Arab channels connect people in real time, giving communication a role beyond being merely informative. They became de facto agitators as they reported the dramatic events unraveling in their region. In one of Al Jazeera's promotions of its coverage of the 2008 Israeli invasion of Gaza, a young Arab man says, "When Palestine was attacked in 1948, they told us 'we didn't know' (until it was too late). Today they have no such excuse."

It has come naturally to Arabs of different dialect, gender, and generation to work for the satellite television industry and collectively create a trans-border and transnational pan-Arab space. Not a day goes by at Al Jazeera when I don't run into Arab colleagues from each of the twenty-two Arab states that collectively make up the Al Jazeera identity. It is an identity that has grown to become the virtual public space of the Arab world, commanding the loyalty of tens of millions in any given week. A similar situation exists with other satellite channels in the region. It's a dream realized for those pan-Arab nationalists who long argued that their common language—alphabetical and political—was at the heart of the common Arab identity and culture. Today, not only does the "land speak Arabic," so do the airwaves, figuratively and literally.

Arabs no longer needed visas to travel across borders in order to come together to discuss, debate, and share fears and aspirations, as satellite connectivity and common preoccupations transcended geography, ethnicity, and narrow regime interests. In that sense, Arab networks have been a modernizing influence. They are advancing spoken Arabic language and the public sphere with male and female professionals. There is little or no tribal or sectarian bias, no monopoly over the truth, or right and wrong. These diverse and pluralistic professional platforms have helped raise consciousness without being ideological, even acting as "moderating" forces, particularly among the poorer, more reactionary and more subaltern sections of the population. Indeed, according to one poll, watching Al Jazeera led to less stereotyping and a better understanding of countries such as Israel and the United States.

Just as television produced a common social, cultural, and artistic platform on which to discuss anything from poverty to "honor killings," it also paved the way for the prominence of so-called common Arab causes such as Palestine, Iraq, and Lebanon, where Arab lands were attacked or occupied by non-Arab powers. But raising awareness about them became not only a journalistic function but a *defacto* political act as well.

AN ARAB VISION IN FOCUS

New and social media have played vital roles in coordinating, sharing, and transmitting information and images. They have been effective, especially among the young and connected middle classes, but satellite television reaches most homes 24/7, providing hundreds of Arabic-speaking channels. Unlike new media, it requires no interactivity and tends to reach its target audience with much ease and little resistance. If it's on the news, it must be real. More importantly, reporting the facts has an empowering effect on those sitting on the sidelines. For the tens of millions who've watched the revolution unfold live, change became real and probable. As satellite television transmitted images, disseminated information, and provided analysis, background, and debate, change became a reality. The extended and rolling coverage by the Arab news networks proved indispensable for organizers and activists as they transmitted their eyewitness accounts to the general public at little or no effort or cost.

When the regimes tried to jam Internet-based communications, or block certain social media outlets, television played an important role as the information bridge between protestors in different parts of the country. The satellite networks projected real, dramatic images of the evolving protests while conservative and censored state media brought ever more ridicule and contempt upon themselves.

The emergence of satellite networks broke the Arab state's hold on media as satellite networks competed in the political and religious playing fields and through the use of entertainment and pop culture. In denial or under orders to tame its coverage, official outlets presented the upheavals either as exaggerated media fantasy or as instigated from the outside.

For decades the regimes have spread lies and spewed propaganda. They turned their defeats into televised victories along the lines of "the mother of all battles" when referring to Iraq's forced ejection from Kuwait, and justified their internal repression against minorities and peaceful opposition under the guise of "ensuring stability" and "citizen safety" against fifth columns, using brutal force against civilians to "protect" the population. The visits of foreign officials were projected as elaborate state pageants that underlined the strategic importance of the regime for regional security. Once a regime lost its control over the message, it lost control, period. From then on, it was a question of public will and time.

The same could be said, perhaps, about the early Western monopoly over the airwaves. When satellite television first emerged, Arabs, among others, were more likely in 1991 to hear CNN's Bernard Shaw reporting from Baghdad, followed by American generals, and in between commercials for McDonald's, Nike, and Jeep. By the time of the 2003 U.S. war in Iraq, satellite television had become the enterprise of the Arab public and private sector, with masked resistance fighters, bearded Islamic scholars, angry intellectuals, and bitter Iraqis dominating the screens.

The affordability and popularization of television technology allowed dishes and antennas to proliferate on every other rooftop, rendering hundreds of television stations accessible with the mere flick on a remote control. While hardly a sign of renaissance, they've underlined and strengthened the Arab collective. In the process, the satellite television market became pluralistic, diverse, and competitive long before new media took root in the Arab world. Since the founding of the Middle East Broadcasting Center (MBC) in the early 1990s, but more strategically since the introduction of Al Jazeera in 1996, hundreds of satellite networks tore through the curtains of state censorship to enter Arab living rooms. They also upstaged the likes of CNN and the BBC, which presented themselves as viable alternatives to local media. Paradoxically, many of these channels were subsidized through Gulf money in search of influence and commercial gains, but were run by Arabs from each and every country in the region, adding to the plurality of accents and perspectives.

Arabs Got Talent

Regionalization or so-called perverse globalization has become the norm in the Arab world as culturalization took precedence over Western-driven globalization. Arabic took over from English and French, and Al Jazeera and Al-Arabia pulled ahead of CNN and the BBC on the charts, just as Rotana pulled ahead of MTV among Arabs, including the English-speaking elites. Satellite television has brought the Arab-speaking world together for better or worse. They mostly advanced Arab rather than Western brands, explored Arab desires instead of U.S. preoccupations, Arab drama and soap operas, rather than French literature and British sitcoms. Even when they adopted Western pop culture, they succeeded in adding their own flavor to it, prompting regional and global powers from Iran to China through France, Russia, and the United States, to establish satellite networks that broadcast in Arabic.

With their own pop stars, Arabic series, and video clips transmitted on specialized satellite networks, the choice was no longer limited for Arabs. Arab pop culture pulled ahead of its Western counterpart, Amr Diab became more popular than Prince, Nancy Ajram became the Arabs' own Mariah Carey, singing words they understood and felt. The youth reclaimed Arab pop stars and even their stars' physiques. Frequently aired and widely circulated, the video clips of Ruby, a young Egyptian student turned singer/dancer, became a pan-Arab phenomenon. Shakira had to step aside as many marveled at the way Ruby moved her hips and went as far as to discuss her bottom on satellite television. In a bitter response to the "Ruby phenomenon," a conservative Muslim commentator ridiculed her fans, claiming she was no more than an ass! Ruby's body parts and talents notwithstanding, Arab pop culture, Westernized or otherwise, had become a unifying and somewhat liberating factor for young Arabs, a mirror for their aspirations. Like their predecessors who united the Arab world through the printing press and the radio airwaves, the mandarins of new media have unified and connected the Arabs like never before.

The success of Arabic networks, which bypassed state borders and broke social taboos, answered two central freedoms: freedom of mind and body. This was clearly represented by the early success of Al Jazeera and the Lebanese Broadcasting Corporation

(LBC), with the former providing an open platform for voicing opinions, discussion, and debate, and the latter providing an entertainment platform that underlines aesthetics and exhibits suggestive sensual/sexual expressions. Many of the hundreds of channels that have sprung up since have either emulated Al Jazeera and LBC, or specialized in sports and religion. The fact that Al Jazeera belongs to the Qatari state and LBC is financed by Saudi businessman Waleed Ben Talal, adds another paradox to the complicated world of Arab television.

Beyond news and sports, the airwaves have been polarized between the liberal and the conservative camps with a few hundred presenters, stars, and symbols on each side of the cultural divide. The tele-evangical side presented a wide range of opinions, from the less conservative Sharia'a preachers to the hardline Wahhabi apologists that defend the rulers of Saudi Arabia. All the while, the liberal camp presented everything from erotic video clips to the latest catwalk shows by head-scarfed models. By 2010, the airwaves were dominated by hundreds of populist clerics preaching the virtues of living piously and hundreds of mostly female hosts, artists, and pop culture stars. Both sides of the divide were financed primarily by, and based in, the Persian Gulf, Egypt, and Lebanon.

Virtual Pluralism

Satellite television networks have also revealed the "invisible Arabs" for the caged political animals they were. They provided a virtual public square for debates and discussions among secularists and fundamentalists, liberals and leftists, feminists and conservatives, officials and opposition never seen or heard before in the region. Along with the Doha-based Al Jazeera and other twenty-four-hour news organizations such as Al Arabia, there were entertainment, religious, general, or specialized networks that have long presented the Arabs with a wide range of views, perspectives, and information beyond their borders and region that contrast sharply with the authoritarian regimes and information distributed on their local channels. No longer were Saudis subjected to the joy of watching endless hours of their king receiving those paying their respects to him, nor the Libyan leader forcing the state television channel to broadcast the image of his hanging shoes as a signal of his dissatisfaction with their programs. News was no longer prioritized according to hierarchies. Urgency and importance mattered because news no longer had to begin with kings and presidents and end with the commoner. An editor at a state-run television or newspaper had to remember the exact hierarchy of the ruling family so as to start from the top down, regardless of content. If a king or president's picture came after or below that of a "less significant" person, the journalist was all but condemned.

Democracies make civic studies mandatory in the classroom and incorporate courses on universal values, democracy, and the separation of powers in the curriculum, but not in the Arab states. Familiarity with freedom of expression, civil and human rights, and voting had to be acquired through television. At times it had the feel of a political circus or a "tower of Babel," but voicing the most outrageous of opinions has long proved more productive than taming them. Indeed, there is no point in defending those we agree with; it's the right of the most unconventional and disagreeable voices that are preserved by a liberal media and society.

When the television program *Star Academy* was featured on the MBC channel a decade ago, hundreds of thousands of young people from the Atlantic to the Gulf voted for their favorite stars, and as far as we know, their votes counted. For many, this was a revelation; it was the first vote they'd ever cast, albeit in a virtual democratic ballot run by a station. The same was repeated on Abu Dhabi Television, where a popular program featuring competition among poets was aired. But when, after weeks of live competition, an Emirati won the people's vote through phone texting, many suspected this was more of the same rigged elections they had grown to hate.

Paradoxically, undemocratic countries that tried to liberalize their economies and commercialize their satellite networks, such as the United Arab Emirates, Saudi Arabia, and Qatar, in addition to Lebanon and later Egypt, have paved the way for a more liberal, albeit consumerist media in the Arab world. Television and other forms of marketing provided abundant competition and multiple choices in consumer products and services, an abundance that became terribly scarce when it came to the political and social spheres. Eventually, people, especially the younger generation, couldn't see why they had a choice among laundry detergents and television sets, but not textbooks; news networks, but not political leaders.

Autocracies, sensing the disadvantage of being left out, allowed for a relative opening that underlined Arab culture and history, presenting nationalist and historic series that depicted Arab heroism and pride. Bab al-Hara or "The Neighborhood Gate," a Syrian soap opera shown on MBC during Ramadan in 2010, recounted the proud and steadfast resistance to the French occupation in the early part of the twentieth century. The month-long series was reportedly watched by more viewers than any other. The courage and dignity expressed by its characters couldn't have been lost on a new generation of repressed and humiliated Syrians and Arabs across the region.

THE AL JAZEERA EFFECT

"What Al Jazeera is doing is vicious, inaccurate, and inexcusable."

—DONALD RUMSFELD,
FORMER U.S. SECRETARY OF DEFENSE

One could hardly speak of change in the Arab world without invoking the "Al Jazeera effect" in nurturing democracy and connecting people from all walks of life and of all philosophical, ideological, and religious persuasions. A Western colleague once told me, "At times I catch myself watching Al Jazeera, not because I understand anything that it is saying, but because I love watching the pictures and the lively debates that draw me in like nothing on Western networks."

When it was first founded in the mid-1990s, Al Jazeera was seen as a positive development in the West and was praised in U.S. and European capitals for presenting Westerners, Israeli spokespersons, and politicians of all stripes for the first time to an Arab audience. But soon after its coverage of the 1998 U.S. bombing of Afghanistan and its extended coverage of the second Palestinian Intifada against the Israeli occupation in 2000, Al Jazeera was criticized for providing an open forum for popular sentiments and anti-Israeli and anti-American views.

The network's detractors multiplied afterward. U.S.-Middle East scholar and an apologist for the Bush administration, Fouad Ajami, wrote, "Al Jazeera, which claims a global audience of 35 million Arabic-speaking viewers, may not officially be the Osama bin Laden Channel, but he is clearly its star, as I learned during an extended viewing of the station's programming in October. On Al Jazeera (which means "the peninsula"), the Hollywoodization of news is indulged with an abandon that would make the Fox News Channel blush. . . . "[1] And Fox news anchor Bill O'Reilly didn't blush or flinch when he said, "That anti-American operation is spurring on the revolt. Many Arabs get their information from Al Jazeera. That network is extremely powerful and is encouraging uprisings all over the Muslim world. Al Jazeera very rarely condemns the jihadists, and I believe the network would be happy to see them take power."[2] Ajami at least understands Arabic; O'Reilly doesn't.

Al Jazeera's coverage of the U.S. invasion and occupation of Afghanistan and Iraq after the 9/11 attacks exacerbated Washington's already hostile attitude toward Al Jazeera's uncensored and at times unfiltered coverage of the wars. Demonizing the Arabic channel became the order of the day for the Bush administration with Secretary of Defense Donald Rumsfeld blaming Al Jazeera for the escalation of violence. President Bush had reportedly discussed with British prime minister Tony Blair bombing Al Jazeera's bureau in Baghdad. The election of Barack Obama after eight years of Bush toned down the criticism, and the United States began to see the network with more objectivity. Secretary of State Hillary Clinton characterized Al Jazeera as "real news" that was winning against U.S. media outlets. She stressed, "Where you've got a set of global networks that Al Jazeera has been the leader in, that are literally changing people's minds and attitudes and like it or hate it, it is really effective."[3]

Indeed, the Arab Spring has underlined the importance of Al Jazeera as a free media outlet in a sea of authoritarianism. As the *New York Times*' David D. Kirkpatrick wrote, "As the protests accelerated this month, some Tunisian officials protested that Al Jazeera was hyping the unrest because of its anti-Western agenda: its managers wanted to see a 'moderate' Arab regime fall, even if the protesters were not Islamists, like those in so many earlier revolts. But that seems unlikely. Al Jazeera's producers knew they had a story line that their audience would love."[4]

ABC News Washington correspondent Sam Donaldson told my colleague on *ABC This Week* in January 2010, "Thank you for what you're doing. People say Al Jazeera fanned the flames here by bringing the fact that democracy is in existence and that people are being suppressed. That's what we need. We need more communication in the world. It's not Al Jazeera's fault that Mubarak is under siege now."[5] Similar sentiments were echoed by Frank Schaeffer, in the *Huffington Post*, who asked "Why Aren't you Watching Al Jazeera?"

> If you care about anything more on the news than celebrity trivia join me in saying: Thank God For Al Jazeera! We Americans are so isolated from the larger world that we will always be a dollar short and a day late unless we find alternatives to our "media." Al Jazeera is that alternative. . . . If freedom and democracy comes to countries ranging from Egypt to Libya future historians will note that the freedom of information provided by Al Jazeera (at great cost) played a huge role, a bigger role than the increasingly irrelevant U.S. media that is too busy worrying about Charlie Sheen to notice that the planet is changing.[6]

Indeed, some book titles on Al Jazeera are more than sufficient to give you an idea regarding the role of the Arab network: Mohammed el-Nawawy's *Al-Jazeera: The Story of the Network that Is Rattling Governments and Redefining Modern Journalism* and *Al-Jazeera: How the Free Arab News Network Scooped the World and Changed the Middle East*, and Hugh Miles's book *Al-Jazeera: The Inside Story of the Arab News Channel that Is Challenging the West*.

Al Jazeera's reach has been its most important asset and source of legitimacy. It allows it greater access to more people than many other media outlets, old and new. Its viewing numbers jump to the tens of millions during major news events. And during the early days of the Arab Spring it captured the spirit of the revolution like no other network. Admittedly as with any vibrant news organization Al Jazeera has seen serious internal disagreements within its editorial leadership and made some poor calls of judgment during its years of continual round the clock coverage. But ultimately, Al Jazeera's success lies in its capacity to report the facts uninhibitedly, provide an open forum for debate, and continuously correct and renew itself relatively free from commercial and geopolitical pressures.

As Marc Lynch, a leading American Middle East media observer said in the *New York Times* at the end of January 2010, "The protests rocking the Arab world this week have one thread uniting them: Al Jazeera, whose aggressive coverage has helped propel insurgent emotions from one capital to the next."[7] Indeed, Al Jazeera became the Arab public square where everyone met, and where updates from the centers and the flanks were watched and heard, unfiltered and uncensored. Robert Malley and Hussein Agha wrote in the *Washington Post* the day Mubarak fell, "Al Jazeera has emerged as a full-fledged political actor because it reflects and articulates popular sentiment. It has become the new Nasser. The leader of the Arab world is a television network."[8]

7 | Islamists and Democracy

"REVOLUTION HALAL"

The most influential Islamist movement in the Arab world—
the Egyptian Muslim Brotherhood—chose Mohammed Badï'e
as its General Guide, or leader, in January 2010. He was unequiv-
ocal about the movement's pursuit of a peaceful social and political agenda—how, under no circumstance, would it seek power
through violence. Indeed, since its founding in 1928, the Brotherhood, which has branches and offshoots throughout the Arab
world, has evolved into a social and charitable movement that has
often been reluctant to take the political lead, even though it was
marginalized and persecuted by the Sadat and Mubarak regimes.
The leadership of the once outlawed Brotherhood—which boasts
an estimated half million members in Egypt and is said to command the support of one-fifth to one-third of the country's
population—has begun to debate the need for a greater, albeit
indirect, role for the movement in Egyptian political life.[1]

Badï'e is no young man. At sixty-three, this medical doctor,
who was first imprisoned with the Brotherhood's hawkish leadership in the 1960s, belongs to the older, conservative wing of

the movement. (All told, he was imprisoned four times for more than thirteen years over the last four decades.) His election came at a time of rift between the conservatives, who insist their organization must remain an evangelical religious charity that works toward Islamizing society, and the younger, more industrious mid-level leaders, who reckon it is time to make a decisive entry into politics to effect change. The movement's serious gains in the 2005 elections, when the group's supported candidates won one-fifth of the seats in parliament, encouraged the politically minded members to make their mark on the movement. They hoped to continue the détente with the Muburak regime while making incremental gains in the sociopolitical spheres.

However, this optimism proved short-lived, as the regime shunned the Brotherhood and rigged the 2010 elections in an attempt to take full control of parliament and pave the way for Mubarak to transition power to his son Gamal. Although the Brotherhood was left in a very difficult situation, Badi'e sensed a "great opportunity" for the opposition forces "to unite, to join together in a popular political movement," as he told his discouraged adherents.[2] He may have been a movement conservative, but even he was responding to its younger, more liberal base to enter the poli⁺ical arena. He knew that the Brotherhood's involvement in the 2005 elections—as "independents"— had given its political wing new power. Though he had no intention of spearheading a revolution, he was keen to cajole the restless and embittered mood of the opposition to see the silver lining in the black cloud that was hovering over Egyptian political life. The fact that Mubarak succeeded in angering just about everybody outside his immediate clique had made the Brotherhood less isolated and more capable of confronting the regime together with the disgruntled secular opposition.

Revolution, it must be emphasized, is not a commonplace in the history of Islam. In fact, contrary to conventional wisdom, revolutions are rarely encouraged or praised, even when Muslims are faced with unjust Muslim leaders. Revolution, or *thawra*, in the contemporary Arab world is a positive pursuit of justice, but its closest equivalent in Islamic history—*fitna*—was perceived as disorderly and unruly and its results too messy and costly to justify. Better to survive injustice than cause chaos that could turn into tyranny. That's why the Muslim Brotherhood, the single largest Islamist movement in the Arab world, has historically supported reform and incremental peaceful change.[3]

However, following an attempt on President Gamal Abdul Nasser's life in 1954, Muslim Brotherhood leader Sayyid Qutb called for the removal of the pan-Arabist leader, referring to him as an apostate. This prompted a bloody crackdown on the movement by the regime. After Qutb's execution in 1966, the Brotherhood split on the interpretation of his ideas, summarized notably in his book *Ma'alim fi'l-Tariq* (Signposts on the Road). The traditional leadership embraced peaceful jihad, and the extremist militants split and waged violent jihad to oust who they considered apostate rulers. The terrible cost paid by the Brothers has further polarized the proponents of peace and violent jihad. In response jihadi movements condemned the Brotherhood's laxity and tolerance of secular dictators; the Brotherhood did not hesitate to condemn those who carried out terrorist attacks in Egypt and the rest of the world.

All of this helps explain why the Brotherhood leadership didn't spearhead confrontations with the regime over the years and why it didn't lead the revolution on January 25, 2011. Indeed, when the January upheaval got underway, the Muslim Brotherhood was almost nowhere to be seen, except for its younger activists who joined the marches without the support of the group's elders. The Brotherhood's Egyptian branch dragged its feet, just as it had in Tunisia weeks earlier, and remained on the sidelines, even as the protests showed signs of success. The same happened in Syria and Yemen, where the local Muslim Brotherhood didn't join the youth until their protests became serious and widespread. But as soon as its leaders realized the scope and momentum of the popular uprisings, the Brotherhood decided to join; better late than never.

The group was able to link with the protesters through its open, connected, and precocious younger activists who were already involved in the uprisings. Once they connected with the protesters, the Brotherhood's participation gave the revolution considerable heft. In Egypt they could flex their organizational muscle in the urban centers, while in Tunisia their strength was concentrated in rural areas. The group remained within the mainstream of the movement and played an important role in daily decision-making. Its long experience in grassroots organization and its wide reach in the region made the Brotherhood and its affiliates a central part of the protest movement. With the decline of *l'ancien régime*, the Islamist movement realized they were poised to make gains in the ensuing political and social vacuum. Within days of the ousting of Ben Ali and Mubarak, the Brotherhood in Egypt and An-Nahdah in Tunisia surfaced as two of the biggest winners. Their grassroots networks, organized structures, and social subsidiaries were essential to win sympathy and support. These factors are likely to play an even greater role in the post-revolution stage.

THE SECULAR-RELIGIOUS GEOPOLITICS

The rise of political Islam in the Arab world was nurtured in context of the regional rivalry between secular Egypt and theocratic Saudi Arabia. After the nationalist Egyptian military officers took power in 1952 and began to speak in the name of the Arab world, Saudi Arabia took exception. It also bristled at the Ba'ath's secular nationalist ideology and the Leftist seculars that had become such a potent popular force in several Arab countries. Unhappy with their secular nationalist agenda for the region, Riyadh found common purpose with Western powers irritated by Egypt's independent foreign policy and its non-alignment in the Cold War.

To offset Nasser's Arab agenda and Egypt's use of the Cairo-based Arab League, Saudi Arabia helped found the Islamic Committee in 1961–1963 that soon became the Conference of Islamic States where the Arabs are a minority. Raising the pan-Islamic banner was Saudi Arabia's best and perhaps only way to confront Egypt's secular nationalism and its leadership in the developing world and non-aligned movement. The rivalry between the two regional powers deepened after their proxy war in Yemen in the early 1960s, with Nasser dispatching troops to support the takeover by secular officers and the Saudi monarch arming and financing the conservative Imamate. There was little doubt where the West stood with the conservative theological state.

But Egypt's timid posture and relative isolation since it signed a separate peace treaty with Israel in 1979 left the door open for Saudi Arabia and its religious fundamentalist brand to mushroom throughout the region, most evidently through the growing anti-secular and anti-nationalist Salafi groups, including the violent jihadis. With Saudi help, private and public, these groups financed their activities in primarily secular societies, as Saudi Arabia opened its doors to religious students and scholars from all over the Arab and Muslim worlds. Some of the new movements boasted of representing the struggle of Arabs and Muslims throughout the world and, in the process, defamed the name of both in the international arena.

Repression and public despair, coupled with rocketing unemployment rates and vast inequalities in the wider region, helped Salafi and jihadi groups to tap into the Arab region's reservoir of fresh recruits, the youngest population on earth. Some went to Afghanistan, Chechnya, and Bosnia to fight under the banner of global jihad.

THE RISE AND DECLINE
OF AL-QAEDA

For all intents and purposes, al-Qaeda's jihadi "holy war" doctrine was established by dissident members of the Muslim Brotherhood, such as Abdullah Azzam, who was the former head of the Jordanian Brotherhood and rejected the Brotherhood's peaceful jihadi doctrine. Al-Qaeda militants are also disciples of Sayyid Qutb, the Brotherhood leader and ideologue who was imprisoned and executed by the Nasser regime in 1966. His clear and uncompromising writings and reflections on the Muslim world (and America) became the cornerstone for young jihadists in search of a holistic Islamic system.

Jihadists abandoned the mother group after its leaders renounced revolutionary violence, following its painful confrontations with Arab regimes, and instead pursued religious, social, and political preaching as a way to win both hearts and minds in the Muslim world. Many of these radical "brothers" found their way to Afghanistan through the Brotherhood's networks, and later through their own "services bureau," all of which were supported by the CIA's effort to reverse the Soviet occupation of Afghanistan at the height of the Cold War, aided by Saudi Arabia and Pakistan.

Once fully organized, following the death of Azzam, al-Qaeda leaders such as Ayman al-Zawahiri, formerly of the Egyptian

Islamist jihad, accused the Muslim Brotherhood of betraying the cause of Islam and abandoning their "jihad" in favor of forming political parties and supporting modern state institutions. With the Soviet withdrawal at the end of the Cold War, al-Qaeda extended its campaign, turning against secular or "apostate" Arab regimes and against any form of Western presence ("Crusaders" and Jewish) in the Muslim world, from Andalusia in Spain to Kashgar in China, in order to establish an Islamic caliphate.

The U.S.'s deployment of half a million American soldiers to Saudi Arabia—the home of Islam's two holiest sites—following the Iraqi invasion of Kuwait in 1990 presented al-Qaeda with an opportunity to rally Arabs and Muslims against the "new crusaders" and their regional clients. In the process, it evolved into a polycentric, theologically connected, jihadi network made up of Arabs and Afghans who fought the Soviets alongside new groups ready to wage jihad under its banner anywhere in the world.

It went on to carry out a number of attacks on U.S. targets including two U.S. embassies in Africa and a military frigate in the Gulf of Aden. Al-Qaeda was also linked to terrorist attacks in various Arab countries such as Saudi Arabia, Egypt, and Morocco, and the escalation of violence in Yemen, Lebanon, and Palestine. The group's franchise also spearheaded a full-fledged civil war in Algeria, which has led to a bitter backlash from the majority of Arabs who rejected the actions and the worldview of al-Qaeda and its affiliates among the "Islamic groups."

Al-Qaeda's failures in the Arab world led it to focus on U.S. and Western targets as a means to rally Arab and Muslim support. Bloodying the nose of empires has always had its fans in the Arab world. The 9/11 attacks and the failure of the subsequent U.S. war on Iraq in 2003 played into the hands of the bin Laden group. The paradoxes that characterized al-Qaeda were part of its success. Its limited capacity and unlimited megalomania, modern organization, and medieval agenda, along with global networking and anti-globalization rhetoric played well in its favor.

America's mistaken reactions to the group notwithstanding, al-Qaeda's Arab-Afghans were generally hated in the Arab world and have had no Arab agenda of any sort that merited even the least consideration. It was only natural after the popular uprising swept through the Arab world that the violent jihadi groups would be the first losers in the upheaval of civil disobedience. The unity among people of all ideological trends, including the "mainstream Islamists," have turned the tables against al-Qaeda's demonizing tactics directed at all other Muslims. Tunisian Islamist leader Rashid Ghannouchi told me in the autumn of 2011, al-Qaeda was "finished" thanks to the revolution in Tunisia.

ISLAMISTS IN THE AGE OF DICTATORS

Relations between Arab regimes and Islamist movements have differed from one country to another but can generally be divided into two categories: confrontation and accommodation. The Muslim Brotherhood and its offshoots have had no problem finding an accommodating division of labor with dictators and monarchies where they could attend to religious, educational, and social matters, while accepting the autocrats' monopoly over power. They joined coalition governments in Jordan, were active participants in Kuwait's parliament, partnered with the regime in Sudan and Yemen, and joined the post-Iraq coalitions after the invasion.

In other countries, the Islamist movements faced repression either because of their growing popularity or in retaliation for attacks on the regimes. The Muslim Brotherhood was suppressed violently in Egypt in the 1950s, in Iraq in the '70s, Syria in the '80s, and Algeria in the '90s.

Sudan became a refuge or a hub for many of the Islamist leaders looking for a safe haven to consult, organize, and plan future moves during the 1990s. They included such extremist Salafist leaders as Osama bin Laden and liberal Islamist leaders and thinkers as al-Ghannouchi, as well as Islamist resistance leaders of the Palestinian Hamas and the Algerian Salvation Front. This didn't last long as Sudan's own dictator soon turned against his Islamist partners.

Sudan's case is illustrative of the complicity between a dictator and his Islamist partners going sour. Hassan al-Turabi, the head of Sudan's Islamist movement, is a savvy thinker and political operator who was imprisoned by President Jaafar Nimeiry on charges of sedition in the 1980s. After the 1989 coup d'état by unknown army officer Omar al-Bashir, Turabi became the intellectual force behind the new regime, and in the 1990s served as the parliament speaker and head of the ruling National Congress Party (NCA). When Turabi tried to overshadow him and amend the constitution to reduce his powers, President Bashir declared a three-month state of emergency as "a measure to restore discipline and order."

The move was supported by Egypt's Mubarak and Libya's Gaddafi. Bashir was also nudged by the United States to get rid of his Islamist partner, who also headed the pan-Islamist National Islamic Front, an offshoot of the Muslim Brotherhood. Eventually, Bashir accused the popular Turabi of attempting to overthrow his government and detained him for thirty-two months, followed by a two-year prison sentence for treason, and purged much of his Islamist movement's leadership. As late as 2009, Turabi was detained once again for calling on President Bashir to give himself up to the International Criminal Court.

This wasn't the first time the secular dictators rallied in support of a crackdown over an Islamist movement. Following the Islamist Salvation Front's electoral victory in 1991, the Algerian situation alerted its neighboring Tunisian and Egyptian regimes, making them more watchful of the rise of their own Islamists. The three North African autocracies mounted a coordinated effort to preempt solidarity with Algeria and tame what they saw as a transnational religious threat challenging their monopoly on power. In the following two decades, the "Islamist threat" became their alibi to repress peaceful political opposition and tighten their grip on society. Indeed, the only practical and productive meetings of the Arab League were those of the interior ministers' discussion of security cooperation against their Islamists.

DEBATES WITHIN
THE ISLAMIST MOVEMENT

Contrary to the monolithic version of political Islam presented by Western media, the Islamic world and its Islamist movements have gone through a long and deep transformation over the last several decades that has involved sharp theological and political disagreements as well as friction among its various components along sectarian and generational lines. There have been countless public debates and lively exchanges among Muslims over the means and ends of political Islam or the role of Islam in politics, state, and society. The Muslim Brotherhood and its various trends and scholars, the Wahhabites and their Salafi offshoots, the Sufis and their various popular voices, the so called second Islamic international around Sudan's Hassan al-Turabi and Tunisia's Rashid al-Ghannouchi, the populist Muslim televangelists, Sheikh Qaradawi of the Association of Muslim Scholars and the extremist jihadis aligned with bin Laden and Ayman al-Zawahiri, aside from countless religious and secular scholars and thinkers, have all been part of the great debate over Islam and governance.

From its outset, the idea of politicizing Islam in the context of the modern state has provoked much controversy and created new gray areas between religion and politics. Secular dictators and parties have been as interested in filling in the blanks as their Islamist rivals, with each side arguing how best to accommodate governance with Islam. Secular regimes rejected on principle the religion-based political parties when the majority of the population was Muslim, accusing Islamist leaders of stratifying "good" and "bad" Muslims through politics. They also argued that considering Islamic Shari'a law was already either "a source" or "the main source" of legislation in their countries—there was no point in further Islamization or organized political Islam.

On the opposite side, after decades of evolution, the influential Egyptian Muslim Brotherhood that was formed soon after the breakup of the Ottomans, has accepted the alternation of power through democratic elections and embraced pluralism in social and political life, but stopped short of supporting liberal democracy—a concept that has been practiced primarily by Western nations and increasingly stripped of its liberal component elsewhere in the developing world.

While some of the Brotherhood branches and leaders remained vague on the subject of a civic democratic constitution, more Brotherhood affiliates accept the principle of an elected female or Christian leader in the civic state. The Palestinian Hamas, for example, won the legislative elections in 2006 on the basis of a civic Palestinian Basic Law that functioned since 1997 as a temporary constitution and was ratified by Arafat in 2002. Likewise, the Lebanese Shia group Hezbollah has entered the political fray and accepted the democratic rules of governance while retaining its armed-wing for defense against any Israeli invasion.

The rapprochement between Islamism and democracy was rejected by the Saudi-supported Salafis and other fundamentalist religious groups across the region who insisted on the literal interpretation and implementation of the Shari'a in future Islamic states or in a grand pan-Islamic caliphate. And it wasn't all a matter of principle. Those who long benefited from their partnership with Islamists to maintain their monopoly on power, as in the extreme case of Al-Saud and fundamentalist Wahhabite Islam, or exploited the fear of religious extremism to hold onto power, as in the case of the totalitarian regimes, the debate over the role of Islam was no more than a camouflage to conceal their true motives.

And invoking Islam has often been the parlance of hypocrites. A secular Tunisian leftist commented sarcastically on the paradox of interests and values thus:

> Ben Ali's son-in-law, Sakhr el-Materi [hardly religious], bought a large estate and named every road on the property after one of the Prophet's 99 names. He founded the Zeitouna Islamic bank and a radio station with the same name, broadcasting religious programs only. Where did the Islamist leader, Sheikh Rashid Ghannouchi, seek refuge when he fled from Ben Ali's repressive regime? In the U.K., a secular state. And where did the secular Ben Ali seek refuge when he fled from the revolution? In Saudi Arabia. . . . Facts are better than theories.[4]

One of the foremost of modernizers among the Islamist groups has been the Tunisian An-Nahdah under the guidance of Rashid al-Ghannouchi. The seventy-year-old Islamist was imprisoned twice in the 1980s and went into exile until after Ben Ali's departure. He espoused egalitarian views with an emphasis on social and economic justice. Since its founding, the movement accepted the principle of political diversity, alternation of power, and the rule of the majority under a democratic constitution. Ghannouchi, who commands considerable respect among Arab Islamists, went further than the Brotherhood leaders to interpret "the rule of God" as ordained in the "will of the people." An-Nahdah remained loyal to its principles despite Ben Ali's and his predecessor Bourgiba's attempts to uproot the movement's members and purge its leaders through repression, imprisonment, and exile. Soon after Ben Ali's ousting, Ghannouchi told Al Jazeera that he supports democracy and is categorically opposed to an Islamic caliphate. During an hour-long conversation two days after his party's victory in the Tunisian elections—they won almost 40 percent of the vote—al-Ghannouchi summarized his vision of democracy to me:

> Democracy is when the people rule themselves by themselves through an authority that represents them. They should be able to constantly oversee it and overthrow it when they want. It is when citizens can enjoy their personal freedom, regardless their color, wealth, religion, and way of thinking. It is when the state is built on citizenship basics, which means the state does not belong to a certain family, person, or party. It belongs to all its citizens.

Another An-Nahdah leader, Ali Laaridh, explained that the group's openness wasn't a tactic to gain power, but rather the culmination of long and bitter experiences that involved suffering from police repression and was affected by other views and cultures while in exile: "We have suffered abuse. We know what the violation of human rights means. We have lived in 50 different countries. And we have learned about democracy and women's rights. So we should be judged by the long way we have come. See how we live, us and our families: My wife works, my daughters study, one of them does not wear a veil."[5]

Many in Tunisia remain doubtful of An-Nahdah's commitment for democratic principles and skeptical of its plans once it took power. They argue that in Tunisia and elsewhere the only true guarantee in the long term could come with the adoption of a civic constitution with universal principles at its core. Indeed, it is over this issue that the most important battle of ideas is being fought.

OPENING A NEW CHAPTER

The ousting of Ben Ali, Mubarak, and Gaddafi has dramatically changed the political equation for the Islamist movements. A proverbial Pandora's box had opened up, as the long-suppressed Islamists have started to play a leading role in the revolutionary events of the last year. They included the Saudi-supported Salafi groups, which have sprung up in different parts of the Arab world since the end of the 1970s, as well as the homegrown Sufis that long avoided politics but have now joined the political process out of worry for their own religious rights. Even the reformed al-Qaeda and jihadi militants have thrown their hats into the ring in Egypt and Libya.

As soon as President Mubarak was ousted, the Egyptian Brotherhood moved to establish its first political party—the Freedom and Justice Party—under the leadership of three members of its strong Shura (Consultative) Council: Mohamed Mursi, the party leader; Essam Elarian, his deputy; and Mohamed Saed el-Katatny, secretary-general. In August 2011 the group held special elections to replace the three in order to maintain organizational separation between the political party and the movement. These were the first open and public elections in the group's history. It was no less telling of the change in the political atmosphere that the vote was followed by a Ramadan Iftar reception that included members of the Supreme Military Council and government officials, something unheard of in previous decades.

The priorities and programs of the Islamist movements have varied over time and geography. Prior to the revolution, the Brotherhood divided their effort on social and political advocacy, whereas the Salafists were mainly concerned with enforcing punitive religious dogma and spent very little time calling for political change. The Sufis, for the most part, lived peacefully under the regime so long as they were allowed to practice their religion. This changed with the advent of the mass protests as the Brotherhood became active in the revolutions against Arab autocracies, while other movements like the Salafists, Sufis, and jihadis remained on the sidelines until after the ouster of Ben Ali and Mubarak, when they emerged to take advantage of the new opening.

Be that as it may, the Islamist groups have emerged in 2011 as important pillars of change in Tunisia, Egypt, and across the region, as they struggled shoulder to shoulder with liberal, leftist, and nationalist groups. Their participation in the revolution in Yemen, where they previously partnered with the regime, and in Libya and Syria where they were banned and imprisoned but later released, has also been substantial. In Libya they organized and fought the Gaddafi forces along with other revolutionaries, and in Yemen they joined other popular forces leading the protests in Sana'a. They also became an integral part of the "co-ordination entities" that have sprung up in various parts of Syria, and in the end of the summer they joined the Syrian National Council, the coalition of Islamists, Liberals, and Leftists, under the leadership of secular opposition figure Burhan Ghalyoun.

210 | THE INVISIBLE ARAB

The Islamists were helped by the fact that the biggest protests were generally held on Fridays when they emerged from mosques after prayers. Although on many occasions it was the secular, leftist, nationalist, or liberal activists that spearheaded the protest movement, Friday's prayers gave the events a religious or conservative aura, at least to those watching from afar as many chanted "there is no god but God." As Muslims from all quarters visit the mosque on their day off, Friday had become the most convenient meeting point for many of the organizers taking advantage of people assembled in mass without need for official permission. Islamist movements have also used mosques as a source of financial support and recruitment. Attempts by secular progressives to use schools as alternative safe houses for assembling protestors didn't work.

The theological approach to politics was also opposed by a number of main opposition parties and movements from the secular right, to the liberal and the radical left. Indeed, some were more worried of a "totalitarian Islamist" takeover than of "secular dictators." That was the case in Algeria when the military purged the Islamic Salvation Front, after its 1991 sweep in the municipal and early parliamentary elections. Opposition groups in Algeria, like their peers in North Africa and other Arab countries in the east, looked from the sidelines, at times complicit, as dictators violently repressed Islamist movements. For decades, Arab autocrats were relatively successful in playing on and exploiting the suspicion between their secular and Islamist oppositions.

The 2006 elections in the occupied Palestinian territories notwithstanding, the Tunisian elections at the end of October 2011 are the first free competitive elections in an independent Arab nation between secular and Islamists trends. Most likely, the Palestinian Hamas, the Tunisian An-Nahdah, and Egypt's Freedom and Justice party have opened the way for more such popular competitions that will have major influence over national identity and governance in the Arab region.

Internationally, and notably in Western and U.S. circles, the Islamists—and at times Muslims in general—are demonized as aggressive, bloody, paranoid, terrorist, and imperialistic in their outlook. They see the implementation of Islamic Shari'a as a form of totalitarianism that's worse than dictatorship, when, Shari'a, agree with it or not, is simply a body of principles. While other Arabs judge the rise of Islamist political power on the basis of their vision for governance and commitment to democracy and pluralism, much of the Western fear is based in clichés of anti-quated views of Islam and the Islamists, or disinformation regard-ing the view of Muslims and Islamists in general of al-Qaeda and the 9/11 attacks.

Meanwhile, Islamist movements the likes of the Egyptian Muslim Brotherhood have already opened dialogue with the mili-tary and with Western powers on the basis of mutual interest and respect. This might be seen as a positive development that allows for a new sort of regional order on the basis of a new accommoda-tion among Islamists, the generals, and Western leaders. However, this triangle could eventually be as oppressive and totalitarian as the previous dictatorships. As I will argue in my final thoughts, the Islamists must make sure that their representatives reconcile with the principles of democracy and modern statehood anchored in the Arab lands, not a division of labor with the mili-tary and its Western support system.

EPILOGUE | The Visible Arab

*If you think you're too small to make a
difference, try sleeping with a mosquito.*

—AFRICAN PROVERB

SOMEWHAT POSTMODERN:
REVOLUTION EN DIRECT

Video clips and images of the revolutionary dramas have passed from cameras and cell phones to laptops and satellite television networks, making the Arab uprising perhaps the most filmed and communicated revolution in the history of the region, or indeed the world. Images took over from the reality on the ground to present a magnified and, at times, sensational representation of the upheaval, which in turn encouraged new protestors to join the spectacle.

The images of young revolutionaries overcoming brute force seduced the entire Arab nation and, arguably, people around the world. The cyber and television images were effective in conveying, molding, and transforming events. In fact, these images were so potent that they shaped revolutionary change.

In a world dominated by a multimedia culture, images are more effective than rhetoric, and human stories are more real than analysis and easier to accept because they humanize and familiarize social and political movements. In recent memory, images have on a number of occasions ushered in new eras. For example the image of a young man trying to block a tank with his body in Tiananmen Square became the symbol of a defiant new generation of Chinese. A woman drowning in her blood after being shot during the recent Green Revolution symbolized the crackdown in Iran. And certainly the images of a tortured Iraqi prisoner with his head covered and another naked one being dragged like a dog on a leash by a woman exposed the brutality of the U.S. occupation of Iraq. Earlier on, other iconic images went on to frame their respective conflicts. Pictures of a Vietnamese girl fleeing with her torn and burnt clothes from a U.S. napalm attack; the dead Salvadorian nuns whose bodies were found after being buried by the regime's death squads; the journalist killed on live television in Nicaragua by the regime's soldiers; and that of a boy and his father under fire during the Second Intifada.

The widely televised Arab revolution produced countless images of unarmed Arab youth defying tanks and soldiers, reinventing the public space, tearing down larger-than-life portraits of dictators, and erecting new platforms surrounded by millions, chanting slogans and inaugurating a new era.

In that spirit, the images of Muslims and Christians praying together in Tahrir Square have had a decisive effect on the people of Egypt who had suffered from inter-religious violence, and on many others in the Arab world where sectarian and ethnic tensions have wrought havoc in recent years. The symbolism of this widely televised togetherness in Tahrir and other freedom squares went a long way in averting religious tensions within the various revolutions and countries, all the while denying the regimes the capacity to stir sectarianism. People watching such prayers felt they were part of something bigger than life itself, something perhaps divine; *Mash'Allah*, God willed it, had indeed overtaken *Insha'Allah*, God's willing, in the hearts of many.

The interactive dynamics of satellite and social media in communicating and transmitting images have helped shaped the revolution's postmodern features more than anything else. And the ultimate revenge of history, the symbolic closure with the past, came in the image of the pharaoh behind bars as a frail Mubarak stood trial lying down on a stretcher.

The majority who did not participate in the actual, real revolution "participated" through watching, or rather testifying as an eyewitness. Their emotions revolved around their fascination with what they saw, not with what they physically experienced on the ground. Their experience was, however, real, and so were their emotions as they joined the revolution from their living rooms and laptops. Most might have watched from the sidelines, but the continuous flow of images from multiple sources kept them transfixed. They got involved through their TV remote controls as they explored various angles and perspectives of the same revolution. But that popular "participation" through media representation helped prepare people and attain their consent for the aftermath, which is crucial for the success of any change.

Invisible Arab citizens suddenly became citizen-journalists, thanks to their cell phones. Their captured images became indispensable to 24/7 TV coverage, as network journalists found themselves banned from reporting or violently harassed. Many protestors could watch themselves in real time on their iPhones, blurring the lines between real and virtual, form and content, image and reality.

It was never clear to me whether the fighters who captured, humiliated, and killed former Libyan leader Muammar Gaddafi were busier exacting revenge on the former dictator or taking countless pictures of an injured man and of his corpse.

In the age of celebrity, marketing, and television, people want to be remembered, preserved, shelved, and when needed, recalled and celebrated on demand. Images immortalized. If it was televised, it must have been real! Be that as it may, reality is much more complex than camera shoots and messier than packaged images.

ANTI-TOTALITARIAN, POST IDEOLOGICAL

I doubt the Arab revolution could have taken down regimes if it were not for its pluralistic, diverse, and creative nature, and I believe more of the same is needed for the post-revolutionary stage of the revolution to succeed. Nationalists, leftists, Islamists, and others put their differences aside as they were led by an ad-hoc coalition of young activists, students, the unemployed, labor unions, bloggers and artists, the religious and the Marxist, and women and men, who adapted to emerging realities.

The 99 percent have spoken on behalf of the collective. Long invisible, these Arabs have made themselves visible; they are the marginalized and the voiceless citizens from Morocco to Bahrain who broke the chains of fear and marched peacefully and proudly, announcing the dawn of a new era. Dignity has replaced humiliation.

They avoided deterministic statements, bombastic promises, and dogmatic goals that did not reflect the views of the Arab majority, such as "workers of the Arab world unite" or "Islam is the solution." Indeed, the genius of the revolution has been to use real needs and realistic demands to destabilize dictatorships and attain improbable results. Fulfilling these basic needs will be the test of their long-term success.

No longer are the Arabs bound by what they stand against—or the "populist negativism" that defined previous generations, to cite the late Arab thinker Mohammad Abed al-Jabri. Rather, what started as a social revolution calling for real reform soon turned into a political revolution demanding regime change that maintained its focus on freedom of expression, economic security, and social justice. Most agreed the Arab future would need to be democratic in nature.

The young revolutions haven't been directed against dictatorships only, although that was certainly their hallmark. They were also a cry against all that represents, justifies, or defends repression and injustice. For years, the new generation of Arab activists, girls and boys, men and women, had gone online to communicate, brainstorm, and organize as a way to escape conservative familial and societal norms, and to confront rigid hierarchal political, social, and religious structures.

The young, educated, and interconnected middle class in the region rooted for a revolution beyond "high politics," one that affected their immediate lives, including education, employment, and culture. After all, authoritarianism exists not only at the top of the political structure; it is ubiquitous in schools and textbooks, where it blocks motivation and discourages creativity and initiative. The youth have broken the elites' paternalistic trusteeship on politics and power and instead embraced alternative models and modes of living that release talents, build stamina, and encourage dissent.

The young Egyptian Muslim brothers and sisters have set the bar high for their peers in the Arab word. Theirs is a dual challenge, to continue to play a major role in the youth movement while playing a greater role in molding the future of the Muslim Brotherhood. In recent years, they protested against the regime, and confronted their conservative older leaders with surprising zeal. Their role in Tahrir Square was indispensable in terms of planning and organizing the demonstrations as part and parcel of the youth movement, as was the pressure they exerted on the Brotherhood's leadership to join at a later stage. Thanks to their connectivity, the Islamist youth opened up to teachings and inspiration beyond their immediate clerics that helped them reflect more creatively and liberally about Islam and society.

The revolutionary youth, men and women, were also vehemently opposed to the authoritarianism of the opposition leaders who've been no more democratic than the regimes as they held onto their positions. Their monopoly on dissent had led to intellectual and political stagnation among the elites, leaving the young activists little or no capacity to affect the agenda of the opposition parties. The latter's holistic ideologies and antiquated programs led much of today's youth to revolt against a whole "old" order and mentality that blocked the way to new blood. Their distaste for authoritarianism and absolutism has made the long-invisible youth and women the most eager to break from the shackles of the past.

Regrettably, the post-revolutionary Egyptian and Tunisian elections make it clear that change hasn't sunk in deep enough or spread wide enough, yet. The older male domination of the political parties and security apparatus remains intact. But this can't and won't last long. Owing to the revolutionary social transformation that has taken place, I am convinced the future belongs to the democratic majority of youth and women as they make up more than four-fifths of the population.

While much has been accomplished, serious challenges lie ahead to reverse decades of dictatorship. The Arab revolution needs to maintain its main objective: democracy, not ideology; democracy in which ideological trends compete freely.

GROOMING DEMOCRATS

In the absence of a majority of democrats, the skeptics argue, democracy is a pipe dream. How could the Arab nations produce democrats without democracy, and how could a democracy be attained without democrats? After all, democracy is not a television discussion, a slogan to be chanted; it's a system of values, a system of government; it's a culture and a mentality.

The Arab revolutions have provided a great opportunity to break out of this vicious circle. Revolutions are the nourishment that allows aspiring democrats and young self-declared democracies to grow and evolve together and feed off each other. The high turnout in the Tunisian elections to vote for tens of parties and thousands of candidates underlines the thirst of people to exercise their democratic rights peacefully. It's a great beginning on the long journey to writing laws, building institutions, and grooming a new generation of responsible citizens.

Alas, some of the political movements, mainly the Islamists, have not committed themselves unequivocally to the democratic principles, and it's not clear what they would do if or when they take power. Many of the Islamists I spoke to reckon that if they have a majority they have a democratic right to change the constitution and govern as they see religiously fit. They don't recognize democracy as first and foremost a system of governance based on democratic values that go beyond the right of majority to rule, to ensure that the rights and privileges of the minorities are respected and preserved—just as gender, religious, ethnic, and other basic rights are universally respected. And yet, having these parties within the political process is far more beneficial to the long term than keeping them outside it through coercive means. It's high time for inclusionary, not exclusionary, politics in the Arab region that take all opinions and concerns into account.

That's why a civic constitution that enshrines universal human values is paramount. It protects the rights of secular and religious alike, just as it preserves the rights of those political forces not in power, and allows for clear legal reference to major disputes. As a social contract, such a constitution should be written not only by male legal scholars as we saw in the Egyptian transitional process, but rather benefit from other sectors of society as well. A bill of rights of sort is what the Arab world needs as it traverses the challenging years ahead where many might feel obliged to take exceptional measures in case of socio-economic failure.

Although I personally attach importance to the liberal component of liberal democracy in terms of individual liberty, the degree of liberalism or conservatism in any future constitution will have to be worked out among the Arabs themselves in each and every country without interference from the outside. But constitutions need to be immune from outbreaks of populism and anchored in the long-term interest of a country. They need to be protected by an independent judiciary to guarantee their respect by the executive branch. Egypt's old Court of Appeal (Mahkamat al-Ist'inaf) is an interesting model to build on. A source of irritation to the Egyptian dictator, the court made headlines when it judged the November 2010 elections as rigged. The court's judges are elected by other judges of a lower court and hence are not beholden to politicians for their appointments.

Democratic constitutions not only keep religion out of the business of state (not the individual), they also keep the latter out of religion—its beliefs and practices. There have been countless discussions about the role of Islam and Shari'a in the state and constitution. To name Shari'a a source of legislation could be a welcomed compromise by all as a constructive way forward; Shari'a is a body of laws, after all. Some defend the Islamic concept of Shura (consultation), when speaking of democracy, as authentic to Muslims. But that shouldn't be an excuse to impose Shari'a as the only source of laws.

Much of the fear and hesitancy of Arab democrats and open-minded Islamists in actively calling for democracy was grounded in the negative association many in the Arab world have with liberal democracy. Democracy is cursed by its association with Western imperialism—recall that George W. Bush's neoconservative war agenda used the pretext of promoting democracy in the region. Some of the secular Arab dictatorships had degraded the term democracy by claiming to be democrats. So many genuine democratic activists invoked Shura or other such religiously inspired concepts instead. They needn't have been so cautious. As I mentioned earlier, many of the new non-Western democracies have separated democracy as a process and system of government from liberalism as a Western-centric philosophy over the last few decades, rendering democracy more universal than before. The ruling AK Party in Turkey has shown the way forward in accepting the parameters of the secular civic state, and it seems An-Nahdah, the party that won more than two-fifths of the Tunisian parliamentary seats, will follow in its footsteps. Interestingly, the AK Party was also influenced by the writings of Al-Ghannouchi, the head of An-Nahdah.[1]

Arabs shouldn't limit themselves to any religious-centric political culture. Nor should they tackle political differences on the basis and degree of religious beliefs. Opening to other people and benefiting from their experiences is what has long enhanced

Arab and other cultures and enriched human civilization. After all, it's the Arabs and Muslims who translated and preserved the Greek civilization for the West to benefit from.

DEMOCRATIC DEVELOPMENT

This is the time for creative thinking about the future where investment and sustainability—not consumerism and militarism—are the bedrock of Arab development. This is one of the advantages of a new beginning; the Arabs can learn from the mistakes and failures of other nations as well as from their successes. It's a time to open up to the world, not shield ourselves from it.

While economic development and modernization are no guarantee for democracy, poverty and underdevelopment are a recipe for tyranny. That's why new leaders need to enact new laws that do away with corruption and nepotism and, instead, encourage initiative and investment in people and the economy—one that creates and protects jobs, safeguards social justice, improves infrastructure and education, and attracts capital.

Wide-based economic development nurtures social conscience and strengthens social relations, two indispensable ingredients of an Arab political culture conducive to peaceful democratic competition. The wider and stronger the Arab working and middle classes, the more stable would be their democracy.

Even rich authoritarian economies that have tried to provide economic security and a degree of economic and social liberalism will continue to see their economy slip in comparison to others if they forego democratic development. The recent Gulf Cooperation Council (GCC) invitation to the monarchies of Jordan and Morocco to join its regional coalition of authoritarian regimes as a buffer against changes in their neighborhood will not, ultimately, protect them.

Meanwhile, if certain Arab monarchies persist in their attempt to resist or sabotage reform and change, the new Arab democracies will need to rally together as a league of Arab democracies.

In the long term a democratic Arab world would be more committed to pan-Arab unity on the basis of popular, representative democracy than it would a dictatorship. A democratic Arab world will be the fruit of common interests and societal binds, not the peddling of populist ideology from above. As Arab States rebuild their nations and reconnect with the rest of the world, they will soon realize that there is no escape from promoting "regionalization" or Arab cooperation to fend off global pressures. Arab integration is also the answer to ethnic and sectarian divisions, fragmentation, and tribalism. The Arabs' strength lies in their popular unity.

INTELLECTUAL FREEDOM

Arab intellectuals have gone largely missing in recent times. Critical of political power, many intellectuals have been coerced, tortured, or exiled; in other words, they have been absented from the public life, or they bartered their principles for posts or prestige. But more than a few spoke courageously about a new way forward in the region.

Such true intellectuals are indispensable to transforming the primarily social and political revolutions into a cultural revolution that affects all aspects of Arab life. Along with educators, scientists, journalists, and others, they need to imagine and construct an alternative Arab educational and cultural landscape. Arab school curricula are in dire need of rewriting and restructuring to reflect the spirit of the democratic revolutions and of the times. An entire generation, from the first grade to the university level, needs new textbooks, libraries, laboratories, and more if the future is to outshine the present. This can't be realized by slogans and demonstrations; it takes tedious hard work away from the cameras.

During these revolutionary times, some intellectuals will naturally find themselves critical of the newcomers to power. And that's a healthy attitude toward the new leaders. But there is also a need for a constructive, intellectual critique that not only deconstructs and demolishes but also plans and builds. No longer is it enough to signal what's wrong; it's important to show the right alternatives.

In addition to expertise in economics and development, the Arabs are in need of cultural and artistic renewal. Half a century ago, Egypt's economy was equal to that of Turkey, and its cinema, theatre, and literary contributions competed with the French. Today, Egyptians are far behind and will need decades to catch up. Artists, poets, and architects are as important as economists, engineers, and doctors for the health of nations in need of renewal. The caged Arab imagination needs to be freed from the chains of the past.

FASTEN
YOUR SEATBELTS

The next few years promise to be difficult. The revolution's aftershock could be dangerous if people are not prepared to combat the looming forces of counter revolution, which manifest in the region's pervasive dictatorships, in its reactionary political and religious movements, sectarian groups, and with the cynical regional and international powers. The revolutions have added new elements of unpredictability to a region bridled with instability and conflict that the nascent revolutionaries will find hard to turn their back on. The festering instability I mentioned at the outset in the likes of Sudan, Somalia, Lebanon, Iraq, Palestine, and Israel's threats of war against Iran has changed little since the outbreak of the revolutions.

This is especially true, as the seasons have turned on the Arab revolution. The Arab spring in Tunisia and Egypt gave way to a heated summer in Libya, Syria, and Yemen, leading to the deaths of tens of thousands. The regimes' violent crackdown, the militarization of the revolutions and the international intervention in Libya have derailed the uprisings from their original popular, democratic course. Now there is every likelihood that change will come only through military struggle. The week I finished writing this essay, Tunisia held its first free elections, Gaddafi was brutally murdered by opposition fighters, and Syria seemed to be heading for a final, bloody showdown. Though the Arab Maghreb and Egypt might be beginning to see the light at the end of the tunnel, the Arab Mashreq around Syria and Iraq isn't looking too bright.

Over the last several decades, the Arab region, which comprises 6 percent of the world population, has accounted for 20 percent of its armed conflicts. War, instability, and conflict have had their toll on the region's development and must be dealt with accordingly. That doesn't mean surrendering pan-Arab security—rather the contrary: peace will come through strength. But strength itself doesn't come through expensive military purchases, let alone war.

If they must rebuild their military, it's worth recalling that Arab militaries were defeated on the battlefield because their regimes' backwardness rendered their armor brittle. A military power not backed up by know-how and modern organization is useless. Power is a reflection of development; underdevelopment leads to humiliation and defeat. Having said that, the most potent power is deterrence and the more united the Arab nations, the more they are capable of deterring aggression against any one of them.

For all practical purpose, national sovereignty, personal liberty, social progress, and regional security are entwined. Attempts at piecemeal dealing will fail utterly.

In the short run, it doesn't seem regional powers like Israel, Saudi Arabia, and Iran would like to see the Arab revolutions succeed. If a strong democratic Egypt regains its regional influence, it could eclipse Saudi Arabia, put Israel on notice, and curtail Iran's regional ambition. Fortunately for the Arabs, the regional powers' conflicting agendas will prevent them from jointly conspiring against them.

Speaking of conflicting agendas, I hereby declare the politically charged terms "moderate" and "extremist" null and void. Referring to corrupt, authoritarian, and oppressive regimes as moderates because they are friends, allies, or clients of Western powers is ridiculous. It's time we reverse this old and misleading imperial construct. No longer will rogue regimes be defined according to their proximity to Western powers; rather Washington and other influential centers will be seen as extremists if they continue to support oppressive clients and undermine popular uprisings in countries like Bahrain or Yemen. The same applies to Israel's colonial dictatorship in Palestine.

Even the pundits and Zionist apologists understand that Israel cannot continue to rule over another people after sixty years of dispossession and forty years of occupation. Fatah and Hamas, too, should end their semi-totalitarian control over their population centers, many of which are refugee camps. The way forward will need to go beyond the last two decades of U.S. monopoly over the "diplomatic process" in favor of greater regional and international role. Increasingly, representative Arab governments will be more reflective of their public opinion than Washington's opinion as the latter loses more of its strategic leverage in the region with destabilizing consequences on the short term.

ARABS REIMAGINED

National reconstruction begins with people's reconciliation. The Arab world is in need of restoring justice that is fair and measured, not retributive justice that resorts to the excessive means of past regimes. Revenge, retaliation, or the uprooting of everything that's associated with the old regime—on the lines of de-Ba'athification in Iraq—might help bury the past, but it will also kill the chances for a better future.

Freedom will thrive when Arabs free themselves not only from dictatorships but also from their legacy. People aren't free if all they do is reverse the past or define themselves in negation to the former rulers. This is especially true when, for whatever reasons, past policies were not necessarily wrong. Gaddafi's role in the establishment of the African Union and Assad's position on Palestine, for example, shouldn't be renounced merely because they were adopted by dictators. Indeed, gender equality, health care, and beneficial social programs mustn't be reversed because they were developed under a despot.

The challenge is to make decisions on the basis of the good of future generations, not what avenges the ugly past. It will take time, but more importantly it will take political maturity. After long decades of authoritarian rule, the future will be defined by more than bricks and ballots. Bruised nations need to reconcile with their past in order to build a better future.

Moreover, the plurality of the social and political forces behind the revolutions that contributed greatly to their successes in Tunisia, Egypt, and Libya should be preserved and strengthened in the years to come. Unlike many twentieth-century revolutions, Arab revolutionaries must avoid settling scores among themselves through coercion and violence. It's up to the people, not the multiple leaders of the revolutions, to decide the future course of their nations.

I have seen many victims becoming victimizers and the prosecuted embracing prosecutor roles in the region and elsewhere. Fascinated or obsessed by those who had control over theirs and their families' lives, or determined "never again" to allow gruesome injustice against them, they rush to wear their victimizers' sunglasses, earpieces, and outfits before holding their weapons and occupying their torture chambers. Arab revolutionaries and future leaders must ensure first and foremost that injustice does not happen under their watch.

Change doesn't come by substituting national flags and the names of internal security services, or by growing or shaving beards. It comes by changing the power structure prevailing in Arab societies. Dictatorship, theocracy, aristocracy, tyranny, democracy, and "communism" are variations on the division of power in a society where individuals, elites, a party, or specific groups monopolize and abuse power. The same goes for discrimination, chauvinism, racism, and slavery, where unequal power relations are camouflaged by skin color, gender, class, or ethnicity.

Democracy is a system where power is shared relatively fairly among the citizens. But even in older democracies, fairness has been undermined by competing claims. In the United States, for instance, powerful corporations that are treated like citizens during elections manage to push for laws that favor them over people's interests.

Arabs have learnt the hard way that democracy cannot be imported, parachuted, imposed, or outsourced: its success will ultimately depend on their awareness, participation, and commitment to the public good. The invisible Arabs have become visible, and in the process they have the potential to become invincible.

"YOUTH OF THE WORLD UNITE": FROM TAHRIR SQUARE TO LIBERTY PLAZA

"Another world is possible for all of us."

—Young Egyptian activist Asma Mahfouz
speaking at the Occupy Wall Street
movement in October 2011

Like millions around the world at the end of 2011, we have been eagerly following the emergence of a new international movement for social and economic justice inspired by the Arab uprisings.

Less than one year after youth peacefully occupied the public squares of the Arab world, American, European, and other youth movements have sprung in different parts of the world demanding economic security and political accountability. Economist and Nobel Prize winner Joseph E. Stieglitz remarked after a tour of some of these countries:

> The protest movement that began in Tunisia in January, subsequently spreading to Egypt and then to Spain, has now become global—with the protests engulfing Wall Street and cities across America. Globalization and modern technology now enables social movements to transcend borders as rapidly as ideas can.

The youth movements are spreading horizontally on the SPIN model—segmented, polycentric, ideological, networked groups—

making them hard to contain and harder to defeat. Organized non-hierarchically similar to the environmental, feminist, and other global movements, these youth movements are bound by similar grievances and aspire for comparable objectives.

For example, the increase in youth unemployment in the prosperous West is comparable to the impoverished Arab world. In Spain unemployment among youth stood at 48 percent in 2011, Greece at 43 percent, Italy at 29 percent, and 22 percent in the United Kingdom. Sooner or later, this often translates to pent-up frustration and the potential for major public protests.

Likewise, the steep inequality in relatively poor Egypt or Tunisia is not so different from the United States—the world's richest and more powerful country—where 1 percent of the people take 25 percent of the income. The similarities in their economic disparities and the lack of political accountability of their elites has not been lost on observers in Europe and United States, who have drawn parallels between the spirit in Cairo, Madrid, and Portland.

And this of course isn't unique to the West. Burma's democracy leader Aung San Suu Kyi called the Arab Spring an "inspiration" to the Burmese, saying "the universal human aspiration to be free has been brought home to us by recent developments in the Middle East. The Burmese are as excited by these events are as people elsewhere."

Curiously, China's leadership tried to contain or ignore the excitement about the Tunisian and Egypt protest movements. Worried about a repeat of the 1989 Tiananmen Square youth protests, the Chinese authorities blocked all Internet searches of the word "Egypt" during the early stages of the revolution, banned discussion of the protests on media sites, and even blocked Al Jazeera's Web site to Chinese readers and viewers. The time when

Mao Tse-tung boasted "the world is gripped with revolutions; the situation is excellent" is long gone, as China's ruling party tries to maintain maximum control of its antsy youth as the gap widens between rich and poor with the proliferation of new Chinese millionaires and billionaires.

While numbers speak loud and clear, it's the political and economic culture behind the economic disparities that are drawing out the masses. The global financial and economic crisis of 2010–2011 has exposed a culture of impunity, despotism, and corruption that has become rampant throughout the world, blurring the old fault lines between rich democracies and poor autocracies and drawing new fault lines between indifferent ruling establishments and their alienated public.

As the United States and other Western governments doll out trillions of dollars from public funds for inefficient and reckless banks at the advice of their former and present executives, people detect foul play, not to say corruption. What is the difference, they wonder, between Ahmad Ezz of Ezz Steel, the corrupt millionaire and business associate of the Mubarak regime, and the bank executives in and outside U.S. administrations? While Ezz is finally in jail, the latter continue to make policy and generate billions.

The Occupy movement in the United States, the student demonstrations in Britain, the youth protests in Spain, the riots in Greece, and the union protests in France, Italy, Portugal, and Belgium, all feed on the same frustration and aggravation that inflamed the Arab youth: politics devoid of ethics, economics dominated by corporate and special interest, wars devoid of logic.

The Arab Spring has come at an important crossroad in global affairs when the failure of the U.S.-led neoliberal policies of the

"Washington consensus" have given momentum to the ill-liberal "Beijing consensus" among many of the world autocracies. However, the Arab youth, as with their peers around the world, have rejected such false choices. At the end of 2011, by the millions, they dare imagine a better world and a brighter future, and they are beginning to take matters into their hands.

ACKNOWLEDGMENTS

Writing this essay while working as Al Jazeera's senior political analyst had its ups and downs. It's been one of our busiest years (2011), which has meant lots of extra pressure. But while this was my choice, those closest to me had to bear the brunt of my frustrations, preoccupations, and demands. I thank them for tolerating my moods and for their support in more ways than they realize. Writing is a habit that requires solitude; writing under pressure is unfriendly.

However, the heat of the news beat has made it all very enticing. Working out of Al Jazeera's newsrooms and bureaus across the globe provides perspectives like no other. Much of this book is based on notes I have accumulated over the last year, and more generally since I joined Al Jazeera five years ago.

I've been blessed by the company of so many wonderful journalists and colleagues whose observations and comments have been paramount to help me think through the breathtaking events that have been sweeping the Arab world. My team at *Empire* and those on Al Jazeera's Web site have gone out of their way to accommodate my needs.

It's difficult to mention all the names and even harder to select a few. I will just say that this essay is the culmination of discussions, debates, and even provocations and bitter disagreements with colleagues and friends alike. They all have my appreciation and thanks.

The dramatic speed and scope of the transformation sweeping through the Arab world made the intelligent brainstorming

234 | ACKNOWLEDGMENTS

sessions and the academic papers by the Arab Center for Research and Policy Studies all too indispensable for accessing Arab perspectives on the revolutions.

Nowadays, I especially miss and, all too often, remember two very special people who are no longer with us: Joseph Samahaand and Mohammad El Sayyed Said. Their visions and discourse were prophetic.

—*Marwan Bishara*

SUGGESTED READING

Ali, Tariq. *The Clash of Fundamentalisms: Crusades, Jihads, and Modernity* (London: Verso, 2003).

Amin, Samir. *Le Monde Arabe dans la Longue Durée* (Alger: Editions APIC, 2011).

———. *Monde Arabe: Le Printemps des Peuples?* (Editions Les Temps des Cerises, Sept. 2011).

Ashour, Omar. "Ex-Jihadists in the New Libya," Brookings Institution online, August 29, 2011.
http://www.brookings.edu/articles/2011/0829_libya_ashour.aspx.

Aswany, Al. *On the State of Egypt: A Novelist's Provocative Reflections.* (Cairo: The American University in Cairo Press, 2011; Edinburgh: Canongate Books, 2011).

Bergen, Peter. *The Longest War: The Enduring Conflict between America and Al-Qaeda* (New York: Free Press, 2011).

Blanc, Pierre. *Revoltes Arabes: Premiers Regards* (Paris: L'Harmattan, 2011).

Brehony, Noel. *Yemen Divided: The Story of a Failed State in South Arabia* (New York: I. B. Tauris, 2011).

Browers, Michaelle. *Political Ideology in the Arab World: Accommodation and Transformation* (New York: Cambridge University Press, 2009).

Brown, Nathan, and Amr Hamzawy. *Between Religion and Politics* (Washington, DC: Carnegie Endowment, 2010).

Brown, Nathan, and Emad Shahin. *The Struggle over Democracy in the Middle East: Regional Politics and External Policies* (London: Routledge, 2009).

Byman, Daniel. *A High Price: The Triumphs and Failures of Israeli Counterterrorism* (New York: Oxford University Press, 2011).

Chatty, Dawn. *Displacement and Dispossession in the Modern Middle East* (New York: Cambridge University Press, 2010).

Chin, Felix. *Political Developments & U.S. Policy in the Middle East* (New York: Nova Science Publishers, 2011).

Cleveland, William L., and Martin Bunton. *A History of the Modern Middle East* (New York: Westview Press, 2009).

Cook, Steven. *The Struggle for Egypt: From Nasser to Tahrir Square.* (New York: Oxford University Press, 2011).

Corm, Georges, and Hala Khawam. *A History of the Middle East: From Antiquity to the Present Day* (London: Garnet Publishing, 2010).

———. *Fragmentation in the Middle East* (Longon: Unwin Hyman, 1989).

———. *Histoire du Moyen-Orient: De L'Antiquite a Nos Jours* (Paris: La Decouverte, 2007).

———. *Le Nouveau Desordre Economique Mondial: Aux Racines des Echecs du Developpement* (Paris: La Decouverte, 1993).

———. *Le Nouveau Gouvernement du Monde: Ideologies, Structures, Contre-Pouvoirs* (Paris: La Decouverte, 2010).

———. *Orient-Occident, la Fracture Imaginaire* (Paris: La Decouverte, 2007).

———. *Le Proche-Orient éclaté 1956–2010* (Paris: Gallimard, 2010).

Council on Foreign Relations. *The New Arab Revolt: What Happened, What It Means, and What Comes Next* (New York: Council on Foreign Relations, 2011).

Delacoura, Katerina. *Islamist Terrorism and Democracy in the Middle East* (New York: Cambridge University Press, 2011).

Elbadawi, Ibrahim, and Samir Makdisi, editors. *Democracy in the Arab World* (New York: Routledge, 2011).

Esposito, John L. *The Oxford History of Islam* (New York: Oxford University Press, 2000).

Fahmy, Shahira. "Contrasting Visual Frames of Our Times: A Framing Analysis of English- and Arabic-Language Press Coverage of War and Terrorism." *The International Gazette* 72.8 (Dec 2010): 695–717. *Sociological Abstracts*.

Feiler, Bruce. *Generation Freedom: The Middle East Uprisings and the Remaking of the Modern World* (New York: William Morrow, 2011).

Filiu, Jean-Pierre. *The Arab Revolution: Ten Lessons from the Democratic Uprising* (London: C Hurst, 2011).

Fisk, Robert. *The Great War for Civilization: The Conquest of the Middle East* (London: Harper Perennial, 2006).

Freedman, Lawrence. *A Choice of Enemies: America Confronts the Middle East* (New York: Phoenix, 2008).

Freeman, Chas. *America's Misadventures in the Middle East* (Charlottesville, Just World Books, 2010).

Gardner, David. *Last Chance: The Middle East in the Balance.* (London: I. B. Tauris, 2009).

Gardner, Lloyd. *The Road to Tahrir Square: Egypt and the United States from the Rise of Nasser to the Fall of Mubarak* (London: Saqi Books, 2011).

Gerges, Fawaz A. *The Rise and Fall of Al-Qaeda* (London: Oxford University Press, 2011).

Habib, Randa. *Hussein and Abdulla: Inside the Jordanian Royal Family* (London: Saqi Books, 2010).

Hirst, David. *Beware of Small States: Lebanon, Battleground of the Middle East* (New York: Faber and Faber: 2011).

Hitti, Philip K. *History of Syria Including Lebanon and Palestine, Vol 2* (Piscataway, NJ: Gorgias Press, 2002).

Hitti, Philip K, and Nabih Amin Faris. *The Arab Heritage* (Westport, CT: Greenwood Press, 1985).

Hitti, Philip K., and Walid Khalidi. *History of the Arabs* (New York: Palgrave Macmillan, 2002).

Hourani, Albert, and Ruthven, Malise. *A History of the Arab Peoples: With a New Afterword* (Cambridge, MA: Harvard University Press, 2010).

Jacobs, Matthew F. *Imagining the Middle East: The Building of an American Foreign Policy, 1918–1967* (Chapel Hill: University of North Carolina Press, 2011).

Kawczynski, Daniel. *Seeking Gaddafi: Libya, the West, and the Arab Spring* (London: Biteback Publishing, 2011).

Khalidi, Rashid, and Ibrahim Abu Lughod. *The Arab Rediscovery of Europe: A Study in Cultural Encounters* (London: Saqi Essentials, 2011).

Khalidi, Rashid. *Resurrecting Empire: Western Footprints and America's Perilous Path in the Middle East* (Boston: Beacon Pess, 2005).

———. *Sowing Crisis: The Cold War and American Dominance in the Middle East* (Boston: Beacon Press, 2009).

———. *The Iron Cage* (Boston: Beacon Press, 2006).

Kurzman, Charles. *The Missing Martyrs: Why There Are So Few Muslim Terrorists?* (New York: Oxford University Press, 2011).

Levy, Gideon. *The Punishment of Gaza* (London: Verso, 2010).

Lewis, Bernard. *Arabs in History* (New York: Oxford University Press, 2002).

———. *The Crisis of Islam: Holy War and Unholy Terror* (Waterville, ME: Thorndike Press, 2003).

———. *The Middle East: 2000 Years of History from the Birth of Christianity to the Present Day* (New York: Oxford University Press, 2001).

———. *The Political Language of Islam* (Chicago: University of Chicago Press, 1991).

———. *Political Words and Ideas in Islam* (Princeton, NJ: Markus Wiener Publishers, 2008).

———. *What Went Wrong? Western Impact and Middle Eastern Response* (New York: Oxford University Press, 2002).

———. *What Went Wrong?-Western Impact and Middle Eastern Response* (London: Phoenix, 2002).

Maalouf, Amin. *Disordered World: Setting a New Course for the Twenty-first Century* (London: George Miller, 2011).

———. *Le Dérèglement du Monde* (Paris: Grasset & Fasquelle, 2010).

———. *Origines* (Paris: Grasset & Fasquelle, 2004).

MacLeod, Scott, ed. *The Cairo Review of Global Affairs*, Journal of the AUC School of Global Affairs and Public Policy (No. 2), Aug 2011, Oxford University Press.

Maksoud, Clovis, and UNDP. *The Arab Human Development Report* (New York: UN Press, 2005).

Massad, Joseph. *Colonial Effects: the Making of National Identity in Jordan* (New York: Colombia University Press, 2001).

Mearsheimer, John, and Stephen Wait. *Lobby and US Foreign Policy* (London: Penguin, 2008).

Milton-Edwards, Beverly. *Contemporary Politics in the Middle East* (Cambridge, UK: Polity Press, 2011).

Nasr, Vali. *Forces of Fortune: The Rise of the New Muslim Middle Class and What It Will Mean for Our World* (New York: Free Press, 2009).

Nunns, Alex, and Nadia Idle. *Tweets from Tahrir* (New York: OR Books, 2011).

Osman, Tarek. *Egypt on the Brink: From Nasser to Mubarak* (New Haven, CT: Yale University Press, 2010).

Pappe, Ilan. *The Modern Middle East* (London: Routledge, 2010).

Pargeter, Alison. *The Muslim Brotherhood: The Burden of Tradition* (London: Saqi Books, 2010).

———. *The New Frontiers of Jihad: Radical Islam in Europe* (London: I. B. Tauris, 2008).

Petras, James. *The Arab Revolt and the Imperialist Counterattack* (New York: CreateSpace, 2011).

Pollack, Kenneth. *The Arab Awakening: America and the Transformation of the Middle East* (Washington, DC: Brookings Institution Press, 2011).

Reynolds, A. *Designing Democracy in a Dangerous World* (New York: Oxford University Press, 2010).

Riedel, Bruce. *Deadly Embrace* (Washington, DC: Brookings Institution Press, 2011).

Rode, Gideon, and Jonathan Tepperman, eds. *The U.S. vs. Al-Qaeda: A History of the War on Terror* (Washington, DC: Council on Foreign Relations, 2011).

Rogan, Eugene. *The Arabs: A History* (London: Allen Lane, 2009).

Rosen, Nir. *Aftermath: Following the Bloodshed of America's Wars in the Muslim World* (New York: Nation Books, 2010).

Sadiki, Larbi. *Rethinking Arab Democratization: Elections without Democracy* (New York: Oxford University Press, 2009).

———. *The Search For Arab Democracy: Discourses And Counter-Discourses.* (London: C Hurst, 2004).

Sardar, Sheheryar and Adeel Shah. *Sandstorm: A Leaderless Revolution in the Digital Age* (Jul 2011) Global Executive Board LLC.

Tayara, Bassam. *Le Printemps Arabe decode: Faces cachées des révoltes* (Paris: Editions Albouraq, 2011).

Van Dam, Nikolaos. *The Struggle for Power in Syria: Politics and Society Under Asad and the Ba'th Party* (New York: I. B. Tauris, 2011).

Walker, Chris S. *The Revolution Will Be Tweeted?* (London: Lulu, 2011).

Weaver, Mary. *A Portrait Of Egypt: A Journey Through the World of Militant Islam* (New York: Farrar, Straus and Giroux, 2000).

Werfalli, Mabroka. *Political Alienation in Libya.* (Plymouth: Ithaca Press, 2011).

West, Johnny. *Karama! Journeys Through the Arab Spring* (London: Heron Books, 2011).

Williams, Brian Glyn. *Afghanistan Declassified: A Guide to America's Longest War* (Philadelphia: University of Pennsylvania Press, 2011).

Wright, Robin. *Rock the Casbah: Rage and Rebellion Across the Islamic World* (New York: Simon & Schuster, 2011).

Ziadeh, Radwan. *Power and Policy in Syria* (London: I. B. Tauris, 2010).

Zurayk, Rami, and Rashid Khalidi. *Food, Farming, and Freedom: Sowing the Arab Spring* (Charlottesville: Just World Books, 2011).

NOTES

Introduction

1. Ramy Nasr, "Tunisia in the WikiLeaks," Ramy Nasr's Web site, Jan. 19, 2011. Accessed at http://www.ramynasr.com/2011/tunisia-in-the-wikileaks/.

2. "Egypt Set for Runoff Polls," Al Jazeera online, Dec. 5, 2010. accessed at http:www.aljazeeracom/news/middleast/2010/12/201012521 536155637.htm.

3. The same sentiment was echoed in Jordan during November 2010 elections there, when opposition parties boycotted an electoral process that was, in their view, destined to deliver an unrepresentative body.

Chapter 1

1. Rashid Khalidi, *Resurrecting Empire: Western Footprints and America's Perilous Path In the Middle East* (London: I. B. Tauris, 2004), 58.

2. Ghassan Salameh, *State and Society in the Arab Mashreq* (Lebanon: Centre for Arab Unity Studies, 1987, Arabic edition).

3. Ibid.

4. Gaddafi's surrealism of course knew no limits, and in one of the most memorable stories pertaining to *The Green Book*, his buddy, Silvio Berlusconi, the prime minister of Italy, arranged for Gaddafi to preach to several hundred Italian women about his philosophy. Short on interested Italian females, a modeling agency filled the hall for the speech, after which copies of the book were distributed to the paid audience.

5. Sabry Hafez, "Torture, Imprisonment, and Political Assassination in the Arab Novel," *Al Jadid* magazine, 38 (Winter 2002). Accessed at http://www.aljadid.com/content/torture-imprisonment-and-political-assassination-arab-novel.

6. "Fact Sheet: Extraordinary Rendition," ACLU, Dec. 6, 2005. Accessed at http://www.aclu.org/national-security/fact-sheet-extraordinary-rendition.

7. "Creating Opportunities for Future Generations," *Arab Human Development Report 2002*. Accessed at http://hdr.undp.org/en/reports/regional/arabstates/name,3140,en.htm

Chapter 2

1. Mohamed Habib, "Egyptian Universities' Student Unions Dissolved," Ahram Online, Feb. 27, 2011. Accessed at http://english.ahram.org.eg/NewsContent/1/64/6504/Egypt/Politics-/Egyptian-universities-student-unions-dissolved.aspx.

2. After the revolution, the police were put on trial, and in October 2011 they were sentenced for manslaughter with seven years in prison.

3. "Revolutions, Reform, and Democratic Transition in the Arab Homeland: From the Perspective of the Tunisian Revolution," Arab Center for Research and Policy Studies, Jan. 6, 2011. Accessed at http://english.dohainstitute.org/Home/Details?entityID=5ea4b31b-155d-4a9f-8f4d-a5b428135cd5&resourceId=254442df-f575-46eb-b86d-324d862f43d9.

4. "Civil Movements: The Impact of Facebook and Twitter," *Arab Social Media Report*, Dubai School of Government, May 2011. Accessed at http://www.dsg.ae/portals/0/ASMR2.pdf.

5. "Internet World Stats: Usage and Population Statistics," accessed at http://www.internetworldstats.com/middle.htm; "ASDA'A Burson-Marsteller: Arab Youth Survey," March 7, 2011. Accessed at http://www.slideshare.net/AlHaqqNetwork/arab-youth-survey2010

6. Highlights of the second "ASDA'A Burson-Marsteller Arab Youth Survey," accessed at http://www.arabyouthsurvey.com/2009/highlights.html.

7. Tawakkol Karman, "Our Revolution's Doing What Saleh Can't—Uniting Yemen," *The Guardian* online, April 8, 2011. Accessed

at http://www.guardian.co.uk/commentisfree/2011/apr/08/revolution
-saleh-yemen-peace-historic.

8. Global Media Journal online. Accessed at http://www.gmjme
.com/gmj_custom_files/volume1_issue1/articles_in_english/volume
1-issue1-article-3-15.pdf

9. Evgeny Morozov, *The Net Delusion* (New York: Public Affairs, 2011).

10. Philip K. Hitti, *History of the Arabs* (New York: Palgrave Macmillan, 2002), 374-375.

11. "A Beautiful Mind," *Al-Ahram Weekly*, Oct. 15-21, 2009. Accessed at http://weekly.ahram.org.eg/2009/968/fr3.htm.

12. Ibid.

13. George Ziyad, "Egypt: A Writer's Rejection," *World Press Review*, January 2004. Accessed at http://www.worldpress.org
/Mideast/1712.cfm.

14. Chris Toensing, "Tunisian Labor Leaders Reflect Upon Revolt," *Middle East Research and Information Project*, MER258. Accessed at http://www.merip.org/mer/mer258/tunisian-labor-leaders
-reflect-upon-revolt-0.

15. "Unions and National Consciousness," in *The Development of National Consciousness in the Arab Maghreb*, Center for Arab Unity Studies, 1986, 243-252.

16. Testimony delivered to the Arab Center for Policy Studies' conference on Tunisia, website.

17. Quoted by Joel Benin in Rabab El Mahdi and Philip Marfleet, eds., *Egypt: The Moment of Change* (London: Zed Press, 2009).

18. Philip Rizk, "Egypt's Labor Movement: Four Years in Review," *Al-Masry Al-Youm*, Feb. 5, 2010. Accessed at http://www.almasryalyoum.com/en/node/38453

19. Ibid., 80-81.

20. Karman, "Our Revolution's Doing What Saleh Can't—Uniting Yemen."

21. Xan Rice, "Egyptians Protest Over 'Virginity Tests' on Tahrir Square Women", *The Guardian* online, May, 31, 2011. Accessed at http://www.guardian.co.uk/world/2011/may/31/egypt-online-protest
-virginity-tests.

22. Guardian, June 1, 2011, Amnesty International March 23rd, 2011.

23. "Revolutions, Reform, and Democratic Transition in the Arab Homeland: From the Perspective of the Tunisian Revolution," Arab Center for Research and Policy Studies, Jan. 6, 2011. Accessed at http://english.dohainstitute.org/Home/Details?entityID=5ea4b31b -155d-4a9f-8f4d-a5b428135cd5&resourceId=254442df-f575-46eb -b86d-324d862f43d9.

Chapter 3

1. Kauther Larbi, "Tunisia Bans Police from Union Activities," AFP, Google News, Sept. 6, 2011. Accessed at http://www.google.com/hostednews/afp/article/ALeqM5h-J5LJzw788 wECGexCEnZFuKTlNg?docId=CNG.1e1f1c67030c87a81c7d00b92b d972d8.421.

2. "Interview with Syrian President Bashar al-Assad," *Wall Street Journal* online, January 31, 2011. Accessed at http://online.wsj.com/article/SB100014240527487038332045761147 12441122894.html.

3. Michael C. Hudson, "Egypt on the Brink: The Arab World at a Tipping Point?" Middle East Institute online. Accessed at http://www.mei.nus.edu.sg/uncategorized/middle-east-insight-egypt-on-the-brink-the-arab-world-at-a-tipping-point.

4. Anthony Shadid, "Bahrain Boils Under the Lid of Repression," *New York Times*, Sept. 15, 2011. Accessed at http://www.nytimes.com/2011/09/16/world/middleeast/repression -tears-apart-bahrains-social-fabric.html?pagewanted=all.

5. "I'm the King of Kings: Gaddafi Storms out of Arab Summit and Labels Saudi King 'a British Product,'" Daily Mail online, March 31, 2009. Accessed at http://www.dailymail.co.uk/news/article -1165858/Im-king-kings-Gaddafi-storms-Arab-summit-labels -Saudi-king-British-product.html.

6. According to Libya's new leaders, those killed on the side of the struggle against the Gaddafi regime number between 30,000 and 50,000. The number preferred by the new government's minister of health, Naji Barakat, is a more modest 25,000 to 30,000. Yet in the

country's morgues, the war dead registered from both sides so far is mostly in the hundreds of thousands, not the thousands. Those who are still missing total as few as one thousand, according to the International Committee of the Red Cross. These figures may be incomplete, but even if the missing number proves to be three times as high and all are dead, the toll would be far short of what is being claimed. Much of the death toll is based on the theory that there were 30,000 prisoners before the fall of the Gaddafi government. When the prisons were all opened, only 9,000 were found inside. No one actually knows how many prisoners there were, and no one actually counted how many were released.

7. Rachel Kliger, "Weapons Galore in Yemen," *Yemen Times* online, April 22, 2010. Accessed at http://www.yementimes.com /defaultdet.aspx?SUB_ID=33925.

8. Carsten Wieland, "Asad's Lost Chances," Lebanon Wire online, April 14, 2011. Accessed at http://www.lebanonwire.com/1104MLN /11041404MER.asp.

9. "Interview with Syrian President Bashar al-Assad," *Wall Street Journal.*

10. This was the case as this book went to press in November of 2011.

Chapter 4

1. William Young, "Iran Sees Rise of Islamic Hard-Liners," *New York Times*, Jan. 28, 2011. Accessed at http://www.nytimes.com/2011/01/29/world/middleeast/29iran.html.

2. The Ottoman Empire in Turkey was the dominant force in the region from 1299 to 1922, but by the aftermath of World War I, as the great powers divided up the spoils, the once mighty empire was reduced to a fraction of its former glory.

3. Dilip Hiro, "After the Arab Spring, Part III," Yale Global Online, Sept. 26, 2011. Accessed at http://www.yaleglobal.yale.edu /content/after-arab-spring—-part-iii.

4. "Egypt Party Wary of Turkey's Arab Spring Role," Reuters, *Arab News*, Sept. 14, 2011. Accessed at http://www.arabnews.com/ middleeast/article501844.ece?service=print.

Chapter 5

1. Judy Keen, "Rice Reflects on Bush Tenure, Gadhafi in New Memoir," *USA Today*, updated Oct. 30, 2011. Accessed at http://www.usatoday.com/news/washington/story/2011-10-31/condoleezza-rice-memoir-bush/51006960/1.

2. Cited in Elizabeth Flock, "Dick Cheney Isn't the First to Assign Credit for Arab Spring," *Washington Post* Blog Post, Aug. 31, 2011. Accessed at http://www.washingtonpost.com/blogs/blogpost/post/dick-cheney-isnt-the-first-to-assign-credit-for-arab-spring/2011/08/31/gIQAtVQFsJ_blog.html).

3. Charles Krauthammer, "From Freedom Agenda to Freedom Doctrine," *Washington Post*, Feb. 10, 2011. Accessed at http://www.washingtonpost.com/wp-dyn/content/article/2011/02/10/AR2011021005339.html.

4. Fareed Zakaria, "Interview with Henry Kissinger and Zbigniew Brzezinski," CNN Transcripts, Jan. 23, 2011. Accessed at http://www.cnnstudentnews.cnn.com/TRANSCRIPTS/1101/23/fzgps.01.html.

5 "Was George Bush right?" *Economist*, Feb. 3, 2011. Accessed at http://www.economist.com/node/18063852?story_id=18063852.

6. Hossam el-Hamalawy, "Right Time, Wrong Place," *New York Times*, June 2, 2009. Accessed at http://www.nytimes.com/2009/06/03/opinion/03alHamalawy.html.

7. Human Rights Watch, *World Report 2010 - Tunisia*, 20 January 2010, available at: http://www.unhcr.org/refworld/docid/4b586cdd7b.html

8. "Iranians Favor Diplomatic Relations with U.S., But Have Little Trust in Obama," University of Maryland poll, World Public Opinion, Sept. 19, 2009. Accessed at http://www.worldpublicopinion.org/pipa/articles/brmiddleeastnafricara/639.php.

9. Jesse Lee, "President Obama on the Situation in Egypt: 'All Governments Must Maintain Power Through Consent, Not Coercion,'" *The White House* Blog, Jan. 28, 2011. Accessed at http://www.whitehouse.gov/blog/2011/01/28/president-obama-situation-egypt-all-governments-must-maintain-power-through-consent-.

10. "Biden: Mubarak Is Not a Dictator, But People Have a Right to Protest," PBS *Newshour*, Jan. 27, 2011. Accessed at http://www.pbs.org /newshour/bb/politics/jan-june11/biden_01-27.html.

11. Brian Montopoli, "White House: We're Not Taking Sides in Egypt," CBS News *Political Hotsheet*, Jan. 31, 2011. Accessed at http://www.cbsnews.com/8301-503544_162-20030108-503544.html.

12. Roger Cohen, "Score One for Interventionism," *New York Times*, Aug. 29, 2011. Accessed at http://www.nytimes.com/2011 /08/30/opinion/30iht-edcohen30.html.

13. See Maximillian C. Forte's excellent expose in The Top Ten Myths in the War Against Libya, counterpunch.org, August 31, http://www.counterpunch.org/2011/08/31/the-top-ten-myths-in -the-war-against-libya/)

14. "Southern Mistral 2011," Air Defence and Air Operations Command, March 4, 2011. Accessed at http://www.southern-mistral.cdaoa.fr/GB/index.php?option=com _content&view=article&id=54&Itemid=67.

Chapter 6

1. Fouad Ajami, "What the Muslim World Is Watching," *New York Times*, Nov. 18, 2001. Accessed at http://www.nytimes.com/2001/11/18/magazine/18ALJAZEERA.html? pagewanted=all.

2. Bill O'Reilly, "More Danger in the Muslim World," *The O'Reilly Factor*, Jan. 28, 2011. Accessed at http://www.foxnews.com/on-air/oreilly/transcript/more-danger -muslim-world.

3. David Folkenflik, "Clinton Lauds Virtues of Al Jazeera," NPR News, *The Two-Way Blog*, March 5, 2011. Accessed at http://www.npr.org/blogs/thetwo-way/2011/03/03/134243115 /clinton-lauds-virtues-of-al-jazeera-its-real-news.

4. Robert F. Worth and David D. Kirkpatrick, "Seizing a Moment, Al Jazeera Galvanizes Arab Frustration," *New York Times*, January 27, 2011. Accessed at http://www.nytimes.com/2011/01/28/world /middleeast/28jazeera.html.

5. "Crisis in Egypt," ABC News, *This Week*, Jan. 30, 2011. Accessed at http://abcnews.go.com/ThisWeek/week-transcript -crisis-egypt/story?id=12796399&page=14.

6. Frank Schaeffer, "Why Aren't You Watching Al Jazeera?" *Huffington Post*, March 14, 2011. Accessed at http://www.huffingtonpost.com/frank-schaeffer/why-arent-you -watching-al_b_834971.html.

7. Worth and Kirkpatrick, "Seizing a Moment, Al Jazeera Galvanizes Arab Frustration."

8. Hussein Agha and Robert Malley, "In Post-Mubarak Egypt: The Rebirth of the Arab World," *Washington Post* Opinions, February 11, 2011. Accessed at http://www.washingtonpost.com/opinions/ in-post-mubarak-egypt-the-rebirth-of-the-arab-world/2011/02/11/A BYEmrQ_story.html.

Chapter 7

1. Most figures are only rough estimates in the absence of any official count.

2. "Muslim Brotherhood Vows to Take Opposition to Streets," ITN Source, Dec. 26, 2010. Accessed at http://www.itnsource.com/ shotlist/RTV/2010/12/26/RTV3294310/?v=1&a=0.

3. See historic analysis of the revolution in Azmi Bishara, "Revolution and Appetite for a Revolution," Doha Institute, Aug. 22, 2011, Arabic edition; http://dohainstitute.org/Home/Details ?entityID=5d045bf3-2df9-46cf-90a0-d92cbb5dd3e4&resourceId =6a25f83f-63b9-4807-8834-791d4a793d90.

4. Serge Halimi, "Tunisia: Democracy Year One," *Le Monde Diplomatique*, October 2011. Accessed at http://mondediplo.com/ 2011/10/01tunisia.

5. Ibid.

Epilogue

1. For the record, this leading Tunisian party was called by former president Ben Ali as "destructive, danger on democracy, terrorist group, and corrupting"—all in one speech.

INDEX